Leveraging for Success in United Nations Peace Operations

Leveraging for Success in United Nations Peace Operations

edited by

Jean Krasno
Bradd C. Hayes
Donald C. F. Daniel

PRAEGER

Westport, Connecticut
London

Library of Congress Cataloging-in-Publication Data

Leveraging for success in United Nations peace operations / edited by Jean Krasno, Bradd C. Hayes, and Donald C. F. Daniel.

p. cm.

Includes bibliographical references and index.

ISBN 0-275-97883-4 (alk. paper)

1. United Nations—Peacekeeping forces. 2. Conflict management. 3. Sanctions (International law). I. Krasno, Jean E., 1943– II. Hayes, Bradd C. III. Daniel, Donald C. (Donald Charles), 1944–

JZ6374.L478 2003

341.5′84—dc21 2003042009

British Library Cataloguing in Publication Data is available.

Library of Congress Catalog Card Number: 2003042009
ISBN: 0-275-97883-4

First published in 2003

Praeger Publishers, 88 Post Road West, Westport, CT 06881
An imprint of Greenwood Publishing Group, Inc.
www.praeger.com

Printed in the United States of America

The paper used in this book complies with the Permanent Paper Standard issued by the National Information Standards Organization (Z39.48-1984).

10 9 8 7 6 5 4 3 2 1

contents

PART TWO
CROSSCUTTING ANALYSES

PART THREE
CONCLUSION

Illustrations follow page 168

illustrations

acknowledgments

The editors would like to thank the Widgeon Foundation and the Naval War College Foundation for their support in making the writing of this book possible. We would also like to express our appreciation to the United States Institute of Peace for their support of the study on obstructionist leaders. We are also grateful to Edward Luck of the Center for the Study of International Organization and Bruce Russett of UN Studies at Yale for kindly hosting the seminars where the papers were first presented.

Introduction

a conceptual framework for the use of leverage

JEAN KRASNO

Conceptual Framework and the International Context

For the United Nations, the early 1990s were a period of great expectations. The Organization was seen as an important contributor to a new world order through its role in mandating and implementing peace operations. By the mid-1990s, however, disillusionment with the UN's potential had set in. Having failed its mission in Bosnia, the Organization gladly ceded its central role in the region to a coalition of the willing. Its difficulties there and in Somalia threw a pall over its fiftieth anniversary in 1995 and led to a major reduction in its peace-operations profile. Deployed forces in UN operations dropped drastically from nearly eighty thousand in 1993–1994 to fourteen thousand in 1998, and no completely new UN mission was approved until 1998. The UN's image in the media and among many policy-makers was that of a failed instrument where peace operations were concerned, but the fact is that before and after the mid-1990s the UN did have successes and it did learn from its failures.

Coleman and Grene in their chapter aptly explain that not only has the global political environment changed, but the very quality of conflict has evolved from primarily interstate to complex, multiparty violence that is both internal and regional in nature. That makes the work of the UN considerably more challenging, and the institution is undergoing today considerable reform in its peacekeeping capabilities in line with a major and comprehensive report of the Brahimi Panel. In response to international needs, the UN is undergoing a resurgence in its peacekeeping profile with more than 40,000 personnel in operations in 2003. This book aims to highlight UN peace-operation successes for what they tell us about the leverage available to Member States and the Organization when confronted with instabilities that may require a peace operation.

The original purpose of this research was to provide information to policy-makers by examining the use of force to achieve success in UN peace operations, primarily military force. However, we soon came to realize that the actual use of force was much more complicated and that there are an array of diverse instruments or tools for applying pressure to achieve success. Therefore, we decided instead to create a set of questions to establish a research agenda, addressing how government and individual actors, operating with the endorsement of the United Nations, can exercise leverage vis-á-vis parties to a conflict to achieve a positive peaceful solution. We undertook to examine two principal circumstances:

- leverage used to compel warring parties to end the fighting and accept outside intervention in the first place; and
- leverage used to deter parties that have agreed to an operation from returning to conflict and to follow through and comply with the UN mandate.

Leverage can be seen as the use of pressure where actors can utilize a set of instruments that compel others into taking actions, or refraining from undesired acts. A mechanical lever gives the user more power and strength than innate capacity would do alone. Similarly, political, military, and economic leverage offers international actors a means of pressure beyond what can be achieved without these tools.

Peacekeeping is defined as the deployment of military/civilian personnel endorsed by the international community in order to contain a crisis or conflict that threatens international peace and security. A peace operation is one that involves both peacekeeping and other aspects of humanitarian and political assistance to achieve a sustainable and stable peace. The premise of this study is that intervention will happen as a natural outcome of political agendas, and therefore the quality of that intervention and its resulting impact on peace and security depends on having a system in place that can guide the decision-making process and lay out a set of viable options.

This project set out to examine the context of a timely and judicial use of moderate force in concert with other elements of leverage. The use of pressure, the implied threat of force along with economic, political, and other instruments of leverage is the centerpiece of the study, but it is understood that effective leverage does not operate in a vacuum. A variety of elements come into play that may or may not be controllable but that have a dynamic interchange and effect on results that need to be understood. The authors found that using the concept of leverage as an investigative tool uncovered other unexpected sources of pressure that are less obvious, but nonetheless equally effective under the right circumstances.

We hope that a careful analysis of cases along a set agenda of research questions may offer a greater understanding of why certain peace operations are successful or unsuccessful. An understanding of these dynamics would contribute to a base for future policy planning for crises in which the parties are reluctant to reach agreement and that may present hazardous risks.

Initially, the working definition of leverage applied by the authors was the use of, or threat to use, force to inflict harm and/or the offering of incentives in order to compel a change in behavior. Leverage could take the form of: (1) military force, or the threat to use force; (2) economic and political sanctions or incentives; and (3) sociopolitical isolation. The chapter writers, people who have had direct knowledge of experiences in the field, soon began to broaden that working definition. They explained that there were other, less-tangible instruments of leverage like prestige and trust that came into play along with the more visible concrete mechanisms like troop deployment and so on. Therefore the study was adapted to inquire more broadly about what mechanisms of leverage could become available to the diplomatic community to bring about changes in behavior and compliance with a peace process.

Instruments of leverage, whatever their quality or character, are most successful when applied consistently by a common coalition of partners. If there is a split in the partnership or a weakening of will, leverage is less successful and will probably not achieve the desired goal. Orchestrating these factors to achieve a common end within the international context is a complex process. Not only do alliances and the will to act shift, but subtle changes can thwart the timing of diplomatic intervention. It takes tremendous skill and sensitivity to identify these shifts in will and capacity to be able to apply leverage successfully. A sense of timing and knowledge of which instruments to use when will determine whether or not the key actors can manage a successful outcome.

Goals and Structure of the Research Project

The project was organized by scholars at three U.S. institutions of higher learning: the Naval War College, Yale University, and New York University. The papers were initially presented at a series of seminars where scholars and practitioners with knowledge of the cases were invited to comment on the papers and that information was then incorporated into later drafts. The purpose was threefold: (1) to commission a series of case studies of UN peace operations; (2) to provide a forum where representatives of UN Member States, UN Secretariat officials, and research-and-strategy-planning communities could reflect upon the case studies and comment; and (3) to inform decision-makers and their advisors on the results of the findings of this study.

Past analyses of cases too often have ignored what was below the visible portion of the iceberg to explain why actors succeeded or failed in peace operations and have not attempted to view outcomes in terms of leverage. The purpose here was to examine the synergy of leverage forces brought to bear in ways that go beyond work that has already been done to explain the events of the 1990s.

An additional intent was to probe for not only the instruments of leverage but the context into which they can be utilized effectively. We asked the chapter writers to think about the package of leverage (carrots, sticks, enabling resources, information, and so forth) that might be available for negotiating an agreement or implementing the mandate and dealing with leaders that need to be convinced that it is in their best interest to cooperate. We wanted to know if there were appropriate tools of leverage that the international community might develop or that the United Nations might maximize. We wondered if communication played a role in successfully conveying or not conveying pressure. We asked the experts to examine what role Member States play in applying leverage and what the role of the Special Representative of the Secretary-General (SRSG) is in orchestrating leverage with the parties in the field of operation. We also wanted to probe for a greater understanding of the use of force through troop deployment, and ask about the importance of force levels in the theater of operation and the timeliness of deployment.

Each of the chapter writers approached the set of inquiries in a slightly different manner, depending on the case at hand and the point of view they held as a participant, researcher, or observer. No single chapter addressed all the questions, but we discovered that the cases uncovered mechanisms that came into play that were unanticipated at the outset of the study. This is the exciting, discovery aspect of using cases to probe for dynamics that are not available to those outside the inner-circle of decision-makers and that may not have been identified as factors if we had not set out to ask these questions.

The Value of Case Studies Told Firsthand

The great advantage of this series of case studies on country-specific operations and cross-cutting issues is that they are told by firsthand sources. The chapter authors were either present in the field during the events, participated directly in negotiations, or the research was conducted through interviews with people who were directly involved. Some of the chapter authors were Deputy Special Representatives of the Secretary-General. For example, Derek Boothby was the Deputy for the UN Transitional Administration in Eastern Slavonia (UNTAES) and Dirk Salomons was the Deputy for UN Operation in Mozambique (ONUMOZ). Mark Quarterman worked under Ian Martin, the SRSG for the UN Transitional Assistance for East Timor (UNTAET). Diego Arria was the ambassador of

Venezuela to the UN and participated directly in the negotiations on El Salvador. He also has firsthand knowledge on other issues related to the history of Central America in general. Mats Berdal had direct access to the principals involved in the UN Protection Force (UNPROFOR) in both Bosnia and at UN headquarters in New York.

Jean Krasno took her information from direct interviews with those involved in the peace process on Namibia and those involved in establishing the Friends of the Secretary-General mechanism. Both Chris Coleman and Andrew Grene work inside the UN in the Department of Peacekeeping Operations and view the inside workings of peace operations on a daily basis. Don Daniel and Bradd Hayes gathered the information for their piece on obstructionist leaders from workshops with practitioners who had been involved with and have to work with this type of leader in field operations.

Why Begin with Bosnia?

It may seem odd in a book on successful peace operations to begin the case studies with Bosnia, a well-known humiliating failure. But the failures of Somalia, and only a few months later Rwanda, followed finally by the catastrophic fall of the safe havens in Bosnia shook the policy-making community to the extent that we needed to learn from these failures. We felt we needed to reexamine why things went wrong and then compare the failure in Bosnia to a series of forgotten UN successes that came before and after. Bosnia therefore becomes a focal point for comparison that makes success that much more understandable.

We hope that the study of leverage as a conceptual framework and the comparison of successful operations to failures like UNPROFOR in Bosnia will contribute to the understanding of peace operations. The challenge of bringing scholars and practitioners together in this exercise has been mutually informative. We believe that the strength of this book is the practical wisdom brought to light through information gathered directly from practitioners and their collective experiences.

PART ONE

Case Studies

CHAPTER ONE

The United Nations in Bosnia, 1992–1995

faithful scapegoat to the world?[1]

MATS BERDAL

SETTING THE STAGE

The confused, hesitant, and reactive nature of the "international community's" response to the disintegration of Yugoslavia provides the essential backdrop against which the history of United Nations operations in the Balkans during the first half of the 1990s must be viewed. The confusion and hesitation were reflected in the decisions and actions of the UN Security Council—the body that the founding members of the Organization had, nearly half-a-century earlier, solemnly entrusted with "primary responsibility for the maintenance of international peace and security." From the very beginning of the wars in the former Yugoslavia until the late summer of 1995, the Council proved unable to forge a common *strategic* purpose that went beyond a limited set of objectives on which Council members (and indeed troop-contributing countries) could all agree. Partly for this reason, a number of diplomatic mechanisms and initiatives—notably the International Conference on the Former Yugoslavia (ICFY) and the Contact Group—were set up to support efforts to contain the conflict, mitigate its humanitarian consequences, and help the parties themselves to find a negotiated solution to the conflict.[2]

Against this background, this chapter looks at the international community's attempt to leverage the parties to the war in Bosnia. It concentrates, above all, on the attempts to leverage the Bosnian Serbs and their allies across the Drina.[3] The reason for this focus is given in part by what David Hannay, the United Kingdom's Permanent Representative to the UN

from 1990 to 1995, writing in 1996, acknowledged as "the undoubted primary responsibility of Milosevic and of the Bosnian Serbs for the outbreak of fighting and for the brutality with which it was prosecuted."[4] It is also the case, however, that international efforts to cajole and threaten the warring parties—however unsuccessful for much of the period under review—were directed primarily against the Serbs, even though they were not alone in carrying out atrocities nor, indeed, in seeking to obtain territory for themselves by means of "ethnic cleansing" (this, notwithstanding the basic truth of Hannay's observation).

The chapter examines the sequence of events that led to UN resolutions authorizing the use of "all necessary means" to protect "safe areas" in the context of a brutal and ongoing war. A central concern throughout the chapter is the debate that raged, throughout the period under review, about the scope for using military force to impose a solution on the warring parties, an issue that is obviously critical to any discussion of leverage. In this context, particular attention is given to the lessons that should, as well as those that should not, be drawn from NATO and UNPROFOR's use of force in the late summer of 1995 (Operation Deliberate Force).

The story told is essentially one about the failure to apply effective leverage on the parties and thus bring the war in Bosnia to an early end. As such, it points to obstacles inherent in any attempt by outside actors to influence the course of civil or internal wars.[5] While some of these obstacles, as will be argued more fully, proved particularly difficult to overcome in the case of Bosnia, the story of the UN's involvement there between 1992 and 1995 also provides lessons of much wider significance and policy relevance.

The UN Security Council and Mandate Formulation for Bosnia

Consensus about the UN's role in Bosnia until the summer of 1995 among the permanent members of the Security Council, as well as among the principal troop-contributing countries not on the Council, centered around three sets of objectives: (1) relieving as far as possible the human suffering caused by the war; (2) containing the conflict and mitigating its consequences; and (3) encouraging and facilitating an overall settlement. In the course of the mission, the mandate evolved and new tasks were added onto existing ones, yet the deployment of UN troops remained geared toward the achievement of these three purposes.

Helping in the provision of humanitarian aid was the principal way the UN sought to alleviate the humanitarian consequences of the wars. To this end, the UN's Protection Force (UNPROFOR) in Bosnia, made up of troop contributions from Member States, was tasked: "(a) to provide support to the efforts of UN's High Commission for Human Rights (UNHCR) to deliver humanitarian relief in Bosnia and Herzegovina, particularly through the provision of convoy protection when so requested; (b) to provide protection for other humanitarian agencies with the approval of the UNHCR; (c) to protect UN facilities, including UNHCR storage centers, if so requested; (d) to provide protection for convoys of released detainees on request by the International Commission for the Red Cross (ICRC) and with the concurrence of the Force Commander that the request is practicable."[6] Containing the conflict, the second broad objective, was done by imposing various constraints on the warring parties through such arrangements as the "no-fly zone" over Bosnia, the "safe areas," and weapons exclusion zones. The third objective, that of assisting the negotiating process, was pursued "by negotiating local cease-fires and other arrangements, maintaining these where possible and providing support for measures aimed at an overall political settlement," the latter including support for ICFY's activities and welcoming initiatives such as the creation, in

April 1994, of the Contact Group comprising representatives of the United States, Britain, France, Germany, and Russia.[7]

The limited and reactive nature of these objectives reflected disagreements among Member States about the origins and nature of the conflict, disagreements that intensified during the course of the conflict. At the same time, consensus around these objectives, as David Hannay was later to write, also reflected agreement on one other point crucial to limiting the UN's exercise of leverage:

> From the very beginning of hostilities in Bosnia the one common point amongst all the external parties was their determination not to be drawn into the fighting themselves nor . . . to see this as a black-and-white issue calling for enforcement action. There was thus a clear unwillingness to treat it in a parallel way to Iraq's aggression against Kuwait.[8]

As the war in Bosnia continued, an increasing number of Member States, notably the United States and Germany, questioned the wisdom and viability of the early assumptions on which UN involvement had been based. Yet, the "determination not to be drawn into the fighting themselves" persisted, and there was no willingness among troop-contributors to reconfigure the mission to engage in war-fighting or to take action that would expose troops to what Member States considered to be "unnecessary" risks. This meant, in effect, that UNPROFOR in Bosnia remained essentially a "peacekeeping" mission, however unsatisfactory that term was to describe its operations in the midst of an ongoing war. Indeed, the central difficulty in Bosnia was precisely that the war continued in spite of the UN's presence. This ensured an ever-growing number of Security Council resolutions and presidential statements—more than 140 between 1991 and 1995—usually aimed at addressing specific contingencies arising in the field and adopted under the enforcement or Chapter VII provisions of the Charter partly in order to demonstrate resolve on the part of the international community. Meanwhile, divisions among external powers persisted, making UNPROFOR's role on the ground increasingly difficult to sustain as mandates grew "increasingly complex and contradictory." In particular, UNPROFOR remained under constant and conflicting pressures from Member States to take more forceful action without altering the peacekeeping basis of its mandate. It was this tension that prompted an embittered General Francis Briquemont, Force Commander in Bosnia from July 1993 to January 1994, to complain, shortly before the end of his tour of duty, that his mission had been plagued by "a fantastic gap between the resolutions of the Security Council, the will to execute these resolutions, and the means available to commanders in the field."

Yasushi Akashi, much criticized especially in the United States for his performance as SRSG and Head of the UN mission, would later write:

> The competing interests of the Council's permanent members, and the resultant inability of the Council to develop an overarching strategy

> toward Bosnia, resulted in the Council responding to tactical developments, issuing mid-course changes, and passing Resolutions that often reflected the domestic political needs of the Member States rather than the operational and strategic requirements of UNPROFOR. This practice, strategically unwise under any circumstances, was particularly alarming because of the peacekeepers' presence in the midst of an ongoing war.[9]

For all the criticism he received, not all of it unjustified, this is a passage with which it is difficult to quarrel, as the history of the "safe-areas regime" brings out all too clearly.

THE ESTABLISHMENT OF THE "SAFE-AREAS" REGIME IN BOSNIA

Background: The Eastern Enclaves and Mladic's Drina Offensive

The war in Bosnia and Herzegovina began in late March 1992 when fighting broke out between Croat forces, supported by recently formed Muslim militias, and Serb paramilitaries outside Bosanski Brod near the strategically important Posavina corridor linking Serb-inhabited strongholds in northern Bosnia around Banja Luka with Serbia proper. In early April and over the course of the next three months, a murderous onslaught by Serb paramilitary forces, aided by the Yugoslav Army (JNA), resulted in Bosnian Serb forces (BSA) securing control of more than 60 percent of the territory of the newly recognized republic. Starting with the attack by the notorious "Tigers" of Zeljko Raznatovic (better known by his nom de guerre, "Arkan") on the town of Bijelinja, an attempt was made to secure and "ethnically cleanse" a swathe of territory in the north and east of the country. The onslaught, conducted with utmost brutality and before the UN had any significant presence throughout country, was geared towards the wholesale expulsion of the non-Serb, largely Muslim population from towns and cities where, in many cases, non-Serbs had constituted the majority population before the fighting broke out. With JNA support, ensuring an effective logistic system and overwhelming firepower, the campaign succeeded in rapidly cleansing much of the targeted territory, including the towns of Zvornik, Bratunac, Foca, and Visegrad along the Drina Valley.

In isolated places, however, notably around the towns Srebrenica and in Gorazde, the local Muslim population was able to resist the initial onslaught, to organize its defenses, and later in the year, to counterattack. In late September, Muslim forces commanded by Naser Oric attacked out of the Srebrenica enclave and succeeded, over the next three-to-four months, in retaking territory that had been overrun in the spring and even to capture towns and villages that had been predominantly Serb-inhabited before the war. When Oric's forces overran Serb-controlled villages, culminating in the attack on the village of Kravica on 7 January 1993, horrors and acts of revenge were repeated in a vicious cycle of violence—all-too-familiar in the history of the area.[10] By late January 1993, Oric's fighters had acquired military control over nearly 900 square kilometers of territory in eastern Bosnia, from the Drina to a hilltop less than ten kilometers from Government-controlled territory around Tuzla.[11] At its greatest extent the enclave included Cerska in the north, with Zepa in the south physically linked to Srebrenica itself.

It was against the background of these advances that the BSA under Ratko Mladic decided to launch, in early 1993, a major offensive in the Drina valley aimed at forcing back, with a view eventually to eliminating, Muslim resistance in the eastern enclaves. Drawing on its advantages in logistics and firepower, Mladic's forces made rapid progress, soon cutting off Zepa from Srebrenica. With customary brutality, indiscriminate shelling by Serb forces drove a rapidly growing refugee population into an ever smaller piece of territory, centering on the town of Srebrenica. When, in March and April 1993, Bosnian Serb forces intensified their attacks further, the vulnerability of the refugee populations within the enclaves was cruelly exposed to the outside world.

The US Advocacy of "Lift and Strike": Council Divisions Exposed

As the situation deteriorated in the enclaves, the new US administration of President Bill Clinton began to press more forcefully for a policy of "lift and strike" to halt Serbian advances. The idea was to combine the lifting of the arms embargo that had been established under Resolution 713 (1991) as it applied to the Bosnian Government, with, in the words of Secretary of State Warren Christopher, "compensatory air strikes to prevent the Serbs from overrunning the Bosnians while the Bosnians were being armed."[12] During the 1992 presidential-election campaign, candidate Clinton had strongly hinted that "tougher action" of this sort would be taken and, in line with this, the administration withheld even lukewarm support for the Vance–Owen peace plan once it entered office in early 1993.[13] The lift-and-strike option emphatically did not, however, envisage the deployment of American ground troops in Bosnia, either in support of the existing mission or as part of a deliberate transition to an enforcement operation.

European governments, especially those that had made substantial troop contributions to UNPROFOR, did not share American views on the lifting of the embargo and, at a meeting of the European Union (EU) Foreign Ministers in Denmark on 25 April 1993, made their position clear.[14] Britain and France, both Permanent Members of the Security Council with large number of troops on the ground in Bosnia, were most alarmed by the American stance. Their concerns stemmed, in the first instance, from a conviction that the lift-and-strike option, as outlined by Secretary Christopher, simply was not implementable, at least not without troops on the ground that were both capable and willing to engage in war-fighting. And, indeed, as events were later to prove, the UN forces in Bosnia were highly vulnerable to countermeasures from the warring parties. More importantly, no Western government at this stage of the conflict was prepared to accept a level of risk to its soldiers that was substantially higher than existing peacekeeping commitments. Above all, the Europeans stressed that a lift-and-strike decision could not be isolated from the fact that the UN was engaged primarily in a humanitarian capacity on the ground. While these differences explain much of the tension that existed between Member States with troops on the ground and those without, different views on the origins and nature of the conflict served to further reinforce divisions among Council members. Thus while the primary responsibility and brutality of the Bosnian Serb forces were recognized by all, the Bosnian Croat (HVO) war against Government forces in Central Bosnia, which flared up in early 1993, received little attention from US policy-makers, and hardly any from Congress. Indeed, in her review of *The World and Yugoslavia's Wars* (edited by Richard Ullman and produced by the Council on Foreign Relations in 1996), Jane Sharp (herself a fierce critic of European policy in Bosnia) was absolutely right in drawing attention to the "perplexing US blind spot towards Croatia."[15] By May 1993, fighting in Central Bosnia between Muslims and Croats—with the HVO supported by Tudjman and the regular Croatian Army (HV), just as the Milosevic and the JNA had been and still was supporting the Bosnian Serbs—was as intense and as savage as anything to date in the wars of Yugoslav succession.[16] This aspect of the conflict, which the British forces were bound to feel more keenly given their operational deployment in the areas of Bosniac–Croat fighting, reinforced a preexisting skepticism about the advisability of more forceful intervention, especially of the lift-and-strike variety.[17]

It was, then, partly in order to forestall what was perceived to be mounting, and indeed possibly irresistible, pressure for lift-and-strike that both the United Kingdom and France came to argue in favor of formally designating several Bosnian-controlled towns as "safe areas."[18] Calls for "tougher action" against the Bosnian Serb Army came not only, however, from the United States. The Non-aligned caucus of the Security Council, led by Venezuela and Pakistan, played a key role in actions and decisions that led to the creation of the safe-areas regime. The Srebrenica crisis in early April resulted in the adoption of Resolution 819, tabled by the Non-aligned and declaring Srebrenica to be a safe-area. The resolution also authorized a visit to Bosnia by a Security Council mission to "report on the situation." The report of the mission, led by Ambassador Diego Arria of Venezuela, noted that the "actual situation [in Srebrenica] obviously does not correspond to the spirit or the intent of the resolution [819],"[19] and it called for the concept of safe areas to be "extended to other towns in need of safety."[20]

The recommendation provided the basis for a new draft resolution, again presented by the Non-aligned, calling on the Council to expand the safe-areas regime and strengthen UNPROFOR accordingly. This latter point, the need for additional resources, had by this stage become a major concern to the UN Secretariat and, especially, to UN commanders in the field.[21] On 6 May, the Security Council declared that the towns of Zepa, Tuzla, Srebrenica, Sarajevo, Gorazde, and Bihac "and their surroundings should be treated as safe areas by all the parties concerned and should be free from armed attacks or any other hostile act."[22] References to the "enforcement measures"[23] in the original draft resolution, however, had been dropped at the insistence of France and United Kingdom. Instead, the Council authorized a strengthening of UNPROFOR by fifty additional UN Military Observers to monitor the humanitarian situation in the safe areas and declared its "readiness . . . to consider immediately the adoption of any additional measures necessary."[24] None of these developments provided more than a temporary respite from the fighting around the enclaves and, as fighting continued, it became clear that the Council's commitment "to ensure full respect for the safe areas"[25] would have to be addressed. Anticipating this, the Non-aligned countries argued forcefully, in a memorandum presented by Pakistan on 14 May, that the safe-areas concept could only work if security of the designated areas was "guaranteed and protected" by UNPROFOR.[26]

THE "JOINT INACTION PROGRAM" AND RESOLUTION 836

All of these developments, together with the evidence of a worsening of the situation on the ground, led to renewed efforts by Britain and France to find some form of compromise solution between the various positions. The rejection by the Bosnian Serbs of the Vance–Owen Plan increased their fears that American pressure for tougher action in the form of lift and strike would prove increasingly irresistible.[27] Although the Bosnian Government leadership had signed up to the Vance–Owen plan, President Izetbegovic, as Sudetic perceptively observes,

> was convinced that the Serbs would never sign it, and he gambled that if the peace plan collapsed and the Serbs were held responsible for its failure, the UN Security Council, under American pressure, would lift the arms embargo against the Bosnian Government and might even approve NATO air attacks against the Serbs.[28]

It was not an unreasonable gamble. On 18 May, in testimony before Congress, Warren Christopher again reiterated the administration's view that lift and strike was the best way forward.[29]

The following day, France presented its own memorandum suggesting ways of strengthening the UNPRORFOR mandate so as to "give it expressly . . . the task of ensuring the security of the safe areas. To this end a new resolution should provide for the possibility of recourse to the use of force, by all necessary means."[30] The French favored a "light minimum option" involving the deployment of some 5,000 troops to confer credibility on the safe-areas concept. In an effort to bridge positions that had emerged, France, United Kingdom, the United States, Spain, and Russia then agreed in Washington, on 22 May, on a "Joint Action Program," formally abandoning the Vance–Owen plan as a comprehensive solution and calling instead for a piecemeal approach to implement "agreed provisions." The program, agreed to after an embarrassingly unsuccessful European trip by Warren Christopher to persuade his NATO allies about the wisdom of lift and strike, was so obviously a compromise that it was soon dubbed the "Joint Inaction Plan" and was harshly criticized as such by the Non-aligned caucus.[31] The program endorsed the safe-areas concept and resulted in the adoption by the Security Council (with two abstentions, Pakistan and Venezuela) of Resolution 836 on 4 June. The resolution, which was based on the earlier French memorandum, decide to extend

> the mandate of UNPROFOR in order to enable it, in the safe areas referred to in resolution 824 (1993), to deter attacks against the safe areas, to monitor the cease-fire, to promote the withdrawal of military or paramilitary units other than those of the Government of the Republic of Bosnia and Herzegovina and to occupy some key points on the ground. (paragraph 5)

To this end, the Security Council *authorized* UNPROFOR ". . . acting in self-defense, to take the necessary measures, including the use of force, in reply to bombardments against the safe areas by any one of the parties or to armed incursions into them" (paragraph 9), and *decided* that

> Member States, acting nationally or through regional organizations or arrangements, may take, under the authority of the Security Council and subject to close coordination with the Secretary General and UNPROFOR, all necessary measures, through the use of air power, in and around the safe areas in the Republic of Bosnia and Herzegovina, to support UNPROFOR in the performance of its mandate set out in paragraphs 5 and 9 above. (paragraph 10)[32]

The Aftermath of Resolution 836

These operative paragraphs raised the most serious concerns both at the UN headquarters in New York and, especially, among UNPROFOR commanders who feared that the sponsoring states were passing a critical resolution without sufficient regard to its possible long-term consequences.[33] In particular, it was felt that without an adequate number of troops, the safe areas would be impossible to defend as the wording of the operative paragraphs of the resolution, when read in conjunction with one another, clearly seemed to suggest. Partly in order to clarify the operational implications, but also acutely aware of the difficulties it would encounter in trying to raise additional troops, senior officials in the Secretariat raised their concerns with the representatives of the sponsoring states and Canada in a meeting held in New York on 7 June.[34] One source of concern was the lack of troops, since none of the sponsoring countries were prepared to increase their contingents nor were willing to redeploy existing contingents in-theatre to the newly established safe areas. UNPROFOR commanders in the field were also concerned about the lack of any provisions for demilitarizing the safe areas.

At the meeting on June 7, the Secretariat arranged for an oral presentation to the Security Council outlining the findings of a "preliminary military staff study" by UNPROFOR that called for 32,000 additional troops in order "to credibly implement the safe-areas concept." The reaction from members, notably United Kingdom and France, was swift and negative. They emphasized instead their preference for the "light minimum" option that had been drawn up earlier by France, which envisaged the deployment only of some 5,000 troops. As for the wording of Resolution 836, it was made clear that the phrase "to deter attacks against the safe areas" (paragraph 6) had been chosen deliberately, instead of "to defend" and, similarly, that "to promote withdrawal of military and paramilitary forces" (paragraph 5) had been chosen rather than to "ensure or enforce." Preference was expressed by the permanent Council members for a "gradual build-up" in the safe areas, and it was stressed that UNPROFOR`s "deterrent capacity" was to derive from its *presence* in the safe areas rather than from its military strength.[35]

Actual implementation of the safe-areas concept soon ran into difficulties, with the Secretariat unable to secure commitments to meet even the agreed light minimum option. But more serious than this in the long run was the deepening of tensions among the external powers and, with it, a persistent failure to align activities on the ground in Bosnia with the wider diplomatic efforts aimed at reaching an overall settlement.

The only way in which the adoption of Resolution 836 could have been justified, and indeed was justified at the time, was to view the measures introduced as a short-term initiative to stabilize a precarious humanitarian situation. The sponsors of the resolution, even at the time of its adoption, were not blind to what the Secretary-General would later refer to as the "inherent deficiencies of the safe-area regime"; yet, they still hoped in May and June of 1993 that a political breakthrough towards a settlement would prevent these deficiencies from becoming too acute. Ambassador Merimée, explaining France's support for Resolution 836, stated that "the designation and protection of the safe areas [was] not an end in itself, but only a temporary measure: a step towards a just and lasting political solution."[36] Madeleine Albright stated that the resolution was "an intermediate step—no more, no less."[37] David Hannay was later to write that the "safe-areas policy [was] originally seen as a very short-term expedient, [and was] never a viable or sustainable one in the longer term in the absence of progress in the peace process."[38] Yet this is precisely where progress continued to prove most elusive.

Given that UNPROFOR was already over-stretched and unable to meet the expectations raised by the wording of a steadily increasing number of resolutions, the continuation of the war meant that the disjunction between Security Council decisions and UNPROFOR activities on the ground only widened further. In December 1993, Cedric Thornberry, who had recently returned as head of UN Civil Affairs in Zagreb, stressed that a key lesson from his experience was that "the peacemaking or negotiating process, which precedes or accompanies that of peacekeeping, must be very closely coordinated with peacekeeping, so that each can be fully relevant to the actual situation on the ground."[39] Not long after Thornberry had left the theatre, the "European Union Action Plan," the third peace plan to be presented to the parties, collapsed and more than sixteen months were to pass before all three parties to the Bosnian conflict would be present at negotiations. The upshot, as far as UNPROFOR was concerned, was to leave it with the supervision and monitoring of an ever-growing number of agreements, partial cease-fires, military-exclusion zones and ultimatums issued by NATO. By early 1995, the remarkable list of agreements whose implementation the UN was committed to support included: the Sarajevo Airport Agreement of June 1992; the Srebrenica Agreement of April 1993; the Srebrenica and Zepa Agreements of May 1993; the Mount Igman Demilitarized Zone Agreement of August 1993; the Sarajevo Airport Agreement of February 1994; the Agreement on the use of civilian traffic across Sarajevo airport of March 1994; the Gorazde Agreement of April 1994; and the Anti-Sniping Agreement of August 1994.[40] In addition to this came the commitments arising out of the cease-fire in 1994 between the HVO and government forces in Central Bosnia, which included detailed provisions for weapons-control measures and extensive patrolling.

The deepening of tensions between the Americans, on the one hand, and European troop-contributors, above all France and Britain, on the other, provide much of the explanation for the course of events following the creation of the safe-areas regime. The failure to halt the war in Bosnia and to make progress after 836, followed by the debacles in Somalia and Haiti in the autumn of 1993, had a profound impact on US Bosnia policy until the summer of 1995. By the autumn of 1993, the distinctly uneven record of the administration's foreign policy lead to what Madeleine Albright, in the spring of 1994, pointedly described as "a period of recalibrating our expectations."[41] The result of this process was to further increase tensions over Bosnia policy with the Europeans. On the one hand, foreign-policy setbacks made the administration far more sensitive to criticism of its Bosnia policy and therefore also more susceptible to domestic political pressure for "action" to be taken. On the other hand, the events in Somalia only reinforced a determination not to become involved militarily. The result was a pattern of being "in politically and out militarily," which the Europeans, above all Britain, France, and Russia, resented and saw as an obstacle to end the war because it, in effect, provided a disincentive for the parties to stop fighting. Indeed, as long as none of the external powers was prepared to exercise forceful military leverage while, at the same time, continuing to differ profoundly on "the way forward," the warring parties, not surprisingly, were inclined to continue to seek either a decisive political or military advantage.[42]

EVALUATING THE UN'S FAILURE TO USE FORCE IN BOSNIA

This section considers the issue of military leverage in greater detail. Specifically, it examines the question that has been at the heart of debates about the use of force in Bosnia between 1991 and 1995: did UNPROFOR fail to use the degree of force that it was in fact mandated to do and, thereby, did it also fail to influence the course of the conflict in a direction that would have brought an earlier end to the fighting? The view that UNPROFOR did indeed fail in this respect is based on a combination of two arguments: first, that UNPROFOR did not act on a Chapter VII mandate that explicitly enabled it to use "all necessary means," and, secondly, that the events leading to the termination of the UNPROFOR mission (especially NATO's extensive use of air power in August and September 1995, highlighted below) have shown that a more forceful approach had always been an option. Both these arguments are flawed.

UNPROFOR and Chapter VII

In the debate about the UN's role in Bosnia, the argument has sometimes been made that Chapter VII resolutions allowed for "all necessary means" to be employed, and that the failure to use military force against the Bosnian Serbs earlier in the conflict had nothing to do with any restrictions imposed by the mandate.[43] While this is arguably correct in a narrow "technical" sense, it overlooks an important feature of Security Council decision-making with respect to the conflict. Although it is true that several resolutions sanctioned the use of force in defense of specific mandates, the Council was also careful always to *reaffirm* its earlier resolutions. Indeed, as far as those charged with implementing decisions on the ground were concerned,

> no single Security Council resolution on Bosnia [could] be read in isolation from the others. Even in those that allowed for the use of force, the Security Council reaffirmed its previous resolutions on UNPROFOR; in other words, it did not want UNPROFOR to abandon its existing mandates in order to undertake new ones. UNPROFOR thus had the difficult challenge of reconciling its authority to use force with its obligation to perform all the other tasks mandated by the Security Council—tasks which required the cooperation of, and deployment amongst, all parties to conflict.[44]

Moreover, as noted earlier, the Council frequently passed resolutions in response to specific challenges on the ground. Adopting a resolution under Chapter VII might have given the impression of resolve and firm action but it did not, in the minds of its drafters, indicate a move away from UNPROFOR's core mission objectives toward enforcement. Particularly noteworthy in this context was the link created between Chapter VII and the "security of UNPROFOR personnel" (UN Security Council Resolution 807 [UNSC 807]) and the subsequent extension of Chapter VII to UNPROFOR's "freedom of movement" (UNSC 847). It is evident from the circumstances of their adoption that these resolutions did not amount to an abandoning of "peacekeeping" principles in favor of enforcement, however flawed the application of these principles was to the circumstances of Bosnia. Instead, as Shashi Tharoor rightly points out, Chapter VII was used here as a procedural device to "reinforce UNPROFOR's self-defense capability, through the strengthening of equipment and local redeployment of military units, as a result of the increased threat to the security of UNPROFOR personnel."[45]

The End of UNPROFOR's Mission: The Significance of "Operation Deliberate Force"

To many observers, the NATO-led air campaign against the Bosnian Serb Army (BSA) in late August and early September 1995—termed Operation Deliberate Force—is seen as supporting the argument that a more forceful option was always available to UNPROFOR in Bosnia. In this view, it was NATO's belated air campaign that finally "produced the results" that allowed agreement to be reached. This, in turn, has been presented and accepted in some quarters as a wider lesson from the conflict in Bosnia for policy-makers regarding the use of force. It is clear, for example, that Western leaders, in assuming that the shock of an air campaign in late March 1999 would quickly lead Milosevic to back down and abandon his repressive policies in Kosovo, were basing their case on this particular reading of how the UN operation in Bosnia had been brought to an end.

There can be no doubt that weakening the military position of the Bosnian Serbs allowed for progress at the negotiating table in 1995. The NATO air campaign was only one of several factors, however, that helped to turn the tables on the Bosnian Serbs. A major weakening of their position had already taken place before the air campaign was launched. Specifically, the spectacular success of Croatia's military offensives, first in Sector West in May 1995 and later in the Krajina in August, had profoundly altered the strategic predicament of the BSA. The Croat offensives, supported and strongly encouraged by the United States and Germany and eventually resulting in the single largest instance of forced population displacement ("ethnic cleansing" for short) in the period between 1991 and 1995, was one of the preconditions for the effective use of force in September. Another was the fact that by late August, UNPROFOR troops had been withdrawn from the areas of most acute vulnerability in Bosnian Serb–controlled territory to the weapon-collection points (WCP) around Sarajevo and Gorazde, the only remaining safe areas in eastern Bosnia. By this time, both Srebrenica and Zepa had, at a terrible cost, already fallen to Serbian forces and were no longer potential UN "hostages" in the event of further fighting. In late August, the remaining British troops in Gorazde were withdrawn shortly before the air campaign started. General Rupert Smith had initiated the withdrawal of troops from exposed and isolated locations soon after the debacle of the hostage crisis in May 1995. In doing so he effectively took away the "hostage card" from the BSA, thus severely limiting the scope for politically paralyzing action on the part of the Bosnian Serb leadership in the event of renewed crisis.

In addition to removing these points of military vulnerability, British and French forces had deployed a Rapid Reaction Force providing, for the first time, effective and accurate mortar and artillery support on Mount Igman near Sarajevo.[46] This gave UN forces a capability that had hitherto been lacking. Finally, after the disaster of Srebrenica and following the London conference in July 1995, command-and-control arrangements for the use of NATO air power in support of UN forces had been simplified and enshrined in a memorandum of understanding between NATO (CINCSOUTH) and the UN force commander. Specifically, it was now agreed that, henceforth, "graduated air operations would be initiated by a direct threat to or attack on safe areas as determined by the common judgement of NATO and UN military commanders."

Taken together, the combined effect of these developments was to prepare the ground for a deliberate transition to *enforcement* action and war-fighting. The necessary steps, which thus far had been consistently rejected by the Security Council and troop-contributing countries, had been taken for military force to be applied effectively. It signaled a decisive break with the efforts of UN forces over the previous three years to maintain its neutrality and impartiality in relation to the parties.

ATTITUDES TOWARD THE USE OF FORCE

During the entire UNPROFOR mission troop-contributing nations made it perfectly clear to the UN Secretariat—through formal channels as well as informal consultations—that they did not want their troops to die in enforcement action in the former Yugoslavia. Indeed, to the extent possible, they sought to avoid the deployment of their own contingents to high-risk areas, particularly to the safe areas. This deeply held concern about the security of personnel shown by troop contributors provides a reality that simply cannot be wished away in any assessment of the UN's performance.

A telling illustration of this can be found in the events leading up to the

London conference in July 1995, specifically in the reaction and attitudes of the British government. This conference is often portrayed as the occasion when the international community, some ten days after the fall of Srebrenica, finally said "enough is enough" and drew a line in the sand, warning the Bosnian Serbs that any further encroachments on the safe areas would lead to instant and massive retaliation. It is true that the feeling among British ministers was indeed that Srebrenica was a "defining moment," but not only in the sense often portrayed. Their immediate worry following the fall of the enclave was the security of British troops in the remaining eastern enclave of Gorazde, and the ministers were determined, above all, to avoid a repeat of the military humiliation that the Dutch UN contingent experienced in Srebrenica. Whatever the context, there is nothing more likely to damage a government politically than a military humiliation suffered by its own troops, and John Major's cabinet was deeply conscious of this fact. Indeed, the fixation on the fate of British troops in Gorazde was such that the force commander felt obliged, at one point during the London conference, to remind the ministers that his responsibilities as *UN* force commander included but also went beyond the security of British troops in the remaining eastern enclave.[47]

All troop-contributing countries, including such traditionally staunch supporters of the Organization as the Nordic countries, were fundamentally in agreement with the stress on sticking to peacekeeping modes of operation as long as personnel were lightly equipped, exposed, and widely dispersed throughout the theatre of operations. When, for example, the Secretariat requested Nordic troops to be redeployed from Tuzla to the safe area of Srebrenica, the request was turned down, ostensibly on logistic grounds. In fact, the Nordic governments preferred the *relative* safety of Tuzla (not an enclave in Serb-controlled territory) because it involved less of a risk to its soldiers serving with UNPROFOR.[48]

But there is another issue that needs to be addressed, and this is the attitudes of the UN Secretariat and senior officials in the field to the question of the use of force more generally. Specifically, it has been argued that key officials serving with the UN, both in the field and perhaps especially within the Peacekeeping Operations and Political Affairs Departments in New York, were instinctively or "temperamentally" uncomfortable with the idea of using greater force, and that this had the effect of delaying a necessary reassessment of the mission, especially in the spring of 1995. In this view, there was within the Organization a deep institutional attachment to the "classic" principles of peacekeeping, fortified by some very real achievements. The UN's "Srebrenica report" speaks of an "institutional ideology of impartiality" and a "pervasive ambivalence within the United Nations regarding the role of force in the pursuit of peace."[49] In the field this ambivalence was embodied in the attitudes and approach of the SRSG and head of mission, Yasushi Akashi. Coming from the UN mission in Cambodia where the question of enforcement to "flush out the Khmer

Rouge" had briefly been raised but decisively rejected, Akashi was deeply influenced by what one advisor described as an essentially "pacifist" outlook.[50] Others have pointed to statements by senior UN officials, including the Secretary-General, that seemed to suggest that *enforcement* should be ruled out almost under all circumstances. Thus the Secretary General's concluding "personal thoughts" on the future of the UNPROFOR mission in late May 1995 noted that "we must not lose sight of three interconnected objectives which represent the essence of the United Nations: the quest for peace, the protection of human life and the rejection of a culture of death. These objectives take time to attain and they will be attained *only through the successful use of non-military methods.*"[51]

This is a striking passage because it breaks quite sharply with what is otherwise a tightly and analytically argued document; the passage does indeed feel like "personal thoughts."[52] But more interestingly, however, is the apparent failure to recognize that there might be a problem here: is it really the case that the "quest for peace and the protection of human life . . . will only be attained through the use of non-military means"? One powerful counter-example from the UN's recent history is the genocide in Rwanda, which in April and May 1994 was finally brought to an end, not through the tireless pursuit by international officials of a cease-fire, but through the military victory of the Rwandan Patriotic Front against the genocidal regime in Kigali.

In the particular case of UNPROFOR's last year in Bosnia, the record shows that the force commander in Bosnia, Lieutenant General Rupert Smith, rightly deserves recognition for having realized earlier than most in the UN system that a critical juncture had been reached by late March and early April of 1995; consent, such as it was, had been effectively withdrawn and some way of "seizing the initiative" rather than continuing to "muddle through" had to be found. Yet he was also fully aware of the need to obtain the Security Council's and troop-contributing countries' support of any action that might allow him to "seize the initiative." There are *two* recurring themes in the reporting from BHC HQ in the spring of 1995: (1) a plea that the Security Council answer "the fundamental question of whether the UN should enforce and escalate for aims other than self-defense," and (2) if an attempt to "seize the initiative" was to be taken—for example, by launching a helicopter re-supply operation to the eastern enclaves that would also serve to confront and face down the Serbs—approval for such an effort from the troop-contributing nations, along with a clear understanding of the risks involved, would have to be obtained in advance. In both cases, General Smith was to be disappointed. As described above, up until this point there remained an extraordinary reluctance on the part of Member States to become engaged in enforcement action and to risk the lives of its nationals in a conflict where a "compelling national interest" was not deemed to be at stake.

Concluding Thoughts

One may legitimately ask whether nonforceful UN peacekeeping was ever the appropriate response to the particular circumstances generated by the disintegration of Yugoslavia. It is certainly no secret that senior UN officials in 1992 were deeply skeptical about involving the UN in the conflict.[53] Many of the concerns expressed at that time were borne out by events over the next three years. Nevertheless, troop-contributing governments persisted with UN peacekeeping because it allowed them to respond in a way that limited the hazard to their own forces in the field and thus remained within the bounds of what was acceptable at home. In drawing lessons from the events in Bosnia during 1992–1995 there has been a tendency—especially marked in the Op-Ed pages of many Western newspapers and in the recommendations of various high-profile, blue-ribbon committees—to bemoan the "lack of political will" and insist that we need more of it, leaving it at that. Between 1992 and 1995, when challenged by angry journalists to explain setbacks and account for the lack of progress on the ground, beleaguered and harassed UN officials (including the Secretary-General himself) naturally and not unreasonably also tended to emphasize the absence of political will among Member States. While there is undeniably a solid core of truth to this argument, it is also true that troop contributors simply did not believe that a more forceful exercise of will justified the costs to themselves. As the war dragged on, the contradictions and tensions in UNPROFOR's mandate became ever more acute, and by the early spring of 1995 a critical moment had clearly been reached. For reasons explored in this paper, key governments and troop-contributing countries, but also some senior UN officials, even then remained deeply reluctant to face up to this reality. This explains, in part, why it took the Srebrenica and other tragedies, including the humiliation of the Dutch contingent, to bring about a decisive policy shift toward enforcement and confrontation with the Bosnian Serbs.

In short, one of the lessons to draw from the UN experience in Bosnia is that one should have no illusions about the requirements and calculated risks of enforcement action. It is also evident from the above that the UN itself is not, and remains very unlikely ever to become, an instrument capable of organizing and directing enforcement operations. Not only is the Organization structurally ill-equipped to do so, but the political obstacles are even more formidable.

Finally, the experience of international involvement in Bosnia between 1992 and 1995 points to one final conclusion: the choice of instrumentality for intervening in civil-war-type conflicts and the strategic aims that underpin such interventions need to be worked out in *advance* of deployment and should not be left for ill-equipped contingents to sort out once they arrive in the theater.[54] This may, of course, be asking too much of governments whose decisions regarding military intervention have always been, and are bound to remain, influenced by a variety of different motives and pressures. Still, it is to be hoped that a better understanding of what the UN *can* and, crucially, what it *cannot* achieve has emerged from three years of brutal and bloody conflict in the Balkans.

NOTES

1. The question posed in the title is taken from an article by Conor Cruise O'Brien written in the autumn of 1993. In spite of the acute troubles facing the UN in Bosnia and Somalia at the time, O'Brien argues that some credit is nevertheless "due to the United Nations, in its unacknowledged role as scapegoat for the vanities and follies of statesmen." Conor Cruise O'Brien, "Faithful Scapegoat to the World," *The Independent*, 1 October 1993. The author is most grateful for the comments provided by Derek Boothby and David Keen on an earlier draft of this paper.

2. ICFY was set up at the London conference on the former Yugoslavia in late August 1992. The co-chairmen of ICFY's Steering Committee were Cyrus Vance, representing the UN, and David Owen, representing the EU. On 1 May 1993, Thorvald Stoltenberg, a former Norwegian foreign minister, replaced Vance as UN representative and co-chairman of ICFY. The first meeting of the so-called "Contact Group," comprising representatives of Britain, Russia, the United States, France, and Germany, was held in London in late April 1994. It was created in order to establish a "united front" vis-à-vis the parties and its initial efforts focused on securing agreement on a territorial division of Bosnia as a preliminary step towards a political settlement.

3. It follows from this that I am purporting to present a comprehensive or chronologically coherent overview of the UN's involvement in Bosnia. Such an overview would, for example, have required that Bosnia and the UN's mission there be looked at, not in isolation, but as part of the wider conflict and the whole of the UN's mission in the former Yugoslavia. Instead, the focus here is on certain key events and themes that, hopefully, will throw some light on issues central to a proper understanding of the UN's performance in Bosnia, as well as to the overarching theme of applying leverage in peace operations. For the purposes of this chapter, the UN presence on the ground in Bosnia is referred to as UNPROFOR even though, until March 1995, this name was not confined to the mission in Bosnia.

4. Sir David Hannay, "The UN's Role in Bosnia Assessed," *Oxford International Review*, vol. 7, no. 2 (spring 1996): 5.

5. The wars of Yugoslav succession are more accurately described as a mixture of "civil" and "international" war. Therein lays, of course, also one of the sources of disagreement among the external actors seeking to address the conflict.

6. "Report of the Secretary-General Pursuant to Security Council Resolutions 982 (1995) and 987 (1995)," 30 May 1995, paragraph 66.

7. Ibid.

8. Hannay, "The UN's Role in Bosnia Assessed," 5.

9. Yasushi Akashi, "Managing United Nations Operations," in Wolfgang Biermann and Martin Vadset, eds., *UN Peacekeeping in Trouble: Lessons Learned from the Former Yugoslavia* (Aldershot, UK: Ashgate Publishing, 1998), 134.

10. Chuck Sudetic provides the best account of the events in the autumn of

1992; see Chuck Sudetic, *Blood and Vengeance: One Family's Story of the War in Bosnia* (New York: W. W. Norton, 1998), 154–64. It is also briefly covered in the "Report of the Secretary-General Pursuant to General Assembly Resolution 53/35: The Fall of Srebrenica," General Assembly Document, A/54/549 (henceforth "UN Srebrenica Report"), paragraphs 33–37.

11. Sudetic, *Blood and Vengeance*, 164 and "UN Srebrenica Report."

12. Warren Christopher on *Public Broadcasting Service MacNeil-Lehrer*, 1 June 1993 (transcript: interview on MacNeil-Lehrer), *ISIS European Wireless Service*. UNSC Resolution 713 was adopted unanimously by the Council on 25 September 1991, obliging all states "immediately [to] implement a general and complete embargo on all deliveries of weapons and military equipment to Yugoslavia."

13. Mats Berdal, "Fateful Encounter: The United States and UN Peacekeeping," *Survival*, vol. 31, no. 1 (spring 1994): 35–36; Laura Silber and Allan Little, *The Death of Yugoslavia* (London: Penguin Books, 1995), 319–20; and Susan Woodward, *Balkan Tragedy* (Washington, DC: Brookings Institution, 1995), 324.

14. *Keesing's Record of World Events*, 39,426.

15. Richard Ullman, ed., *The World and Yugoslavia's Wars* (New York Council on Foreign Relations, 1996). Jane Sharp's review appeared in *Survival*, vol. 39, no. 2 (summer 1997): 159.

16. For details of this war and Croatia's crucial role in it, see judgement in the case *Prosecutor vs. Tihomir Blaskic*, UN ICTFY, The Hague, 1999. General Blaskic was found guilty and sentenced by the UN Tribunal for "having ordered the commission of a crime against humanity for persecution of the Muslim civilians of Bosnia."

17. In its "end of tour" report covering the period from mid-May to mid-November 1993, the 1st Battalion of the Prince of Wales's Own Regiment reported that the period of the battalion's time as "BRITBAT has been marked by almost continual fighting between HVO and BiH in Central Bosnia. A number of cease fires and political agreements have come and gone . . . there has been little progress towards lasting solution to this country's problems and the population of Central Bosnia has become firmly polarized into Croat and Muslim areas; a polarization which has irrevocably changed the demography of the area."

18. Private interviews in New York and London.

19. "UN Srebrenica Report," paragraph 64.

20. UN Security Council Resolution 824 (1993), 6 May 1993.

21. According to the "UN Srebrenica Report," during Council discussions about the draft resolution on 5 May, Chinmaya Gharekan, Special Political Advisor to Boutros-Ghali, made it clear that "UNPROFOR could not be expected to take on this additionally responsibility within its existing resources and that it would need at least one brigade in each town declared a safe area," and concluded that the Secretary-General "did not have the means to implement the draft resolution" ("UN Srebrenica Report," paragraph 66).

22. UN Security Council Resolution 824 (1993), 6 May 1993.

23. "UN Srebrenica Report," paragraph 68.

24. UN Security Council Resolution 824 (1993), 6 May 1993, paragraph 7.

25. UN Security Council Resolution 836 (1993), 4 June 1993, paragraph 4.

26. Memorandum, Permanent Representative of Pakistan (S/25782), 14 May 1993.

27. The "Bosnian-Serb Assembly" rejected the Vance–Owen plan on 6 May, and

this decision was apparently upheld by a "referendum" organized by the Pale leadership held in Serb-controlled territory on 15 and 16 May.

28. Sudetic, *Blood and Vengeance*, 168.

29. Testimony of Warren Christopher (18 May 1993), 93.

30. S/25800, quoted in the "UN Srebrenica Report."

31. Thorvald Stoltenberg and Kai Eide, *De Tusen Dagene: Fredsmeklere pØ Balkan* (Oslo: Gyldendal Norsk Forlag), 85.

32. UN Security Council Resolution 836 (1993), 4 June 1993.

33. The following account is based in part on interviews with and information obtained from officials at the UN, troop-contributing countries, and Council members.

34. From Annan (DPKO) to Stoltenberg (Zagreb) for Wahlgren, 4 June 1993: Subject: Security Council Resolution 836 (1993), (attached: "Clarifications Required in Regard to Security Council Resolution 836").

35. From Annan (DPKO) to Stoltenberg (Zagreb) for Wahlgren, 7 June 1993: Subject: Implementation of Security Council Resolution 836 (1993)—"safe areas" in Bosnia and Herzegovina.

36. Debate, S/PV.3228, 4 June 1993, in *The "Yugoslav" Crisis in International Law: General Issues*, part I, ed. D. Bethlehem and March Weller (p. 287) (Cambridge: Cambridge University Press).

37. Ibid., 295.

38. Hannay, 6.

39. Cedric Thornberry, "The Lessons of Yugoslavia," paper presented to the Centre for Defence Studies seminar, King's College, London, 7 December 1993. The paper is reprinted in *Brassey's Defence Yearbook 1994* (London: Brassey's, 1994), 167–73.

40. COHA, paragraph 6, 31 December 1994.

41. Statement of Madeleine Albright, *Hearing Before Subcommittee on International Security, International Organizations and Human Rights of the Committee on Foreign Affairs*, House of Representatives, 103rd Congress, 17 May 1994, 8.

42. Adding to the tensions, of course, was also the growing evidence in the second half of 1994 of covert American support, in violation of the arms embargo, for the Bosnian–Croat federation in 1994.

43. Paul Williams and Michael Scharf, "The Letter of the Law," in *With No Peace to Keep: United Nations Peacekeeping and the War in the Former Yugoslavia*, ed. Ben Cohen and George Stamksoki (pp. 34–41) (London: Grainpress Ltd., 1995).

44. Shashi Tharoor, "Should UN Peacekeeping Go 'Back to Basics'?" *Survival*, vol. 37, no. 34 (winter 1995–96): 59.

45. Draft May 95 Report, Office of SRSG, paragraph 13.

46. *Strategic Survey 1995–96* (Oxford: Oxford University Press for Institute for International Security Studies, 1996), 130.

47. Private interviews.

48. Interviews. In private, it was conceded to me quite readily that this was the deeper motivation for the Norwegians to resist relocation to Srebrenica.

49. "UN Srebrenica Report," paragraph 505.

50. "Pacifist" refers here to a general conviction that force cannot solve any problems; indeed, that it is only likely to make matters worse. While this conviction is honorable, it is also questionable.

51. *Report of the Secretary-General Pursuant to Security Council Resolutions 982 (1995) and 987 (1995)*, 30 May 1995, paragraph 80 (my emphasis).

52. It should be added that in terms of general attitudes to the use of force, these "personal thoughts" appear to reflect Akashi's thinking rather than those of Boutros Boutros-Ghali who, after all, had shown in the case of Somalia in 1993 that he was quite prepared to contemplate and encourage the heavy use of military force.

53. This is the case especially with respect to Bosnia. See the report drawn up by Marrack Goulding after his fact-finding mission to Bosnia in May 1992 where he recommended against a UN peacekeeping operation on the grounds that the situation was too "dangerous, violent and confused" (S/23900, 12 May 1992, paragraph 25).

54. The UN's year 2000 deployment to Sierra Leone raises serious question as to whether that lesson has been fully internalized by the Security Council.

CHAPTER TWO

Leveraging Namibian Independence

JEAN KRASNO

A UN SUCCESS

Namibia's independence is clearly one of the United Nations' greatest success stories. However, there is a prevailing myth that Namibian independence was an "easy" UN operation, achieved in the end because everybody wanted it. The purpose of this chapter is to dispel that notion as a simplistic whitewashing of a very complex set of events. In fact, Namibian independence is distinguished by an extended orchestration of the use of leverage over several decades by various actors and groups of actors in the face of shifting, countervailing forces that sought to obstruct the transfer of power to the Namibian people. The convergence of leveraging factors culminated in the implementation of Security Council Resolution 435 in 1989 and the deployment of UNTAG, the UN Transition Assistance Group for Namibia. However, the skillful manipulation of leverage did not stop with the arrival of UNTAG in Namibia in the spring of 1989.

The year 1989 was fraught with violence and intimidation by those who either resisted independence, trying to thwart the entire process, or by those who accepted independence but only under white control. UNTAG under the leadership of Special Representative Martti Ahtisaari, and later with his deputy Legwaila Joseph Legwaila, struggled almost on a daily basis to keep the threat of violence below a level that would have derailed the process. What is often forgotten is that Resolution 435 gave the power to the South African Administrator General to run the voters' registration and the elections. The only power that Ahtisaari had was his right to declare the elections "free and fair." The UN had to manage skillfully the

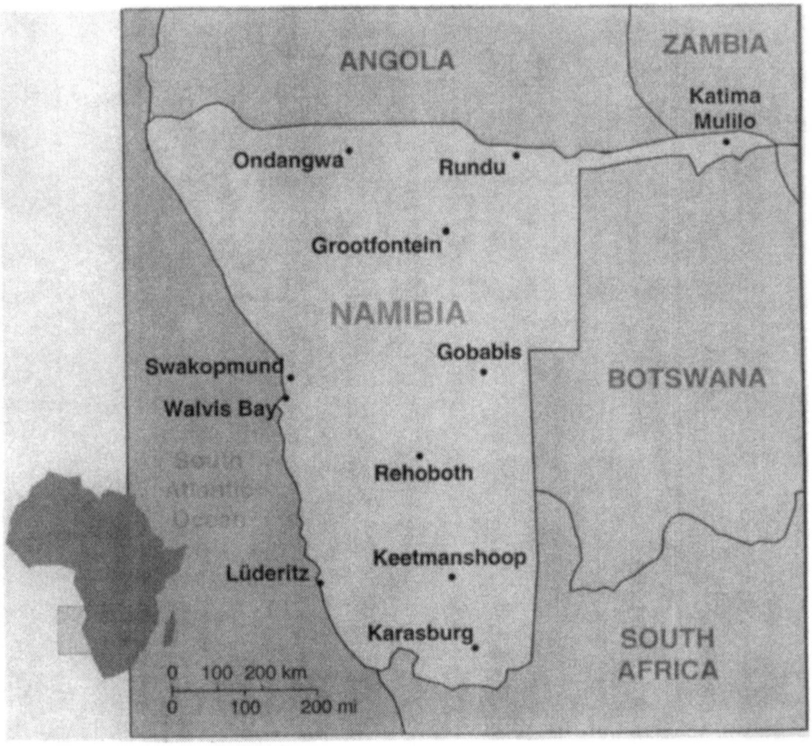

leverage they had available to them to keep the plan on track right up to the moment the votes were counted.

In this chapter, the examination of the use of leverage in the Namibian case is divided into three time periods, each representing different shifts in the centers of power, the type and weight of leverage used, and the opposing forces that sought to obstruct and delay independence: (1) the postcolonial period of 1964–1976, (2) the period between 1977 and 1988, and (3) 1989, the year of the implementation of UNTAG.

As discussed in the introduction to this book, the concept of leverage is defined here as the use of, or threat to use, power to inflict harm and/or the offering of incentives in order to compel a change in behavior. In this case, leverage was brought to bear on South Africa to end its colonial rule in Namibia. Leverage can take the form of: (1) military force, or the threat to use force, (2) economic and political sanctions or incentives, (3) sociopolitical isolation (or in the South African case, ending isolation), and (4) the utilization of less tangible but nevertheless effective qualities such as trust, impartiality, and moral authority. These tools of leverage are most successful when applied consistently by a common coalition of partners. If there is a split in the partnership or a weakening of will, leverage is less successful and will probably not achieve the desired goal. Orchestrating these factors to achieve a common end within the international context is a complex process. Not only do alliances and the will to act shift, but subtle changes can thwart the timing of diplomatic intervention. It takes tremendous skill and sensitivity to identify these shifts in will and capacity to be able to apply leverage successfully. A sense of timing and knowledge of which tools to use when will determine whether or not the key actors can manage a successful outcome. It is like a surfer waiting for the right wave, but then needing the skill to ride it all the way into shore.

The UN, and others who sought Namibian independence, was confronted with a South African government that not only controlled a vast source of wealth but that was also stricken with a deadly fear of losing its control to the black majority. For decades, shifting centers of leverage and domestic pressure continued to sway the balance toward and then away from the objective. This chapter examines the forms of leverage used in the Namibian case, the centers of leverage as expressed by countries or groups of countries, the convergence of this leverage, the weakening of countervailing forces within South Africa, and, finally, the management of these tools during the UNTAG period up to the very end of the transition process.

Historical Background

Early History

Before discussing how leverage was used to achieve Namibian independence and democratic rule, it is important to set the stage on which these events took place. Namibia has historically been a large and sparsely populated region bounded on one side by the Kalahari desert, which spans most of Namibia's eastern frontier, and on the other side by a rugged range of mountainous terrain carving out a largely impenetrable coastline. The northern growing area borders Angola, and the southern diamond region spreads across into South Africa. The summer rainy season, lasting from December to March, brings the only water to this largely arid climate.

The first peoples to inhabit the region were the Bushman and Nama, with the Herero and Ovambo arriving later in the sixteenth and eighteenth centuries.[1] The Germans began to move into Namibia, or what was then called South West Africa, during the late nineteenth century and declared the area to be a German colony in 1884. The German period of colonial control was marked by brutality. As a result, the Herero and Nama, who occupied the most productive land, staged a number of uprisings during 1903–1906 in response to German settlers taking over their communal lands. The Herero uprising of 1904 resulted in the near-extermination of the Herero people, with approximately 65,000 being killed off by the superior German firepower. German control of South West Africa ended in 1915 with the outbreak of the First World War when South Africa was encouraged by Great Britain to invade the territory. At the end of the war, the League of Nations entrusted the region to South Africa as a mandate to prepare it for a transition to independence and to "to preserve the material and moral well-being and the social progress of the inhabitants."[2] However, the brutal labor policies initiated by the Germans were continued by South Africa, which also encouraged white settlers to move onto more of the farmland. South Africa's plan for the region was annexation and control of the rich diamond areas of the south, not independence. While the League disapproved of South Africa's actions, it was too weak to do anything about it.[3]

When the United Nations was created at the end of the Second World War, South Africa informed the Organization that it intended to annex the region. United Nations members rejected this plan, but South Africa began its de facto annexation. In 1948, it granted the South West African white population eight seats in the South African parliament. By the early 1950s the system of Apartheid imposed in South Africa was also implemented in Namibia.

Apartheid in Namibia

During the 1950s, discrimination and oppression of nonwhites continued in Namibia much as it did in South Africa, along with the notorious "homelands" policy. In the capital of Namibia, Windhoek, the native population was moved out of the "old location" and into an outlying "township" called Katutura. The "coloureds" were moved into a separate area located between Katutura and central Windhoek. Each of these "townships" was separated by a wide expanse of highways so that it would be easy to patrol any movement from one area to the other. In Katutura the tribal groups were also separated, and even the addresses on the small houses were marked by a number that was preceded by a letter standing for the first letter of the ethnic group—for example, O for Ovambo, D for Damara, H for Herero, and so on. Separate councils were established for each group as well as separate schools. This "divide-and-conquer" policy was reinforced by a system of competing allocation of funds to councils and their leaders to keep them in control. This was accompanied by systemic repression and impunity for white enforcement mechanisms. A curfew from sunset to sunrise was strictly enforced according to which all nonwhites had to return to their townships. A specific time was not established so that enforcement was arbitrary and left up to the interpretation of the police. One story is told how a black man was shot dead when walking from Windhoek to Katutura while it was still daylight because the police decided that he would never make it back to Katutura by sunset.[4]

The Postcolonial Period: 1964–1976

The Formation of the Independence Movement in Namibia. The pressure for independence and indigenous self-rule had to come from within Namibia, from the Namibian people, as well as from the outside. The Namibian independence movement, therefore, was a key piece of the leverage package that worked to keep the issue alive in the international community and to make South Africa pay a price for its repressive policies. Two leading movements formed in the early 1960s, the South West African Peoples' Organization (SWAPO) and the South West African National Union (SWANU). Many of the leaders of these movements had attended the same high school just north of Windhoek, which was the only secondary school in the country that blacks were allowed to attend. The high school had been started by the missionaries and later taken over by the South African–run administration in Windhoek. Black Africans were not allowed to study science or math and certainly not politics. But black teachers secretly came to the school from Windhoek to teach the students about the political issues of the day and to educate them in forming an independence movement. The current prime minister, Hage Geingob, and the foreign minister, Theo-Ben Gurirab, attended the school.[5] Blacks were not allowed to attend college in Namibia, and this factor, along with political repression, forced many of the future black political leaders to leave Namibia to study abroad and rally support for their movements in capitals around the world.

The Organization of African Unity (OAU), newly formed in the early 1960s, was keenly aware of the need to support independence movements within countries in Africa still suffering under colonial rule. Within about a year of its founding in 1963, the OAU established the Liberation Committee (its full title is the Coordinating Committee for the Liberation of Africa, which was headquartered in Dar es Salaam, Tanganyika [now Tanzania]). The committee called together a meeting of the leaders and representatives of all the existing national liberation movements in Africa, including those of Mozambique, Angola, Rhodesia, Kenya, Uganda, and Guinea-Bissau, all the African countries that were not independent. They were mostly from eastern, central, and southern Africa. The leaders were asked to indicate to the Liberation Committee the ways and means by which they, as the people from these countries, proposed to proceed to achieve freedom and independence for their nations and people. They were asked to go back and prepare so-called programs of action, setting out their objectives and goals. This was done to allow the Liberation Committee not only to recognize movements that in its judgment deserved to be recognized and supported, but secondly and more importantly, to mobilize support for those movements throughout the world.

SWAPO and SWANU, the two Namibian movements, both attended this initial meeting and presented their programs of action. SWAPO, represented among others by Theo-Ben Gurirab, said in addition to seeking support in the United Nations to mobilize the international community for political assistance, it would also organize a military-resistance movement. SWAPO specifically asked the Liberation Committee and the OAU Member States to assist in training SWAPO combatants to launch the armed struggle. The first clashes between SWAPO and South African forces took place in 1966.[6] SWANU felt that the objective conditions in Namibia and the practicalities were such that they did not think the time was right for launching an armed struggle. Initially, both SWAPO and SWANU were recognized by the OAU as justifying support. Ultimately, the OAU decided that SWAPO was undertaking most of the campaigning and had gained international recognition and support beyond the OAU Member States, including the UN.[7] SWAPO was not only leveraging its position through political pressure but also through the threat of violence.

Based on the plans submitted to the Liberation Committee and upon its recommendation, the OAU, at a summit held in Rabat, Morocco, in 1972, decided to recognize those liberation movements that, in the judgment of OAU Member States, warranted support. In the case of Namibia, according to SWAPO member Theo-Ben Gurirab, "SWANU was not de-recognized, per se, but they somehow were not present [at the Rabat summit] and did not do what was expected of them."[8] After that exercise, the OAU, in 1972, recognized several liberation movements as the sole and authentic representatives of their people and it campaigned for their recognition, support, and assistance in the international community.

Leveraging within the UN Context. OAU Member States were also members of the United Nations. Therefore, within the UN context, these African leaders inserted actions taken by the OAU into resolutions introduced in the General Assembly, initiating similar actions and gaining additional support. The OAU utilized its members and influence with other Third World countries in the UN to leverage action in the General Assembly. It was on this basis that in 1973 SWAPO was given observer status within the UN. Theo-Ben Gurirab was directly involved from that point onwards, becoming the UN observer for SWAPO and one of the key players in orchestrating leverage within the UN and the international community. In 1976, SWAPO was recognized by the UN as the sole and authentic representative of the Namibian people. The OAU fostered a concept within the UN that Namibia was essentially under the trusteeship of the UN as a result of its mandate status under the League of Nations and the failure of South Africa to live up to its responsibilities. Namibia therefore was afforded a special status and SWAPO, as the "sole and authentic representative of the Namibian people," was given unique recognition.

SWAPO reached a point where, in 1978, the Organization was recognized as a Permanent Observer, as opposed to the simple observer status achieved in 1973. There is a difference in quality between the two and SWAPO was eventually provided with a seat in the General Assembly. This recognition elevated SWAPO to a level similar to countries like Switzerland, the Holy See that represents the Vatican, and intergovernmental organizations like the Organization of American States (OAS), and the Organization of African Unity. Among the liberation movements, only SWAPO and the Palestine Liberation Organization (PLO) enjoyed that status. In this way, the OAU and SWAPO were able to continue to keep the issue of Namibian independence alive within the international community and to press for action and resolutions in UN bodies.

Between 1966 and 1976 the United Nations passed a series of resolutions and established a number of entities in support of Namibian independence. The October 1966 General Assembly Resolution 2145 ended South Africa's mandate over Namibia and brought the issue directly under the auspices of the UN. The resolution also called for an *ad hoc* committee to study the situation and recommend practical means by which a transition could be administered. The next year, taking the report of the committee into account, the General Assembly under Resolution 2248 created the UN Council for South West Africa consisting of eleven Member States that was to administer the territory until independence and to set up a constituent assembly. A Commissioner for South West Africa was also established in 1967 and Martti Ahtisaari of Finland, who was later to become the Special Representative for UNTAG, was eventually chosen for that position.

The Council for Namibia, as it was later called, played somewhat of a mixed role. Because South Africa viewed the body as a tool of SWAPO, it refused to acknowledge the Council, which, therefore, in reality had no power to affect policy in Namibia. Also, the Council was prohibited from taking any role whatsoever, once UNTAG was implemented. However, the Council continued to meet and take positions on behalf of Namibia in consultation with SWAPO leaders, particularly Theo-Ben Gurirab, Sam Nujoma, and Hage Geingob. In addition, on behalf of Namibia, the Council signed international accords and entered into negotiations on UN General Assembly business. Later, when Namibia became independent, the country took over the commitments made under the Council without having to renegotiate these international arrangements.

While most of these decisions and resolutions were emanating from the General Assembly, the OAU, SWAPO, the African Group, and the Front-Line States (bordering on Namibia and South Africa) continued to seek leverage on the Security Council. By 1969, forty UN Member States requested an expedient meeting of the Security Council to address atrocities being carried out in Namibia under Apartheid. Security Council Resolutions 264 and 269 finally recognized the revocation of the South African mandate on South West Africa and demanded its withdrawal. Great Britain and France abstained on Resolution 264, and the United States, Great Britain, France, and Finland abstained on 269. With Great Britain, France, and the United States having strong economic ties with South Africa and serving as Permanent Members on the Security Council, it had been difficult to achieve any cooperation from that UN body. Therefore throughout this period it was the General Assembly that continued to take the lead. However, in 1970, the Security Council passed Resolution 283, calling on Member States to cease dealing with commercial and industrial enterprises in Namibia. With this action, the UN began to impose economic leverage against South Africa on the Namibian issue. At this point, it must be remembered that the UN was also taking a stand against South Africa on its Apartheid policies at home as well. By 1976 the Security Council was beginning to realize that it was being embarrassed by the moral authority that the General Assembly was creating for itself. The United States was also facing pressure in Congress from the Black Caucus, which had begun to strongly influence the American position. Now, finally armed with leverage from a decision by the International Court of Justice, numerous General Assembly resolutions, a growing moral authority, and constant lobbying from groups of Member States, the OAU through the African Group, with help from the Non-Aligned, pressured the Security Council to adopt Resolution 385 that called for elections in Namibia under UN supervision.

The culmination of efforts through this period demonstrated the constant search for leverage to achieve Namibian independence by the OAU, SWAPO, and others. The issue was kept alive and the big powers were gradually being coerced into taking a hesitant but declared stand on the issue. Nevertheless, the status quo remained in place because while there was significant leverage-building, the countervailing force of South African resistance and the weak will of the major Western powers on the Security Council continued to block any real action.

The Role of the International Court of Justice. The legitimacy of a cause also enhances the ability to leverage action. Therefore attempts were made several times to gain legal backing for the Namibia case within the International Court of Justice (ICJ). In 1949, the General Assembly passed Resolution 338 seeking an advisory opinion from the ICJ in The Hague on the Namibia issue. After a lengthy period, in 1950 the court ruled that "South West Africa is a territory under the international mandates assumed by the Union of South Africa." With the court backing South Africa's claim, the General Assembly failed to achieve the ruling they were seeking, even though the court also stated that this mandate should be under the supervision of the UN.[9] The ICJ essentially leveraged the South African position, and South Africa continued to ignore UN resolutions regarding Namibia.

The General Assembly tried again to gain leverage through the court by persuading Ethiopia and Liberia, as former members of the League of Nations, to bring the Namibian case before the ICJ in a lawsuit against South Africa. The court again failed to give the General Assembly what it wanted, saying that Ethiopia and Liberia did not have sufficient "legal interest to pursue the claim," because they did not border Namibia and hence did not directly suffer from the situation. The court also stated that the right to sue was exclusive to the League itself and not individual members. With the League no longer in existence, this left the UN again with no legal leverage on Namibian independence. Following the second attempt to gain legal authority and the court's avoidance of taking any action against South Africa's illegal activities, the General Assembly in 1966 passed Resolution 2145, which terminated South Africa's mandate and placed South West Africa under the direct responsibility of the United Nations. It wasn't until 1971, with changes in the judges on the court, that the ICJ finally upheld the General Assembly's revocation of the mandate and declared that South Africa was obliged to withdraw from the territory. Finally, the OAU, SWAPO, and other supporters in the UN had the legal legitimacy and leverage they were looking for.

The Period between 1976 to Early 1989

Leverage Appears to Succeed and Then Falls Apart. While much had been accomplished by 1976 within the UN, support among the Western powers for the many resolutions adopted by it was still weak. SWAPO and the African Group had leveraged decisions in the General Assembly and the Security Council, but this pressure was still not enough to break South Africa's intransigence. SWAPO had to keep up the pressure. It defined the struggle on three fronts: first, the national or peoples' resistance—that is, the Namibian people themselves rejecting colonialism and Apartheid and demanding freedom and independence. SWAPO had leaders who were a contingent of the people outside the country, but the credibility of the movement was dependent upon a clear demonstration of dissatisfaction and resistance inside Namibia. Therefore the peoples' resistance was the first front. The second front was diplomatic, which consisted of making connections within the UN, with international organizations, sympathetic parliamentarians, church leaders, and liberation support groups. SWAPO leaders campaigned around the world, explaining the aspirations of the Namibian people to these "friends" that provided them with assistance, including weapons. With this support they launched the third front—the armed struggle.[10]

With this plan they attempted to pull together four types of leverage: (1) physical force and the threat of violence through the armed struggle, (2) economic leverage through attempts to place economic sanctions on South Africa related to Namibian independence, (3) political pressure and political isolation through the continuing flow of resolutions that condemned South Africa for its actions, and (4) moral/legal leverage through the World Court and UN declarations. But SWAPO's resources were limited and still no match for those of South Africa and its supporters in the West, who still maintained economic and trade ties with the South African regime. While the moral authority for SWAPO's position was growing internationally, the United States was itself in a weakened state because of Watergate and its consequences and was unable to assume any kind of leadership role. SWAPO had to garner more resources on its side in order to overcome the countervailing forces it faced. Events outside its control continued to thwart its efforts. Even the sudden independence of neighboring Angola in 1975 had no effect for Namibians, who launched massive anticolonial demonstrations inside the country, only to be beaten down by a wave of deadly repression.

A decisive break came with the election of President Jimmy Carter in the United States, and as a consequence, the positioning of Andrew Young, former leader of the black movement in the United States, as ambassador to the UN and Cyrus Vance as Secretary of State. These people had a different approach to African issues than their predecessors. It was they who initiated consultations among the members of the Security Council—initially the Western members of the Security Council. The Western "permanent" members were the United States, Britain, and France, but at that time (1977–1978) West Germany and Canada were "nonpermanent" members representing the West on the Security Council. These five started what is now known as the "Western Contact Group on Namibia," which commenced a long, drawn-out negotiating process that eventually culminated in the adoption of Resolution 435. While the West in general abhorred Apartheid and South Africa's illegal actions in Namibia, many also feared SWAPO's leanings toward the communist world, where it had received much of its support. However, South Africa's intransigence and flagrant violations of human rights had become an embarrassment and world opinion was pressing for action. Nevertheless, the United States wanted to make sure that any decision emanating from the Security Council would be a product of the West that avoided input by the Soviet Union and China, now represented by the Peoples' Republic of China. More importantly, South Africa had refused to negotiate with the Security Council. Therefore the Contact Group (or Western Five) "operated outside the Security Council."[11] In a visit to South Africa, the Contact Group managed to convince South Africa that the pressure to impose economic sanctions was growing.[12] It then presented a report to the Security Council. Martti Ahtisaari, along with forty-six advisers, made a trip to Namibia in August 1978 to establish the role of the UN in the country's eventual independence. As a result of the two reports, on September 29, 1978 Security Council Resolution 435 was passed, establishing the United Nations Transition Assistance Group (UNTAG) that would oversee Namibian independence.

The initial optimism that blossomed following the passage of 435, however, soon died. There were a number of factors that continued to thwart independence. Primarily, South Africa still believed that it had other options: (1) the belief that it could militarily defeat SWAPO and its allies in Angola, (2) the belief that it could foster a white-dominated government structure within Namibia that would be accepted by the international community, and (3) the belief that SWAPO, if the elections were held immediately, would win and would impose socialist policies that might include the nationalization of white-owned industries and farms. South Africa needed time to build alternative political parties within Namibia to oppose SWAPO. In other words, South Africa was not ready to let go. The South Africans used the argument that the UN had been supporting SWAPO for years and was therefore not impartial. The personality of South African President P. W. Botha, who continued to intensify policies of Apartheid at home, was also a factor.

With South African delays blocking the process, the Carter administration ran out of time before it was voted out of office. The election of conservative Ronald Reagan, whose anti-Soviet/communist policies were to dominate U.S. foreign policy for the next eight years, brought an end to hopes for Namibia—for the near future at any rate. The Carter administration attempted a last-ditch effort by calling a meeting in Geneva in January 1981 to draw up a plan for a new constitution in Namibia. This included a "bill of rights" and other mechanisms for protecting private property that were later included in the final constitution adopted after independence. But the Reagan and Botha administrations found common ground in a pervading fear of communism, and the United States encouraged a position of "linkage" that tied the withdrawal of Cuban forces from Angola with Namibian independence. The presence of Cuban troops in Angola had not been a concern of South Africa at the time of Resolution 435. "The U.S. policy was used by the South Africans as a very important delaying tactic, enabling them to argue that they were actively engaged in negotiations with the United States, while in fact they were attempting to draw out negotiations and pursue an internal settlement."[13]

Shifting Factors End in Success. With Cubans troops still fighting in Angola, "linkage" continued to ensure the status quo in Namibia through 1988; however, a confluence of factors merged at that time that forced the issue to be addressed. In 1988, after suffering a series of defeats, the socialist Angolan government backed by the Soviet Union and armed with Cuban troops launched an offensive attack against the South African Defense Force at Cuito Cuanavale, causing heavy casualties. Cuban troops came very close to the Namibian border and a number of white South African soldiers were killed. The South African public began to question the cost of the war in Angola both in lives and money spent, estimated at about (US)$2 billion a year.[14] Military force was now playing a greater role in leveraging a weakening of South African resistance. An additional source of political leverage was now growing from within the country of South Africa itself in reaction to not only the war but also the effects of economic and military sanctions that were beginning to take hold and be felt. The National Party, which was losing supporters to the Conservative Party within South Africa, needed to take the initiative or it would lose its domestic control.

Pressure was converging within Namibia itself in 1988 as well. Early in the year, a bomb had exploded in the north of the country in a bank right at the time that people were in line to cash their paychecks. Many people were killed in the blast, including the daughter of Bishop Dumeni, a prominent religious leader of Namibia. Shortly after that event, students at a secondary school in the same region went on strike, protesting the presence of a South African military base near the school that not only housed the Defense Force but also the notorious Koevoet special forces. Bases had been strategically placed around Namibia next to schools, hospitals, and churches so that these public places could be used as shields against

SWAPO fighters. The students would often get caught in the cross-fire and be killed or wounded. Also, the Koevoet would use their position of power to rape and harass the girls. Finally, the students at the Ponhofi Secondary School had had enough and called a boycott. Within a few weeks, students throughout the north were boycotting classes in solidarity with the Ponhofi protesters. The brutal efforts of Koevoet to end the strike inflamed further outrage around the entire country. By June 1988 the student boycott had spread to Windhoek and from there to the rest of Namibia, joined by a massive workers' strike. All of this seemed disconnected with the efforts outside Namibia that were, in fact, beginning to reach a resolution to the removal of Cuban troops and an agreement with South Africa to end its colonial occupation.[15]

While SWAPO appears not to have directly organized the uprisings, the demonstrations played into its efforts to keep the pressure on South Africa and also to keep up the costs of maintaining its colonial presence in Namibia. Student demonstrations were something that had been going on since the 1970s. The first mass student uprising started during 1974 and 1975 with the collapse of the fascist regime in Portugal and the independence of Angola; it created a large wave, with thousands of young people openly pressing for independence. It was a tradition that had remained. The more the country was militarized, the more the students were refusing to cooperate with the South African regime. Over the years, schools had been taken over by the government across the country, and in the north were taken over by the army. It was the soldiers, armed with AK-47 rifles and other machine guns and wearing military fatigues, who were teaching the children.[16] While some of the student organizers must have known about the negotiations going on outside, very little information appeared in the Namibian press. What was printed in the media was dismissed as just being more of the same.[17]

In addition to the uprisings in Namibia, the shifts in the military situation in Angola, and the domestic scene inside South Africa, there were also changes in the political atmosphere of the cold war that were beginning to affect the Namibian issue. Under Gorbachev, the Soviet Union started to seek ways to improve its relationship with the West. It was beginning to understand that it could no longer afford to support wars of liberation around the world, and even though Cuba was stepping up its offensive in Angola, the Soviets were giving signs that they wanted to end their involvement. The Reagan administration had been holding a series of negotiations that included Cuba, Angola, and South Africa (but had excluded SWAPO). Only a few days after a number of South African soldiers had been killed, negotiations among the warring parties began to make headway in July 1988. South Africa was now looking for a way to get out of Angola; an agreement to withdraw all forces from Angola was reached in Brazzaville, Congo, in December 1988.[18] Having accepted the linkage policy, South Africa was now left with the other half of the deal: Namibian independence. Also, a key factor for the Angolans was the removal of the South African Defense Force from Namibia that had posed a threat to the cease-fire arrangement. Roger Hearn makes an important point that throws light on the events that followed: "It is important to note that South Africa's agreement to abide by R435 was essentially not related to a 'change of heart' about Namibian independence but from the domestic and international pressures impacting upon it."[19]

Other domestic factors began to converge at the same time. Cold-warrior Ronald Reagan was replaced by his vice president, George Herbert Walker Bush, who was elected in November 1988. Bush immediately put his foreign-policy team in place and instructed them to seek out peaceful solutions to conflicts not only in Africa but also in Central America. In South Africa, hard-liner President P. W. Botha was replaced by F. W. de Klerk who, a year later, in an effort to make peace at home as well, released Nelson Mandela from prison where he had spent some twenty-five years. With these changes, the countervailing forces that had blocked independence finally gave way to the convergence of leverage that was brought to bear by the OAU, SWAPO, the Front-Line States, the General Assembly, and, finally, the Western Five and the Security Council.

1989: Not a Piece of Cake

Getting off to a Bad Start

With the Brazzaville Protocol completed on December 13 and the Tripartite Accord signed in New York on December 22, 1988, the settlement plan, cease-fire, and the phased withdrawal of Cuban troops from Angola were established. The protocol agreement also created the Joint Commission to oversee the implementation of the accord, which consisted of Angola, Cuba, and South Africa as the three parties to the agreement and the United States and the Soviet Union as observers. The Security Council waited until after the Christmas holidays to return to work and establish a date for the deployment of UNTAG. On January 16, 1989 the Security Council passed Resolutions 628 and 629, which set April 1 as the start date for Resolution 435 and the United Nations Transition Assistance Group (UNTAG). However, in the following weeks, an argument broke out between the African Group backed by the Non-Aligned, who wanted to maintain the original budget and troop levels at 7,500 established by Resolution 435 in 1978, and the Western countries led by the United States who wanted to reduce the budget and troop levels by about a third. The African Group and Front-Line States believed that the violence on the ground in Namibia still called for a significant show of force, while the United States and its supporters believed that South Africa was cooperating to the extent that the originally planned force level was not necessary.

A compromise was finally reached through a proposal by Secretary-General Pérez de Cuéllar, who basically laid out a plan by which the implementation of 435 would begin at the lower level of 4,650 troops at a budget of $416 million but with an increase in police monitors from 350 to 500, with the caveat that increases could be made if necessary. The General Assembly finally approved the budget on March 1, 1989, only a month before deployment was to take place. The start date of April 1 was necessary because at least seven months was needed to prepare for elections that had to take place before the rainy season began at the end of November, at which point most of the roads in Namibia would be impassable. But the delay in approving the budget proved disastrous. By April 1 only a handful of troops were in place, and none were in the north of Namibia or near the border with Angola.

The April 1 Crisis. On March 31 and April 1, as Martti Ahtisaari, the Special Representative, was arriving in Windhoek amid celebratory demonstrations amassed along the lengthy stretch of road connecting the airport with downtown Windhoek, he was informed by South African Foreign Minister Pik Botha that SWAPO forces had crossed over the border from Angola, against provisions in the Brazzaville Protocol, and fighting had broken out in the north. Because of the delays in New York, the UN had no troops and no observers in the north and therefore had no independent source of information about SWAPO's movements or about the fighting. In a telephone call to Pérez de Cuéllar, Foreign Minister Botha threatened to pull out of the independence process if the UN did not allow South Africa to release its Defense Forces that had been confined to base in northern Namibia to repel what was being termed as a "SWAPO incursion."[20] Faced with a total dissolution of the transition process before it had even begun, Ahtisaari, with additional pressure from British Prime Minister Thatcher who happened to be in the region and the approval of Pérez de Cuéllar in New York, acquiesced. The UN was blind on the ground at the very moment that it needed critical information. The South Africans had complete control of the sources of information and the media. The "incursion" was presented as "thousands of heavily armed SWAPO troops" engaged in massive fighting in the north. The truth about those days in which over 300 people were killed, mostly SWAPO members, did not become apparent until weeks, months, or even years later.[21]

Briefly, according to interviews conducted for this research, what appears to have happened is that a combination of SWAPO forces from Angola and from inside Namibia gathered openly with their weapons ready to be demobilized by the UN. While Marrack Goulding and others within the UN claimed that there were no SWAPO fighters inside Namibia,[22] others like Bishop Dumeni who lives in the north and later helped to return some of the guerrillas to Angola disagrees by saying, "Yes, they were here. You cannot see them because they were civilians. But their weapons were here. Maybe some crossed the border. But there is also a matter of fact that some were already here."[23] When the SWAPO fighters were unable to find the UN, they suddenly found themselves under attack by South African police, which was in fact an antiguerrilla paramilitary force, and special-forces units, the Koevoet, who under the agreement were not confined to base. Historically, the role of these South African forces was to seek out SWAPO fighters and sympathizers and kill or torture them for information. Generally, their policy was "take no prisoners." Koevoet were paid a bounty for every SWAPO member killed.[24] Therefore they were glad to have the opportunity to open fire on these groups of guerrilla fighters who were caught out in the open. With the release of the South African Defense Force the slaughter increased and in the end about 314 SWAPO were killed and about 38 captured, with only 30 South African police and soldiers killed. Other innocent people were killed and wounded in the cross-fire, allegedly at the hands of the South African forces. South African troops hurriedly buried many SWAPO fighters in mass graves, making it difficult to obtain a final count.[25]

SWAPO leaders admit that everybody is in one way or another responsible for the tragedy of April 1.[26] As stated earlier, SWAPO had not been invited to become a part of the negotiations on the removal of Cuban troops that led to the agreement on Namibian independence. In addition, SWAPO had never accepted the linkage concept and therefore had not wanted to participate. This situation led to different interpretations on the issue of SWAPO demobilization and where this was supposed to take place. The Joint Commission had agreed that SWAPO would be confined to an area above the 16th parallel in Angola, but SWAPO itself had never agreed to that. SWAPO continues to maintain that the issue had never been resolved.[27] The language was "confinement of forces to base." South Africa maintained that the SWAPO terrorists did not have military bases inside the country and that the West should not try to accord SWAPO an advantage by allowing them to build military bases inside the country that they did not have at the time. South Africa maintained that SWAPO came into Namibia to carry out terrorist activities and then ran back into Angola.

SWAPO claimed that it was a guerrilla army, not a conventional army, and therefore operated in small units and was everywhere in the country. Its leaders drew attention to the fact that on a weekly basis the South African government itself complained about activities carried out by SWAPO inside the country. Since guerrilla armies do not operate from bases, SWAPO claimed that the United Nations, the Western Contact Group, and the Front-Line States should have ensured that those SWAPO military units that were inside Namibia should have been informed through channels that they were to gather at two or three locations and be confined to specified camps. SWAPO argued that it was inconceivable that they were asked to withdraw their troops inside Namibia across terrain, which had been accepted as a "no-go" area, into Angola. They could not just walk through the area with their forces.[28] This came as a surprise to the Western countries, because they felt that they had solved that problem in the negotiations with South Africa, Angola, and Cuba in 1988.

After the protocols had been signed, SWAPO leaders still argued that the UN and Western countries had wrongly interpreted the situation to mean that the Angolans, the Cubans, and the Soviets would take care of SWAPO.[29] This meant that the Angolans were supposed to guard the SWAPO encampments with support from the Cubans and the Soviets. SWAPO was frustrated by what it perceived as the Western Five buying the South African argument that SWAPO was *not* inside the country. SWAPO considered the issue unresolved. Nevertheless, SWAPO leaders clearly knew the nature of the agreement by the Joint Commission and that SWAPO fighters were expected to demobilize inside Angola whether they had agreed to it or not. However, some feel that SWAPO leader Sam Nujoma still wanted to make the point that it, SWAPO, had a right to demobilize inside its own country. Therefore SWAPO can also be blamed for not informing its people about the dangers of crossing openly into Namibia.[30]

Leveraging an End to the Fighting. With no independent information of its own on the situation in the north, the UN took several days to assess the crisis and sort out the disinformation coming out of Pretoria. The fighting had to be stopped and the operation salvaged. The UN membership as a whole was still somewhat confused by what had happened. But the members of the Joint Commission were quite clear on what had occurred and why.[31] At this point, it was in the interests of both the United States and the Soviets to get the Namibia issue off the international agenda. The Soviets no longer were interested in paying for the war in Angola, and the United States was being pressured on human-rights grounds to end South African repression in Namibia. By April 8 Sam Nujoma had been reached in Angola and convinced to agree to call SWAPO fighters back across the border. In a press statement released on April 8, 1989, in Luanda, Angola, the president of SWAPO, Sam Nujoma said:

> We believe South Africa needs every pretext to stop Namibia's independence process. Therefore, although we are very clear in our minds that the UN Plan for the independence of Namibia provides very clearly for the confinement of SWAPO troops to assembly points inside Namibia after the cease-fire came into effect, we have decided to make a concession on this issue because we realized that South Africa fears that such assembly points will make SWAPO win the planned UN supervised elections.

This statement was the result of pressure that had been brought to bear by members of the Joint Commission (led by Cuba) who had called on Nujoma and convinced him that it was imperative to bring the fighting to an end.[32] A delegation of the Joint Commission also met that weekend (April 8–9) inside Namibia at a resort called Mount Etjo, which is about two hundred miles north of Windhoek. The UN had not been invited to attend on Saturday, April 8, and only joined the group on Sunday. By that time the five had already agreed on a cease-fire arrangement that included the return of SWAPO fighters to Angola.[33]

With the Cuban-led delegation exerting leverage to gain SWAPO concessions as expressed in the statement made by Nujoma on Saturday, the Joint Commission had only to pressure South Africa to return its forces to base and renew the independence process. This was achieved at the discussions at Mount Etjo, and Thornberry and Pienaar were tasked to compose the final agreement. Thornberry relates that Chester Crocker, the U.S. observer to the Commission, having taken the leading role in the Tripartite Agreement, took up that position again at Mount Etjo. Foreign Minister Botha and others came by occasionally as Thornberry and Pienaar were writing the final draft to make comments, but the day, in fact, was anticlimactic, the agreement having been achieved the day before. While a few incidents occurred during the following days, the fighting essentially ended that weekend.[34] It was clear that Angola, Cuba, and the Soviets could leverage an agreement from Nujoma, who had been dependent on them for support. It was also clear that the United States, with the capacity to strengthen sanctions in the Security Council, had leverage over the South Africans. UNTAG was back on track but the crisis delayed implementation by several weeks.

An Atmosphere of Intimidation

What continued to be misunderstood outside Namibia was the fact that while the South African government had agreed to independence, there were many South Africans and white Namibians who did *not* go along with this decision and tried to either sabotage the process in general, or manipulate it in order to attempt to maintain white control. This was done through intimidation, violence, and assassinations by using the Koevoet special forces and the political party DTA (Democratic Turnhalle Alliance)[35] to carry out the policy. The South African–controlled media, especially radio and television, continued to use systematic disinformation and biased reporting to manipulate the process.

The Koevoet continued to be a source of violent intimidation throughout the process, primarily in the north where over a third of the population live, but also in Windhoek, even up to the final few weeks before the elections. Ahtisaari and Secretary-General Pérez de Cuéllar, operating at the highest levels, continued to complain to the South Africans about Koevoet intimidation. Koevoet had not existed when Resolution 435 was created in 1978. Koevoet members had been recruited specifically to put down SWAPO "terrorist" activities in reaction to the outside pressure brought by 435 and during the P. W. Botha and Reagan administrations. The forces were composed of black Namibians primarily recruited in the north, but all the officers were white South Africans. Koevoet personnel, who were primarily uneducated, went through an intensive training in which they were psychologically conditioned to kill. One of the commanders of Koevoet training stated to a commission of inquiry held during July 1989 that recruits needed no academic qualifications and were trained to combat SWAPO insurgents but could not really distinguish the difference between the armed insurgents and the local SWAPO supporters:

> It was little wonder that the intimidation of SWAPO supporters by former security force members continued on almost a daily basis throughout May, June, July, and August. Koevoet squads continued to patrol in their dreaded Casspirs and, although supposedly stripped of all weapons except for pistols, the "police officers" often stashed automatic rifles and heavy weaponry inside the armoured vehicles.[36]

Following the incidents in the north in April, the administrator general and other South Africans continued to make claims that SWAPO guerrillas were about to invade Namibia. "In this way, patrols and searches by Koevoet and police units could be justified."[37] Koevoet and the South West African Police (SWAPOL) had a formidable presence, using large, heavily armed, armored personnel carriers called Casspirs that were built to travel very fast and able to withstand land-mine explosions. Koevoet-operated Casspirs were known to drive through villages in the north, running over children or anyone in their way.

Only a few weeks into UNTAG's presence there were over 50 reported cases to UNTAG of intimidation and assaults in the north, including an accusation that an army vehicle had deliberately killed a woman attending a SWAPO memorial service. In early June, "a large contingent of police had attacked, arrested, and fired upon SWAPO supporters."[38] The results of the O'Linn Commission, an internal mechanism for investigating acts of intimidation, were that this incident "revealed the extent to which the police would organize and practice deception to harass and intimidate SWAPO supporters."[39] In early September 1989, the UNTAG office in Outjo was attacked by machine guns and grenades, killing a civilian security guard. Death threats were regularly being made against SWAPO members and a hit-list was later found with the names of SWAPO leadership targeted for assassination. Ironically, on September 12, the day that a "code of conduct" was signed among the competing political parties, a prominent SWAPO leader, Anton Lubowski, was shot dead in front of his house in Windhoek, followed the next day by graffiti written on walls around the capital saying that Nujoma, who was due to arrive in the country on September 14, was next.[40]

The political party DTA was a creation of white Namibian Dirk Mudge and the South African regime that was used during 1989 to keep SWAPO from gaining the two-thirds majority it would need to completely control the writing of the new constitution. It was later admitted that South Africa had provided (US)$35 million to the DTA and others opposing SWAPO during the campaign, but Dirk Mudge has explained that DTA needed funding from South Africa to counter the resources that SWAPO had raised from its international funding campaign and the OAU. DTA later revealed that it had over 3,500 people on its payroll in the Ovambo area in the north before the elections.[41] Often the interchangeability between DTA and Koevoet was blatant and they were seen working together during attacks and acts of intimidation.[42] UNTAG was constantly under pressure to keep the level of violence and intimidation under control so that it did not derail the process.

Leverage and the Role of the UN Civilian Police

The role of the UN civilian police (CivPol) in UNTAG was to monitor the activities of the local police but not to take over the policing duties of the local authorities. In fact, it must be remembered that UNTAG as a whole did not have the authority to administer the country or run the election process. It was established as an "assistance group," which meant that the South African administrator general continued to run the country with UNTAG oversight. UNTAG had the ultimate power to declare the elections "free and fair," but the process was one of constant negotiations with Louis Pienaar and his staff.

As discussed above, the South West African Police were more of a colonial policing mechanism, particularly the special unit Koevoet, which operated as a counterinsurgency force. The white-run police held attitudes toward black ethnic groups, particularly SWAPO, that were incompatible with the goals of the UN settlement plan under Resolution 435. The goal of UNTAG "was to create and sustain conditions whereby individuals, groups and political parties could organize, assemble and rally in public places, without fear of threat, assault or other intimidation."[43] Therefore the main task of UN CivPol was to keep SWAPOL and Koevoet under control. This was difficult because under the provisions of 435, as monitors they had no direct mandate to exercise control. In addition, UNTAG needed the cooperation of SWAPOL, which was difficult to manage while attempting to coerce it into changing its ingrained, traditional repressive tactics. CivPol, to the extent that it was able, accomplished this by working closely with SWAPOL and providing feedback to those making political decisions for UNTAG so that "improprieties could be dealt with at the highest level."[44]

Initially in 1978, Resolution 435 included provisions for 360 police monitors but as a result of the Technical Mission to Namibia in 1988, the number was increased to 500 by January 1989. By May, however, as the situation on the ground became clearer, the number was increased to 1,000, and then again to 1,500 in September. Originally the plan called for six districts with 33 stations. That was later modified to include seven districts and ultimately 49 stations.[45] CivPol had to increase its numbers in order to apply effective leverage against the aggressive, heavily armed South African police.

CivPol was not only outnumbered by the South African forces but was also outgunned. When CivPol finally arrived in the north, it began to go on patrols with SWAPOL, which was to inform the UN when it was starting out in the morning to patrol an area. Often, the UN was told that the patrol would begin at 10:00 A.M. and the UN would arrive at police headquarters at the designated time only to find that the patrol had left an hour or two earlier. Even when the UN left with SWAPOL, the South Africans would take off through the bush in their four-wheel-drive Casspirs with oversized tires, leaving the UN in their small four-wheel-drive Toyotas behind in the dust. CivPol would eventually arrive in a particular village where SWAPOL had been earlier to find that the South Africans had been intimidating the populace by looking for SWAPO members and supporters. Occasionally it would be reported that SWAPOL had taken prisoners or had beaten people to obtain information.

Deputy Special Representative Legwaila Joseph Legwaila, who had been active in the African Group and the Front-Line States at the UN as Botswana's ambassador in New York, explained that he had been reluctant to authorize the UN to acquire its own Casspirs because these vehicles had been equated over the years with South African repression. However, because the UN had been unable to keep up with SWAPOL in the bush, UN credibility and effectiveness were being undermined. In the end, the UN acquired its own contingent of Casspirs bought from South Africa and painted white with the UN letters. Far from being criticized by the local population, Namibians welcomed the increased UN power.

The leveraging process by which CivPol operated was convoluted but eventually proved to be relatively effective. It operated in several ways. UN patrols would go out with SWAPOL to observe its activities and report any violations to UN district offices and to CivPol headquarters in Windhoek. Local UN CivPol stations would also hear reports of intimidation and assaults from local citizens and report them to their district offices, which passed them on to headquarters. CivPol commanders would also go directly to SWAPOL office headquarters in their districts and make complaints in person to those in charge. If there was no action taken, UNTAG headquarters under the leadership of Special Representative Ahtisaari would then intercede and complain to South African Administrator General Louis Pienaar. Pienaar was clearly sympathetic to DTA and the police and so when he did not take action, the UN would go higher up to those in charge in Pretoria. Pretoria would then put pressure on Pienaar and he would have to call his police districts and tell them to cooperate. If the district officers felt that Pienaar might pressure them on a particular issue, they might decide to go along with CivPol before things got to that level. Therefore the leverage that the UN brought to bear at times would operate horizontally on the local level or might work its way up the UN command and then back down the South African command into the field.[46] The major thorn in the side of the UN was Koevoet, which was not disbanded until about a week before the elections in late November. By November 8, 1989, 929 cases of intimidation had been reported to UN headquarters.[47]

UNTAG Maintains Political Leverage

All the sources of political leverage that had built up over the years continued through the implementation phase in 1989. The focal point of the leverage, however, changed; now there were two hubs of activity, one still located in New York, but with a second hub relocated to UNTAG headquarters in Windhoek in the person of Special Representative Ahtisaari. While Ahtisaari received criticism for authorizing the release of South African troops from their confinement to base during the crisis in the first week of April, he proved to be a brilliant manager of the complex leveraging that was necessary to keep things on track. He used his single source of power, namely, the authority to declare the entire election process "free and fair," with great skill and tireless energy.[48]

Representatives of the various leveraging groups were in Windhoek: the Front-Line States, the ambassadors to Namibia from the Western Five, representatives from the Security Council, and others. Deputy Special Representative Legwaila explained:

> You would have the trade unions from South Africa, from AWEPA in Western Europe, from the Front-Line States whose sympathies lay with SWAPO. Then you have the American ambassador, the British ambassador, the Russian ambassador. Then I discovered at one point that even the ambassador of the GDR [German Democratic Republic (East Germany)] was concerned that we were not going to pull it off because we were being too nice to the wrong side. The people we really depended on, to tell you the truth, to help us carry out our mandate were the permanent members of the Security Council who were there. Because they were in touch with the Security Council here [in New York]. Even the Front-Line States because they could cause a lot of trouble for us. Once we had the members of the Security Council, the British, the Americans, the Russians, and we had the Front-line States, we knew we were on the right track. But always being careful not to kowtow to any of them. Some of them were not even ambassadors. They were sent there just to represent their country for the implementation of UNTAG.[49]

Legwaila and Ahtisaari met regularly with these groups but particularly when they were having difficulties. The pressure garnered by UNTAG was consistently resisted by

> the government of Namibia in the person of the Administrator General. And the Administrator General was an employee of whom? Of the government of South Africa. He got his instructions from Pretoria. We have just mentioned that we had the Front-Line States on this side and the members of the Security Council on this side and the trade unions on this side, AWEPA, this side. I forgot to mention the other side; that is the South African government. The South African government was very pivotal in the implementation of Resolution 435. It was they who had to agree that we implement it. So, at every turn we had to make sure that we were with them. And they had an Administrator General there who

> was not the most liberal on earth, and who sometimes took positions which were not even supported by the government in Pretoria.[50]

It must be remembered that every policy, whether it was the rules for electoral registration or voting, had to first emanate from the office of the administrator general and then go to UNTAG, who had to reach an agreement among the other political parties, including SWAPO, and then had to gain the approval of the Security Council back in New York. This was a delicate process, and many times the administrator general would not approve the changes made by the Council or the other parties. At times when this happened, Ahtisaari or Legwaila (who was also Botswana's ambassador to the UN) or both would go to Pretoria with Pienaar, sometimes in his airplane.[51]

Ambassador Legwaila described what happened in Pretoria:

> When we got there, we would go to the guest house there, a nice guest house in the hills of Pretoria, and then we meet and have lunch. Then we would say the following to South Africa, "There is a danger that the process will be scuttled if you insist on the following things in this proclamation and there is a danger that you might be faced with a meeting of the Security Council to debate your stalling tactics, and so on. Is that what you want?" We always got a positive response from the government of South Africa if we went to Pretoria. We never went to Pretoria and came back empty-handed. When we went to Pretoria, we always made sure that we dramatized the situation. That is, "You will be faced with a situation where we fail. And if we fail, what happens?" And I remember, Pik Botha would always shout, "No, no, no, we must not allow this process to fail. What will happen to South Africa if it fails?" I used to say, "Thank God."[52]

Of course, UNTAG would not go to Pretoria cold. Pérez de Cuéllar would call ahead and prepare the South African government (de Klerk and Pik Botha) for the arrival and make clear what pressures would be brought to bear on South Africa—namely, further sanctions—if the Namibia process failed:

> The Secretary-General would do that. You see, the members of the Security Council in Windhoek would know our difficulties with the South Africans. They were not just sitting there doing nothing. Everytime they discovered that there might be a crisis, they would call Pretoria. The Secretary-General would call Pretoria. So, when we would go to Pretoria we would be going to talk to people who had already been warned that, "If you don't cooperate with UNTAG, there is going to be trouble." I am told that every time we had one of these crises, the members of the Security Council would say, "By the way, if this time something happens and the South Africans are to blame and the process is destroyed, if the Africans come to the Security Council to ask for sanctions, it would be difficult for us not to support sanctions."[53]

This scene would take place in front of Pienaar with UNTAG as a witness. In that way, Pienaar could not pretend that something else had transpired. UNTAG knew that he had been told. Then they would all have to return to Windhoek together, sometimes on Pienaar's airplane, which could be a painful experience. Both Legwaila and Ahtisaari felt somewhat embarrassed for him. The final official decision would be made by President de Klerk and faxed to UNTAG the next day.[54]

There were a number of key issues over which Ahtisaari and Pienaar vehemently disagreed. These included the policies that had to be created governing the registration of voters; the repealing of the discriminatory laws that was necessary in order to allow people freedom to assemble and to campaign for the elections; the biased nature of the South African–run radio and television (SWABC); and the demobilization of Koevoet. Ahtisaari was able to gain leverage over Pienaar to pass registration laws that were acceptable to all the parties, including SWAPO, and was also able to force the repeal of most of the discriminatory laws except for AG-8, which had established the ethnic councils. However, Pienaar was adamant on the Koevoet issue, even though Ahtisaari had stated in a letter to Pienaar on June 9 that Koevoet forces "were terrorizing the local inhabitants."[55] Ahtisaari finally won that battle, but it was only a week or so before the elections were to take place that Koevoet was finally demobilized. The other heated dispute was over SWABC. While UNTAG had its own radio and television programs and was given air time to inform Namibians about the UN role in the elections and educate people about how to register and vote, SWABC was blatantly biased against UNTAG and SWAPO and frequently aired disinformation to undermine the UN.[56] Ahtisaari managed near the end to have the SWABC board fired and replaced, but, again, only shortly before the voting began.

The Important Role of the Churches in Namibia

Another key leveraging factor that became a very important aid to UNTAG and Ahtisaari was the organization of churches called the Council of Churches of Namibia (CCN). The churches were and still are a central part of the lives of the Namibian people. Bishop Dumeni, the head of the largest church in Namibia during the independence process—the Lutheran Church—explained that the church took a holistic approach to its members, providing them with spiritual guidance, education, health care, and even food. It was ultimately the church in the north that returned most of the SWAPO fighters to Angola after the April 1 crisis and then received the refugees when they started to return. "Forty-two thousand Namibians who were exiled in more than 40 countries were resettled in the country between July and mid-September 1989."[57] Bishop Dumeni describes this:

> When they came, the involvement of the church was key. The churches played a pivotal role because those returning, that is the Namibians who

> were in exile, were not willingly received by the South African government. There was no trust. So, the people who were in exile did not even trust UNTAG because they did not know what this cooperation between the South African government and the UN troops might be. Therefore, they decided to be received by the church. Therefore, all the churches under the umbrella of the Council of Churches in the country, regardless of what denomination, took this responsibility. Of course, we had complete cooperation with the United Nations. They agreed to receive these people in the church centers.[58]

UNHCR, UNTAG, and the Council of Churches worked closely together to make sure that the refugees returning to Namibia were received properly and eventually returned to their villages. The churches worked very hard to prepare the local villagers to welcome the returnees despite the fact that many were afraid of the consequences of receiving people who had been labeled terrorists by those in power. Some refugees did not go home but stayed in Katutura or other central locations in Namibia. All of this was carefully facilitated by the church leaders who knew the families and the local communities. The church also worked to calm people when crises erupted.

The Pivotal Role of Individual Courage

It is important to understand that in Namibia, as well as in other peacekeeping operations, there are many examples of extreme courage carried out by individuals fulfilling their duty to the goals of the operation as they understand them. Shortly after the Mount Etjo meeting, an arrangement had been made for SWAPO troops to surrender themselves to the UN at a few designated posts. UNTAG Spokesman Fred Eckhard went to the north and describes this event:

> I myself went up to the border about the time the whole thing had settled down and we had agreed on a plan to repatriate any SWAPO that were still in the country but in hiding because they didn't trust the South African military. We agreed to set up border checkpoints where these people could turn themselves in, and be escorted back across the border to Angola. [In] every place we had a little tent. We had no flagpoles, so we would attach the UN flag to the tallest tree nearest our tent. The South Africans moved in right next door and set up a military encampment that would have been the pride of any modern army: armored vehicles, jeeps, trucks, the whole business. Needless to say, very few SWAPO came to our little site with so many South Africans just next door.
>
> There was a wounded SWAPO guy who came into our tent and the South Africans wanted to interview him. The military guy in charge was a British major and Cedric was also there with me, as I recall. And the South African said, "We want to interrogate the prisoner." The major said, "No way, he's our guy and you can't have access to him." So, the South Africans raised their automatic weapons and pointed at the major and he still said, "Over my dead body." They said, "We'll be back in one hour and if you don't turn him over, we're taking him." So, they left.

> The major got on the horn to Windhoek. The British had Motorolas in their jeeps and they had a communications unit that could talk to those Motorolas. It was the only communications we had at the time. They called the British base which was four miles outside of Windhoek, saying, "Please get to the force commander or Ahtisaari and ask him what we should do." That jeep then called UNTAG headquarters; it was dinner hour. Both the force commander and the Special Representative were having dinner somewhere in Windhoek. The jeep went from restaurant to restaurant. There are only fifteen or twenty restaurants, but still there are enough that you couldn't get to all of them in an hour. So, Cedric took the decision and said to the major, "Tell him your force commander says to hold the line." So, the major went back out and these guys came up with their weapons again and he drew a line in the dirt and said, "You cross that line and we'll shoot." And the South Africans backed off.[59]

Despite the overwhelming force behind the South Africans, this UN officer, with, in reality, no backup, demonstrated the courage and resolve to protect the wounded SWAPO member whom he knew would have been tortured by the South African troops had they gotten a hold of him.

Another example of personal courage was carried out by a UN female staff member who was originally from Senegal. She had volunteered to go to Namibia because, as an African, she wanted to be a part of the independence process that she and others had hoped and waited for so long. She ran the UN post in the township of Katutura:

> In the township you had SWAPOL, and when I arrived they were very much afraid of SWAPOL, and they were always talking about the "Koevoet." The beginning was difficult because one of my tasks was to reduce political intimidation, and so to ask people to come and report on activities of SWAPOL was very difficult. And I know that SWAPOL was doing incredible things. The turnaround for me was when the first returnees started coming back, and there was a law that had not been repealed then that said something ridiculous like "ten black people could not be together." And so many people wanted to go to the airport to receive the first returnees. They were coming to my center and saying, "OK, now we are going to test this . . . we are going to the airport. . . . And I did tell the UN police, and I went to the airport, and SWAPOL was there and armed to the teeth, and there were hundreds of people from Katutura that had gone to the airport, hundreds of black people, and it was essential for me: I had to show that they could be protected. I didn't know how, what I was going to do, but I showed up, and I kept walking between the crowd and the police, the SWAPOL, back and forth, back and forth, to make myself very visible. . . . But just the fact that I was not afraid and I was there—it was pure luck that the SWAPOL police did not turn them back—the crowd . . . waited patiently when the returnees came, the first plane came and they started dancing and chanting. That was really for me the first turning point. From then [on], they would come to the district, the center, to report any time there was a problem. Up to that [time], they did not trust me that much.[60]

These are just two examples of the kind of personal courage that UN staff members demonstrated in Namibia that ultimately contributed to the success of UNTAG and Namibian independence.

The Vote Count: Tension Right Up to the End

The election took place during November 7 to 11, 1989. Koevoet had finally been demobilized and SWABC was under new management. There were fears that violence and intimidation might erupt during the balloting, but, for the most part, people stood quietly in the very long lines awaiting their turn to vote for the first time in their lives. More than 97 percent of those registered voted at 408 polling stations located around Namibia. There were UNTAG personnel as well as officials from the administrator general's staff of civil servants at each polling place, which had UN CivPol and SWAPOL guards at the entrance and exit. Representatives of the political parties were also present but not allowed near the actual voting tables where people filled out and deposited their paper ballots. After the close of the polls on Saturday, November 11, Special Representative Ahtisaari announced that the elections and the entire voting process had been "free and fair."[61]

Everyone waited by their radios to hear the results. Tensions were still high when the first reports started coming in. Ballot accounts were first tallied in the south and announcements over the radio began claiming that the DTA was winning by a landslide. People were in shock. How could this happen? Bishop Dumeni explains the fears that were sweeping over the country in those first days after the polls closed. He had his suitcase packed and next to his desk in the church office as he listened to the radio:

> Then the people here were prepared to take their bags to the border. If the DTA were in the position to win the elections, many of the people were ready to leave before they would be restricted to their villages. I confess that I was ready just to hear who had won the election. If DTA had won the election, many people would have left. There was nobody who would restrict them or tell them not to go. But they were ready.[62]

Then the count began to come in from Windhoek and there were considerably more votes for SWAPO, but DTA was still far ahead. Nevertheless, David Lush, a reporter for *The Namibian*, went to Katutura to interview Sam Nujoma: "Nujoma sat at a small desk reading the morning newspapers. He looked busy but relaxed, dressed in a perfectly ironed white shirt with cuffs buttoned down with chunky gold cuff-links, dark-grey suit trousers and maroon tie which disappeared into his suit waistcoat made complete by a gold watch chain." When Nujoma looked up from his papers, Lush asked him: "You must be a little disappointed with the way the results have gone so far. Do you think Swapo will win?" "'Of course Swapo will win,' he said firmly though still with good humour. 'You don't really think the great Namibian people will put colonial puppets into power do you?' and he laughed." Then Nujoma asked the reporter about the mood of the people in the township and he answered: "I told him that if my landlady was anyone to go by, Swapo's supporters were despondent. 'No, they must have confidence. They will see; Swapo will still win.'"[63] Of course, Nujoma knew the numbers and the geographic distribution of SWAPO supporters, who were primarily located in the north and whose ballots were just starting to be counted. Nevertheless, even UNTAG members were nervous.

On November 14, when the vote count was completed, SWAPO had won a little over 57 percent of the total that entitled them to 41 seats in the 72-member Constituent Assembly; DTA was next with 21 seats. In all, seven parties won seats. SWAPO had taken 92 percent of the votes in the Ovambo district in the north, but it failed to achieve the two-thirds needed to ratify the new constitution on its own. In the end, SWAPO had to make some compromises with DTA, which had at the very least kept SWAPO from completely controlling the constitutional process. Hence, Administrator General Pienaar was satisfied that the years of building up DTA as a political challenge to SWAPO had, in the end, paid off.

Concluding Thoughts

The successful implementation of Namibian independence is a clear example of the fact that the United Nations does not operate in a vacuum. When the UN process works successfully, it is because key actors have orchestrated the leverage provided by Member States and groups of Member States acting cohesively for a common end. When leverage prevails over a period of time, eventually countervailing factors, like South African intransigence, should give way, particularly in this context as the cold war thawed and interest in supporting proxy wars faded. In the Namibian case, many actors deserve credit for continuing to leverage not only for independence but for self-rule by the Namibian people. Each player had a key role during different stages as described in the three time periods outlined above.

In the opening paragraphs of this chapter, three sources of leverage were described; namely, *physical force*, *political pressure*, and *economic sanctions*. These sources of leverage came into play throughout the entire process: Cuban troops with Angolan and Soviet support and SWAPO providing the physical force or threat of force; the UN and groups of Member States (OAU, the African Group, the Front-Line States, the Non-Aligned, the Western Five, and finally the Joint Commission) providing the political pressure and ultimately economic sanctions or threat of further sanctions. The Namibian resistance also provided leverage from the inside, making South African repression costly. During 1989 and the UNTAG implementation phase, Ahtisaari successfully utilized the visibility of UN troops and the vigilance of UN CivPol to deter escalation of intimidation and violence and, when necessary, called on Security Council members and the Secretary-General to convey threats of economic sanctions to the South African government when leverage was needed against the policies of the administrator general.

In addition, there are two other sources of leverage that in the beginning did not seem apparent but that emerged as the analysis developed and the focus on events tightened. These are *moral authority* and *trust*. These psychological factors have a more subliminal effect but played an important role. Without a moral case on their side, SWAPO leaders would not have been able to win the political and financial support they gained over the years throughout the world, through members of parliaments, nongovernmental organizations (NGOs), and civil society in general, which eventually provided the constituent pressure to force the Western democracies to act. Trust became a key factor during the implementation phase when SWAPO had to *trust* that the relationship they had built up within the UN would not fail them. Nujoma had to make concessions during the first weeks of April that were painful to someone who felt so strongly that Namibia belonged to its people and who ought to be able to demobilize within their own homeland. If Nujoma had not trusted the UN and had returned to fighting, the entire process would have been lost. Angola is a clear example of that scenario. Trust in the Namibian churches also played a key role. When Namibians could not fully trust the UN, they always trusted the churches and the church leaders who secretly returned SWAPO fighters across the border in April and were largely responsible for the peaceful return of the refugees. Another factor, as explained above, was the individual courage and resolve demonstrated by people who otherwise had not been leaders in the struggle but who believed strongly in the rightness of its cause.

The freeing of the Namibian people as carried out through the UN and by UNTAG was not, as many people think, "a piece of cake." It was a carefully and persistently orchestrated process of leveraging. Namibia has now passed its tenth year of independence and it may be an appropriate time to look back and study the lessons learned. It is hoped that this chapter will offer a different perspective on the understanding of this success story and may contribute to providing tools for future UN operations.

NOTES

1. Roger Hearn, *UN Peacekeeping in Action: The Namibian Experience* (Commack, NY: Nova Science Publishers, 1999), 35–39.

2. "The League of Nations, Mandate For German South West Africa," Article 2, in D. Soggot, *Namibia: The Violent Heritage* (London: Rex Collings, 1986), 1.

3. Hearn, 37.

4. An anecdote told to the author during an interview in Windhoek, Namibia.

5. Yale-UN Oral History Interview with Theo-Ben Gurirab, Namibian Foreign Minister (November 1999), 3–4.

6. Lionel Cliffe, *The Transition to Independence in Namibia* (Boulder, CO: Lynne Rienner Publishers, 1994), 20.

7. Interview with Gurirab, 6–8.

8. Ibid.

9. John Dugard, ed., *The South West Africa/Namibia Dispute* (Berkeley: University of California Press, 1973), 128–42.

10. Interview with Gurirab, 24–25.

11. Hearn, 41.

12. R. Jaster, *The 1988 Peace Accords and the Future of South-western Africa*, Adelphi Papers 253 (London: International Institute for Strategic Studies), (autumn 1990), 11.

13. Hearn, 44.

14. Ibid., 48.

15. David Lush, *Last Steps to Uhuru* (Windhoek, Namibia: New Namibian Books, 1993), 80–81.

16. Interview with Gurirab, 24.

17. Lush, 80–81.

18. Chester Crocker, "Peacemaking in Southern Africa: The Namibia–Angola Settlement of 1988," in *Herding Cats: Multiparty Mediation in a Complex World*, ed. Chester Crocker, Fen Osler Hampson, and Pamela Aall (Washington, DC: U.S. Institute of Peace Press), 207–44.

19. Hearn, 49.

20. Yale-UN Oral History Interview with Roelof (Pik) Botha on March 5, 2001, 33.

21. See unpublished paper by Walter Dorn on the tragedy of April 1, "True or False Alarm?: UN Monitoring in Namibia in April and November 1989."

22. Yale-UN Oral History Interview with Marrack Goulding, June 30, 1998.

23. Yale-UN Oral History Interview with Bishop Kleopas Dumeni, March 17, 1999, 15.

24. Brian Harlech-Jones, *A New Thing?: The Namibian Independence Process, 1989–1990* (Windhoek, Namibia: EIN Publications, 1997), 40.

25. Lush, 147–48. David Lush and a colleague from *The Namibian* were in the north during the first week of April; see photograph in photo insert of Lush's book, "The bodies of plan combatants killed during the April 1989 incursion being dumped into a mass grave outside Oshakati."

26. Yale-UN Oral History Interviews with Hage Geingob, Mosé Tjitendero, and Gurirab.

27. Interview with Gurirab, 31.

28. Ibid, 27–29.

29. Ibid.

30. Ibid.

31. Unpublished letter of December 14, 1999, by Cedric Thornberry, UNTAG staff member present at Mount Etjo on April 9, 1989.

32. Ibid.

33. Ibid. The delegations included: *USSR:* Deputy Foreign Minister Anatoly Adamashin; *Cuba:* Carlos Aldana, Cuban party secretary; *South Africa:* Pik Botha, foreign minister, and Magnus Malan, defense minister; *Angola:* Ndalu, military chief of staff; and the *United States:* Chester Crocker, assistant secretary of state for African Affairs, and James Woods, assistant secretary of defense. The Adminis-

trator General for Namibia, Louis Pienaar, and Special Representative Martti Ahtisaari arrived on Sunday with Cedric Thornberry and his assistant Ed Omotoso.

34. Ibid.

35. For more information on the creation of DTA, see the Yale-UN Oral History Interview with Dirk Mudge on March 9, 2001, in Windhoek, Namibia.

36. Lush, 214.

37. Harlech-Jones, 97.

38. Ibid.

39. Ibid.

40. Lush, 219–20. Gwen Lister, the editor of *The Namibian*, was also on the hit list: "[E]vidence came to light that there was a right-wing terror group in existence with the purpose of derailing the independence process."

41. It is not clear exactly where SWAPO got its campaign funding, but it was most likely through its international fundraising and the OAU and its Liberation Committee.

42. Hearn, 82–83.

43. Cedric Thornberry, September 1991, unpublished report, *UNTAG: Description and Analysis of the Mission's Operational Arrangements*, 86.

44. Ibid.

45. Ibid.

46. Yale-UN Oral History Interview with Helmer Petterson, former UNTAG CivPol captain stationed in northern Namibia, September 1999, in Oslo, Norway.

47. Thornberry, 106.

48. Thornberry, 30–31.

49. Yale-UN Oral History Interview with Legwaila Joseph Legwaila, Ambassador of Botswana to the United Nations, May 1999, 29–30.

50. Ibid., 31–32.

51. In an unrecorded, informal conversation with Ambassador Legwaila, he explained that they went to Pretoria often but usually on an UNTAG airplane.

52. Ibid., 33–34.

53. Ibid.

54. Ibid.

55. Harlech-Jones, 73.

56. *Nation Building: The U.N. and Namibia*, a report of the National Democratic Institute for International Affairs (Washington, DC [1990]), 54–55.

57. Ibid., iv.

58. Interview with Bishop Dumeni, 11.

59. Yale-UN Oral History Interview with Fred Eckhard on February 16, 1999, 10–12.

60. Yale-UN Oral History Interview with Hawa Binta Dieye, June 23, 1998, 5–6.

61. *Nation Building*, 57–64.

62. Interview with Bishop Dumeni, 25.

63. Lush, 256.

CHAPTER THREE

Bringing Leverage to the Peace Process in El Salvador and Central America

DIEGO ARRIA

INTRODUCTION

This chapter describes the role of a core group of countries in the Salvadoran peace process, beginning first in the context of negotiations in Central America as a whole. The leverage brought to bear by these countries evolved through several reincarnations from bilateral contacts to the group efforts of the Contadora process, Group of Eight, and finally the Group of Friends of the Secretary-General on El Salvador. The role that the core Group of Friends—Colombia, Mexico, Spain, and Venezuela—played in the Salvadoran peace process inaugurated a mechanism that was successfully copied by the United Nations in other situations, notably Haiti and Guatemala.

Before Contadora

In order to understand how the peace and reconciliation process for El Salvador was finally concluded at midnight, December 31, 1991, at the United Nations headquarters in New York, it is essential to preface it within the context of the efforts of several Latin American countries that had been working to bring peace to the Central American region. Their work primarily focused on problems in Guatemala, Nicaragua, and, since 1981, in El Salvador. Even beginning as early as 1977 in Nicaragua, as the only way to ensure a democratic transition in that country, three Latin American leaders tried to persuade General Anastasio Somoza to leave before the end of his presidential term in order to allow an interim gov-

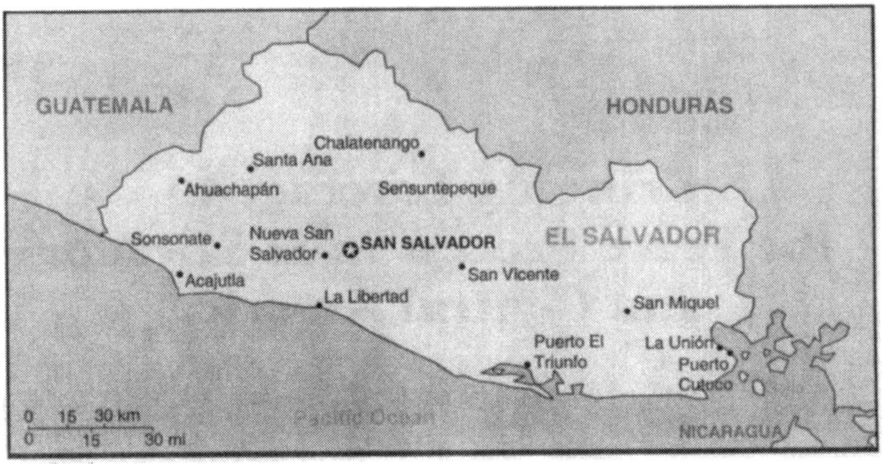

ernment to succeed him. The initiative was not successful because the Carter administration failed to encourage Somoza to leave. President Carlos Andrés Pérez of Venezuela, General Omar Torrijos of Panama, and President Rodrigo Carazo of Costa Rica warned the United States that the Sandanistas would bring down Somoza before the end of his term, which happened as predicted in 1979.

According to President Pérez, in 1978 he had invited General Somoza to a private meeting in La Orchila Island, a small Venezuelan naval base, to discuss with him the need to resign his office before his term was over in order to prevent further confrontation. Pérez had informed the U.S. government of the meeting and its purpose. He told Somoza that the increasing violence of the war would inevitably lead him to bomb most of the cities that were becoming the focus of Sandinista resistance. Several Latin American governments, including Venezuela, were aiding the Sandinistas and Pérez warned Somoza that he risked becoming the biggest murderer in Latin America. Somoza needed to recognize that he had been defeated and should leave as soon as possible. To Pérez's dismay, Somoza replied, "I want you to know that I just received a letter from President Jimmy Carter congratulating me for my human rights record."[1] This was unexpected and extremely unhelpful to the Latin American efforts at encouraging a nonviolent transition in Nicaragua.

U.S. officials have since told me that they were not aware of the meeting in La Orchila and that the letter did not have the intention of trumping Venezuela's efforts. In fact, CIA records from the time show that the United States did not consider the Sandanista threat as serious.[2] In the face of such analysis, it is not surprising that the U.S. administration did not heed the warnings of the Latin American presidents. Anthony Lake, former National Security Adviser, describes the 1979 meeting between U.S. officials and President Pérez:

> Vice President Mondale, Assistant Secretary of State Vyron Vaky, and Robert Pastor of the National Security Council staff met with President Pérez in March 1979. As he [Pérez] has done so often before, the Venezuelan asked how the United States would get rid of Somoza. When Mondale expressed American distaste for Somoza but said that we had no intention of overthrowing him, Pérez lost control of his poker face. You could see the dismay. Vaky says, "Pérez replied: 'In that case, blood will flow.'"[3]

Lake says that Pérez's warnings were unheeded in Washington. The evidence suggests that the U.S. authorities believed that it would be better to have Somoza than a Sandinista take-over. Perhaps someone had reminded President Carter of what a previous American president, Franklin Roosevelt, when faced with a somewhat similar circumstance, had said about Somoza's father: "He's an SOB, but he's our SOB." In this case, history repeated itself, to the detriment of the Nicaraguan people. While this case demonstrates the engagement of Latin American leaders, they were constrained in what they could achieve by the U.S. perception of its interests in the region.

The roots of multilateral diplomacy with regard to Central America predates even this initiative. On March 24, 1975, Presidents Alfonso Lopez Michelsen (Colombia) and Carlos Andrés Pérez met in the Panamanian island of Contadora with the president of Costa Rica, Daniel Oduber, and with General Omar Torrijos of Panama to reach an agreement on how better to support the negotiation process on the Panama Canal between the United States and Panama. The document was called the "Act of Contadora." The strategy agreed upon was to "Latin-Americanize the Canal issue." They asked the other heads of state of Latin America to write to the U.S. president in support of the negotiations. The group strategy proved to be of fundamental value during the process, inasmuch as it became a Latin American issue, not being restricted to Panama.

The group effort also paid dividends when the negotiations neared completion and the supporting nations could weigh in on behalf of Panama. The following and last meeting of this group took place in Bogota, where they were informed by General Torrijos that the treaties would not be signed because the United States had just included a clause that was unacceptable to Panama. The clause in question obligated Panama to contract with the United States on any future canal or the expansion of the present one. Faced with this disturbing development, which meant the collapse of the negotiations, the presidents telephoned President Carter and were able to persuade him to drop the clause. This enabled Carter to sign the Panama Canal Treaty and Neutrality Treaty on September 7, 1977, promising to cede control of the canal to the Panamanians by the year 2000. Presidents Pérez and Michelsen were especially active and effective in moving the process forward. Presidents José Lopez Portillo of Mexico and Daniel Oduber and Michael Manley, prime minister of Jamaica, were also involved. This group of five countries is acknowledged as the precursor of the Contadora Group. This successful effort at group negotiation provided a compelling example of the kind of leverage that could be achieved through regional cooperation.

The Contadora Process

The El Salvador Peace and Reconciliation Agreement of December 31, 1991 was accomplished largely due to previous groundwork undertaken by the Contadora Group. The Group promoted peacefully negotiated resolutions rather than military solutions to the conflicts in Guatemala, Nicaragua, and El Salvador. It also worked to reduce the intensity of the conflicts as well as to limit the extension of war.

The Contadora Group (named for the Panamanian island of the same name where it met) was created on July 23, 1983 by Presidents Belisario Betancourt of Colombia, Miguel de la Madrid of Mexico, Luis Herrera Campins of Venezuela, and General Omar Torrijos, now president of Panama. The aim of the Group was to create an informal and independent Latin American mechanism to intervene in the Central American region where the two superpowers had been entangled in the conflict, and where the Organization of American States (OAS) had proved incapable of taking action. The Contadora countries wanted to help resolve these Central American conflicts themselves. They did not want the United States to unilaterally intervene in the region without their active and direct participation. The efforts of the Contadora Group gained the confidence of Central American countries, who considered the Group to be a reliable and independent multilateral entity capable of negotiating conflicts in the region. Through their joint efforts, the four Contadora countries believed they could apply greater leverage on the parties to the conflict to work for peace. The four also strove to apply this same leverage toward powers outside the region that sought to influence the outcome in favor of one side or the other.

By preserving the dialogue among the parties and preventing the enlargement of the war, the Contadora Group must be credited with laying the foundations for peace in El Salvador as well as for starting the democratic process in Nicaragua and later in Guatemala. For Latin Americans, Contadora was considered a tremendous moral force for political integrity. Most importantly, the Contadora process offered an option to the more radical policies being considered at the time by the U.S. administration. Contadora played an active and influential role, as well as a moderating influence throughout the process. The Contadora presidents worked closely with the Central American leadership to prevent the Nicaraguan Contras, backed by the United States, from invading Nicaragua to overthrow the Sandanista government. Contadora representatives even went to the U.S. Congress to explain that Latin Americans were not pleased with the mining of the Nicaraguan port. Mexico and other countries were also concerned about the flow of refugees from these Central American conflicts.

In 1988, at the request of the South American countries, the Contadora Group was enlarged to include the "Support Group," which included Argentina, Brazil, Peru, and Uruguay, thus forming the Group of Eight and increasing the Group's representation and influence.

Conflict Resolution without U.S. Intervention

The active and coordinated political participation of Latin American countries in conflict resolution in their own region had deep political implications that did not go unnoticed. Some members of the Reagan administration opposed the political self-reliance of these Latin American countries involved in the process. The Contadora Group had cast a wide net by simultaneously dealing with: peace negotiations in El Salvador; political instability in Guatemala; the resilience of the Sandinista regime to open up the political process; and even offering assistance to peaceful and stable Costa Rica whose territory was being abused by irregular forces and neighboring armies. However, the Contadora process was limited by the power of U.S. interests in the region that supported the Contras in the Nicaraguan conflict and the government in the Salvadoran civil war during the Reagan administration. With the pressures of the cold war and the fear of communist influence in the region, the United States had favored a military solution to these conflicts, in opposition to Contadora. Despite failing to persuade the United States of the desirability of a nonmilitary solution and failing to halt the massive Sandinista support for the Frente Farabundo Martí para la Liberacion Nacional (FMLN) in El Salvador, the peace process initiated by Contadora proved durable in the long-run.

U.S. opposition to Contadora was later relaxed due to the new vision of President George Bush's team. It understood clearly that a military solution was not feasible and that the complexity of the problem required the participation of these Latin American countries as well as the full intervention and participation of the United Nations.

The Esquipulas Declarations and the Arias Peace Plan

The Contadora Group's first important achievement was the creation of conditions that made possible the Esquipulas Declaration of May 5, 1986, when the five Central American presidents, while meeting in Guatemala, signed "The Contadora Act for Peace and Cooperation in Central America." The next year, they agreed on "The Esquipulas Declaration II" (signed in Guatemala City) on August 6 and 7, 1987, where the peace plan for the region proposed by Oscar Arias, president of Costa Rica, was considered.

The Esquipulas Declarations were landmarks in building consensus for a peaceful settlement. When President Bush came to power in 1989 he would endorse the plan. The Declarations stated the need to "ask the governments of the region as well as extra-regional ones to discontinue their military and financial support and intervention" as indispensable to reaching a durable peace. The Declarations underline and recognize in the introduction "the visionary and permanent will of The Contadora Group and the Support Group (Argentina, Brazil, Peru, and Uruguay) in favor of peace for the region." It was at this point that the Contadora Group formally ended its activities. Nevertheless, the influence of this group of countries continued to be felt.

In historical terms, it is important to give credit to the Contadora process for building the peace plan. The Arias Plan, in fact, was based almost entirely on ideas previously laid out by the Contadora countries. As Jorge Montaño, Mexico's ambassador to the UN and a very active member of the Group, points out: "If you look at the last document of Contadora and you look at what Mr. Oscar Arias put together, Mr. Arias didn't do anything except to change the name of the act. What Arias did was simply to reproduce all the Contadora statements and put them on different stationary with the national emblem of Costa Rica." It was evident at the time that the United States wanted to move the process out of the hands of the Contadora Group to the Central American presidents. The United States did not want to abandon its military options—options that would be compromised by the Contadora Group's views and influence in the region. The arrival of Bush's team would change the U.S. outlook.

The Arias Plan Is Awarded the Nobel Peace Prize but the War Continues

In October 1987, Oscar Arias was awarded the Nobel Peace Prize in recognition of his peace plan for the region. Yet peace was elusive and the war continued in El Salvador. By the end of December 1988, the Arias Peace Plan was not working and the process faced a dangerous stalemate. At this stage, new presidents were elected in Mexico, Venezuela, and El Salvador: Carlos Salinas de Gortari (Mexico), Carlos Andrés Peréz (Venezuela), and Alfredo Cristiani (El Salvador). A year later, Cesar Gaviria would be elected President of Colombia. The arrival of these new presidents could not have been more auspicious. Their knowledge and commitment to cooperation in bringing peace to the region were quickly established and proven over time. They were essential to the ultimate success of the peace process.

The Declaration of Caracas

The Arias Plan re-energized the peace process for awhile, from 1987 to the end of 1988, when it also reached a stalemate. Pérez was perhaps the most internationally minded of these newly elected presidents; his election in December 1988 occasioned a new impetus to the regional efforts at peace. He used his inauguration to address the Central American conflicts.

Pérez had been vice president of Socialist International, an international association of all the Social Democratic parties throughout the world. He knew all the Social Democrat party leaders in Central America, Latin America, and Europe. He kept his contacts, having nearly daily dialogues with most of the key players in Central America. Two months before he was to take office he decided to consult with the Contadora heads of state and those of the Support Group who would be coming to his inauguration in order to discuss what could be done in Central America. He sent his chief of staff, Beatrice Rangel, to meet with President Sanguinetti of Uruguay, who was the Coordinator of the Contadora and Support Group. Pérez wanted to hold an informal caucus with the eight leaders while they were in Caracas and wanted to clear this with Sanguinetti and have them prepare for the discussions.

The presidents of the Group of Eight visited Caracas to attend Pérez's inaugural, which took place on February 4, 1989. Pérez met individually with each head of state as well as with Fidel Castro of Cuba and Felipe González of Spain who were also there. He asked everyone what it would take to break the stalemate.[4] The eight presidents held an informal meeting that produced the Caracas Declaration, which included the commitment of the Group to cooperate actively in the Salvadoran peace process.

Another significant subject discussed in Caracas was the issue of elections in Nicaragua. The Group warned Sandinista leader Daniel Ortega that the only way to prevent a second Contra invasion supported by the United States was to hold elections as soon as possible. The United States did not believe that Ortega was really committed to holding elections. However, Ortega did not agree with the Group and reaffirmed his position that elections would be held as scheduled in 1993. When the Group failed to convince him, another private meeting was called afterwards with Ortega, Castro, and Pérez. At that time, Castro told Ortega, "I have told you before that you should not hold elections, but if you are going to have them anyway, then you might as well hold them now and prevent another war." This last meeting was ultimately successful. I believe that the relationship between U.S. Secretary of State James Baker and Soviet Foreign Minister Eduard Shevardnadze was also critical in influencing Ortega to hold elections. The Sandinistas knew that Cuban support alone was not enough and when the Soviets pressed Ortega to hold elections, he had to give in. Obviously, neither the Soviets nor Ortega suspected that the Sandinistas would lose. As we know, elections took place under United Nations supervision in 1990 and Violeta Chamorro was elected president.

The Caracas Declaration had an intensive follow-up. The frequency and consistency of the meetings are a testament to the Group's active engagement and enduring influence in the region. In 1989 and 1990, the representatives of the Group of Eight met several times with their Central American counterparts. First in March 1989 at Tesoro Beach, El Salvador; in June 1989 at San Pedro Sula, Honduras; in 1990 in Montelimar, Nicaragua; and in the same year in San Isidro Coronado, Costa Rica.

Cuba's Role

Cuba was a key piece in the puzzle to achieve peace in the region. It was involved in both Nicaragua and El Salvador and also served as a proxy for Soviet influence in the region. The Group of Eight played a key role in leveraging Cuba to support a peaceful solution. It is difficult to see how such a role could have been played by any other organization or any single state. During the same occasion of Pérez's inaugural, members of the Group of Eight had the opportunity to meet with Castro and asked him to support the peace process in El Salvador, which meant discontinuing his assistance to the guerrillas, the FMLN. Castro replied: "We cannot say no when requested to play a role for peace." In fact, to the best of my knowledge, from then on Cuba played a supportive role in El Salvador.

Castro confided to the Group of Eight in Caracas that Cuba's involvement had been such that in his government palace in Havana he had a "Salvadoran War Room" to follow the developments and be more effective in his support for the rebel groups. It should be recalled that the rebel movement in El Salvador was ideologically allied with Cuba, which was not the case in Nicaragua. The Frente Sandinista was the integration of three different movements and only one of them was allied with Cuba. These realities made the Nicaraguan negotiating process less difficult and less complex than dealing with the highly ideologically charged rebels in El Salvador.

After Pérez's inaugural summit, Castro kept to his commitment for peace in Nicaragua. Such a change in Cuba's foreign policy was the logical recognition that the Salvadoran rebels, the FMLN, could not win the war, and with the cold war essentially over, Cuba's ability to influence the outcome was severely diminished. Obtaining Cuban support was an important step since the United States, Contadora, and the Group of Eight had failed to get the Sandanistas to end their support of the FMLN, one of the root causes of the Reagan administration's support for the Contras.

The Soviet Union

The role played by the Soviet Union during the conflict was significant, using Cuba as a conduit. The importance and value of their assistance was well-known. The Soviets were joined by Cuba in supplying aid to the Sandinistas in Nicaragua as well as to other rebel factions in Central America. However, by the late 1980s, the Soviet Union was in economic decline and losing its ability to finance foreign adventures. During the closing months of 1991, this situation started dramatically to change things in Central America. "Perestroika" was beginning to have an effect to the point that the Soviet ambassador to the UN, Yuli Vorontsov (who later became the Russian Federation ambassador to the United States), expressed informally to the Latin Americans the Soviet Union's interest in being part of the peace process. In fact, what later became the "Group of Friends on El Salvador" met with him several times to keep him informed of the developments. This Soviet–Russian relationship became very useful when the Salvadoran resolution was introduced for consideration to the UN Security Council by Spain, the United States, and Venezuela.

The United States

In January 1989, President George Bush replaced Reagan as president of the United States. In December of 1988, Carlos Salinas de Gortari became head of state of Mexico. Both these elections marked a dramatic change in policy concerning Central America. Staff members of the two presidential candidates had several meetings during the two campaigns at which Central America was discussed. Jorge Montaño, advisor to Salinas de Gortari, attended those meetings. An important item on their agenda related to finding ways to solve the Central American conflicts and to remove hostilities that had grown up between Mexico and the United States over these issues. Montaño explains:

> So, the week before the inauguration of Mr. Salinas, let's say about seven weeks before the inauguration of Mr. Bush, we met in Houston in one of the military bases there, and it was a very friendly and very cordial meeting between the two elected presidents. And it was, in a way, replacing the atmosphere—a very poisoned atmosphere—that prevailed from '82 to '88 between the two administrations, between President [Ronald] Reagan and President [Miguel] de la Madrid.[5]

At the meeting in Houston, the possibility that the United Nations could play a greater role in the peace process for the region was also discussed. Montaño relates that UN Secretary-General Javier Pérez de Cuéllar was skeptical, because cold war rivalries had sidelined the UN on Central American policy. The Secretary-General was reluctant to get involved and therefore sent UN official Alvaro de Soto to Mexico for the Salinas inauguration. There, Salinas assured de Soto that Mexico would support the involvement of the UN. De Soto was to become a key player after persuading the Secretary-General to involve the UN in the peace process.

President Bush made further positive steps. Within three weeks of his inauguration, he, together with his secretary of state, James Baker, concluded a bipartisan agreement in the U.S. Congress regarding Central America. The United States would thus speak with one voice on the region. Bush committed the United States to the Esquipulas agreements, agreed to halt arms transfers to the Contras, and to only send humanitarian aid as requested by Congress. Further, he decided to test Soviet foreign policy, using the Nicaraguan case. He wrote to Soviet President Gorbachev in February 1989, asking him to stop sending arms to Nicaragua in the run-up to the elections. Gorbachev agreed. Bush had named Bernard W. Aronson as Assistant Secretary of State for Inter-American Affairs, whose mission it was to travel to Moscow in June 1989 to negotiate with Soviet officials over the matter. Aronson was from the outset much more open, supportive, and flexible about understanding Central American issues and trying to find a common solution.

This new open-and-flexible approach to Central America also benefited from the appointment of Thomas Pickering as the U.S. ambassador to the UN. Having been the U.S. ambassador to El Salvador, Pickering was experienced, knew the region, and spoke Spanish fluently. He was very supportive of a new attitude toward the region and would later play an important role in the last phases of the negotiations when the process moved to UN headquarters in New York.

Elections in El Salvador: Alfredo Cristiani Enters the Picture

A very important event was the election of Alfredo Cristiani as president of El Salvador. He was a prominent and successful business leader and not linked to any of the violent acts that had troubled the country and region. Even though his party, ARENA, had been led by the infamous Colonel Roberto D'Abuisson, the international community quickly recognized that Cristiani belonged to a different league of leaders and he gained their respect and support. A decent, honorable, and courageous man with the will and determination to reconcile his country and achieve permanent peace, Cristiani was undoubtedly the man who anchored the peace agreement for El Salvador.

Shortly after he was elected president of El Salvador in 1989, Cristiani visited President Pérez in Venezuela to ask him for his direct intervention in his country's conflict. Pérez welcomed him, though with reservation because Cristiani had been elected by representing the internationally questioned ARENA Party. After their conversations, Pérez quickly appreciated the fact that Cristiani was not an heir of Colonel D'Abuisson, but that he was quite the opposite. Pérez, like other leaders, came to meet Cristiani immediately, realizing how fortunate it was for El Salvador that a man of his personal and political characteristics had been elected. That first meeting with Pérez was the beginning of a close and mutually trusting relationship that was extremely useful during the next two years of negotiations.

THE ENGAGEMENT OF THE UNITED NATIONS

Events in El Salvador in 1989 brought the shortcomings of the Contadora process to light and demanded a more interventionist role from the international community. Contadora was not in a position to play such a role. The FMLN's major offensive in November 1989 resulted in a severe government reaction to suppress the rebels, but it also created a military stalemate. It was at this point that the Salvadoran government approached the UN to mediate. The countries that had maintained an interest throughout were again central to persuading the UN to assume responsibility for the negotiations.

The engagement of the United Nations was initiated in the fall of 1989 during the opening session of the General Assembly. Presidents Virgilio Barco of Colombia, Carlos Salinas of Mexico, Felipe González of Spain, and Carlos Andrés Pérez of Venezuela convinced Secretary-General Pérez de Cuéllar of the urgency to provide the institutional framework of the United Nations as the only way to reach a firm and durable peace agreement in El Salvador. FMLN leaders also met secretly that year with Alvaro de Soto to try to convince the United Nations to become the peace-broker. Pérez de Cuéllar had been skeptical about the role the UN might play because of the significant involvement of both the United States and Soviet Union in the conflict. However, the Latin Americans clearly understood that their political support was not sufficient to complete the process.

Surprisingly, the Secretary-General included in his memoirs remarks about the Contadora Group that must be addressed to keep the record straight. The Secretary-General says, "In their [the FMLN] view, the Contadora Group (which they had always seen as hostile toward the FMLN) had run out of steam."[6] These remarks are included by the Secretary-General as a sort of justification for UN involvement. This is difficult to understand, because there was no need at all to justify involving the UN; the motivations for Contadora and the UN were the same: peace for El Salvador. Contadora had not been attempting to mediate in the same way as the UN. It is a fact that Contadora could not take the process any further—that was not its role. The purpose of the Group was to fill the vacuum created by the inaction of the OAS (which did not enjoy the confidence of the rebel groups), to counterbalance U.S. intervention in the conflict, and to prevent the expansion of the war. The historic record is clear. Contadora had not "run out of steam," but both Contadora and Esquipulas had exhausted the avenues open to neighboring states. Plainly, Contadora's mission had come to an end as soon as some of its members joined El Salvador in convincing a reluctant UN to assume the process.

The Group of Friends Emerges

The new presidents of Colombia, Mexico, and Venezuela, together with Felipe González, head of the government of Spain, agreed to form the "Group of Friends of the Secretary-General for El Salvador." The creation of the Friends of the Secretary-General for El Salvador (and later for Haiti and Guatemala) profited greatly from the previous Contadora experiences. The four Friends of El Salvador grew out of the Contadora formula, building on the four Contadora countries with the exception of Panama, which had undergone a turbulent period under Noriega, and the addition of Spain in its place.[7] Once the Secretary-General decided to engage the United Nations, the role of the Friends became that of supporters and facilitators of the Secretary-General in his efforts to negotiate and conclude a sound peace and reconciliation agreement.

The addition of Spain is interesting to note here. As mentioned, in November 1989 the FMLN launched a major offensive against the Salvadoran government in the capital city, San Salvador, capturing a good portion of the city. The government responded with force and military death squads[8] took advantage of the situation, killing a number of jesuit priests and civilians. Most of the priests who were murdered at this time were Spanish, one was a Basque, and a number of the civilians killed were also Spanish citizens. Spain began to put pressure on the government for an explanation of the killings. Such an investigation was going to lead directly to the military. Cristiani ordered an investigation and invited the assistance of Spain, the British police, and the U.S. Federal Bureau of Investigation (FBI). These investigations and the results of the Truth Commission's report later led to the conviction of several army officers for human-rights abuses. With additional leverage now coming from Spain, pressure was building against the government to bring the military under control.

The inclusion of Spain in the Group of Friends was also a way to have European participation without France, whose attempt in 1981 to intervene with the Mexicans in the Central American conflict created adverse reactions within the U.S. administration. France seemed to be testing the existence of the Monroe Doctrine and the United States had reacted quickly. In addition, Spain's socialist head of government, Felipe González, had demonstrated Spain's commitment to the region, where he enjoyed great trust and prestige and had a very close political and personal rapport with the other heads of state of the group. Even before he was Spain's head of state, as vice president of Socialists International, González had been a participant in all the committees created to support Central America. Therefore he was very knowledgeable of the situation and knew all the parties involved in the conflict. Time proved that the Euro-Latin American combination was definitely a good one for the negotiation process.

U.S. influence in the region, however, had to be recognized; later the group was referred to as "The Four Plus One" when the United States joined the process. The United States became an informal member, operating behind the scenes through Bernard Aronson or Thomas Pickering. Jorge Montaño explains that the "Plus One" was key because "the 'One' was the most important in terms of being the one-and-only country who had the leverage with the El Salvador government, real leverage with the military."[9]

Leverage with the military was indispensable. Mexico as well as Venezuela had a certain influence with the FMLN, but only the United States had leverage with the Salvadoran military. At certain points when the negotiations were stuck, Montaño relates that the Four Friends went to the "One" and pressured the United States to send someone to El Salvador to use its leverage with the Salvadoran military. Sometimes U.S. officials such as Colin Powell, then chairman of the Joint Chiefs of Staff, would go to El Salvador for two or three hours to talk to the military. Then the Four Friends could move ahead again on the negotiations.[10] The issues under consideration concerned guarantees for the FMLN in the peace process, the National Police, amnesty for both parties, the ultimate disposition of weapons, and other security issues.

It was no surprise that Mexico would take a leading role. For years, many FMLN leaders had been living in Mexico, which had been the first Latin American country to engage itself in the Central American conflict since the 1981 French–Mexican Communiqué ("A Common Position between Mexico and France Regarding El Salvador") by Presidents François Mittterand and José Lopez Portillo. This document recognized the FMLN (the military arm of the rebels) and the FDR (Democratic Revolutionary Front, the political wing of the movement) as belligerent forces that, according to the Geneva Convention, extended to them the protections included in the Convention. The agreement between France and Mexico created serious friction with the Reagan administration.

On the Colombian side, President Virgilio Barco was fighting the FARC (Revolutionary Armed Forces of Colombia) and the ENL (National Liberation Army). By having to deal with these guerrilla groups, Barco had a great deal to contribute to this process from Colombia's painful experiences. An important factor at the time also was the position of Colombia on the Security Council. It could play an important role in communicating with the Council on matters dealing with El Salvador, providing further information to the Council when it needed to get involved.

Venezuela's involvement was due exclusively to the fact that Carlos Andrés Pérez was a very active leader involved in hemispheric issues. Public opinion in Venezuela did not demonstrate much interest in the conflicts in Central America, and the public did not understand the rationale for Venezuela's involvement. Pérez's own history is perhaps more of a determinant here. He had himself led the defense of Venezuelan democracy during the 1960s as the Minister of Government of President Betancourt. A long struggle had continued where the local guerrillas were aided by Castro's Cuba. Pérez's successful role in this conflict led him to his first election as president of Venezuela in 1974. Of all the presidents involved in the peace process he was perhaps the most active, to the ultimate detriment of his own career. The priority and importance that Pérez assigned to these negotiations were such that his chief of staff, Beatrice Rangel, was the official conduit in Venezuela for the parties involved. She enjoyed the trust of all parties, since she had been involved in the process almost since the beginning of the UN negotiations. As a result, the Venezuelan Ministry of Foreign Relations was not involved. During the last year (1991), President Pérez had permanent contact with his ambassador to the UN (myself). There were no limitations on getting the president's attention whenever his participation was needed. This availability was fully utilized and put to good use by all parties, as well as by the Secretary-General and Alvaro de Soto, who became the Secretary-General's Special Representative for El Salvador.

In 1989, in the face of growing pressure to bring the military under civilian control—not the least from Spain—Venezuela arranged a confidential visit to Venezuela by the chief of staff of the armed forces of El Salvador and other officers to meet with their Venezuelan counterparts. The officers spent two days explaining how the Venezuelan military had evolved from one that once supported a dictatorship to a professional one that provided support for a democratic society. This visit proved to be very useful during the negotiations surrounding the draft of the peace agreement, negotiated by the parties with UN intermediation. The FMLN's principal leaders, Comandante Schafik Jorge Handal, Joaquín Villalobos, Francisco Jovel, Eduardo Sancho, and Salvador Sánchez Cerén, had met with President Pérez in Venezuela several times where they learned to trust his independence and good faith in the negotiation process.

Further, many of the meetings under UN direction took place in Venezuela. On those occasions, Pérez never failed to meet with the participants as well as with the Cristiani team and de Soto and his UN team. Frequently, when the process lost momentum, Pérez was called upon to appeal to the parties, conveying the importance of being flexible as well as convincing either side of the need to accept a specific UN proposal. As indicated previously, such fluid and personal communications along with a mutual trust among the parties made the Pérez participation especially valuable, even more so during the last few weeks at the UN when the negotiations seemed to be unraveling. All the parties involved have acknowledged that the rapport and influence gained during those years paid-off handsomely in the end.

Ironically, Pérez was a victim of his own concern for the fate of the Central American region when he was forced to resign the presidency in 1993 for allowing the use of about $250,000 of public funds to be used to train and protect the recently elected president of Nicaragua, Violeta Chamorro. Solidarity with a rising and struggling democracy was something about which the Venezuelans, in general, could not care less and used it as a way to bring Pérez down. Nevertheless, to his credit he has been the most active and committed Venezuelan leader on Latin American issues.

The Group of Friends would work closely and efficiently during the next three years to preserve the process of negotiations to find a peaceful settlement to the conflict, now twelve years old. Their invariable and active cooperation, despite changes in administrations in Colombia, Mexico, and Venezuela, facilitated the international support for the process and added credibility to the efforts being made by the parties. Paramount in their joint effort was to engage the United Nations in the process. Importantly as well, the Group of Friends contributed to changing the role that the United States had been playing for years in the armed conflict, from supporting the Salvadoran government's strategies to one of partnership with the Group. Without the UN's intermediation and U.S. support it would have been almost impossible to conclude the negotiations successfully within the same timeframe.

THE UNITED NATIONS NEGOTIATION PROCESS

In the early stages of the negotiations, the Friends Plus One were an indispensible resource for the UN negotiators. They provided the venue for the discussions and contributed informal advice and support to both parties to keep the process from faltering. The meetings of the parties under the auspices of the United Nations were conducted under the guidance of Alvaro de Soto, a Peruvian UN official appointed by the Secretary-General as his special representative for the Salvadoran peace process. During 1990 and 1991 meetings with representatives of the government of El Salvador and the FMLN/FDR were held primarily in Mexico and in Venezuela, where both governments were equally committed to contributing all the support for the negotiations as well as providing the lodging, meeting facilities, food, and even air travel for some of the participants. Until the very end of the negotiations in late 1991, FMLN/FDR leaders were not allowed entrance into the United States because visas were denied to members of groups that had been designated as rebels or terrorist organizations. Therefore the negotiations could not take place at the UN in New York. Having a neutral and supportive space to get the negotiations off the ground was extremely helpful.

The proximity modality where UN representatives moved back and forth, meeting with the parties, reinforced the UN role as intermediary. For the process to work, both sides had to trust the Organization. There was no alternative. This sometimes resulted in the messenger becoming confused with the message, causing a breakdown of trust in the UN negotiators. The design of the negotiation process was important because neither the FMLN nor the government team could meet face-to-face due to political constraints. When the parties faltered in their trust of the UN, the Friends provided a useful alternative mechanism.

The first hurdle faced by de Soto and his team, comprised of Francesc Vendrell and Blanca Antonini, was the task of overcoming the fears held by the Salvadoran government representatives who often felt that the UN was not being impartial. At times, they felt that the UN was excessively leaning on them in favor of the rebel groups. On some occasions one of the parties, generally the government of El Salvador, would appeal to the Group of Friends for support with the UN mediators. It also happened that the FMLN representatives appealed to the same Friends for similar reasons. In this regard the Friends provided an important function: as an impartial group of observers (with influence). They could defuse tensions and get the parties back to the negotiating table. The UN team must be credited for its extraordinary performance in guiding both sides through a difficult and painful process, especially the new Cristiani government.

A point arrived in mid-1991 when the Secretary-General together with the Friends agreed that it was time to move the final stage of the process to the UN in New York. That decision proved to be a fundamental one for success but first visas had to be obtained for the FMLN negotiating team. The U.S. Immigration and Naturalization Service had placed restrictions on issuing visas to some members of the FMLN. Again, it was important to have the United States involved in the peace process. It was U.S. ambassador to the UN, Thomas Pickering, who helped to convince the right people in Washington that the team *had* to come to New York.[11] Yet the FMLN members did not have freedom of movement once they reached New York. They were restricted to the immediate surroundings of the United Nations' building, basically from 42nd Street along First Avenue to 47th Street or maybe up to 52nd Street. And, going west, they could not go past Third Avenue. This caused problems when meetings had to be conducted outside this area and so they had to be "smuggled" out for some of the consultations.[12]

The process reached a difficult plateau when the United States, during the last months of the intermediation, approached the Secretary-General to express concern about de Soto's handling of the negotiations, arguing that he was not acting in an impartial fashion. Pérez de Cuéllar responded that de Soto had his full confidence. In the last month, when the parties were locked in disagreement, for the same reason Pérez de Cuéllar took the decision to insert on a couple of critical occasions Sir Marrack Goulding, the UN Under-Secretary-General for Peacekeeping, but retaining de Soto's involvement. Goulding, from the United Kingdom, performed admirably, gaining immediately the full confidence of the parties and the Friends Plus One Group. Goulding, with de Soto and the rest of the UN team, was then able to proceed to close the negotiation process with the assistance, once again, of the permanent participation of the five countries acting through their permanent representatives to the United Nations in New York, not only as supporters but also to complement the UN negotiating team.

The Salvadoran Peace Process at the United Nations

Javier Pérez de Cuéllar's second term as Secretary-General of the UN was to end on December 31, 1991. The Four Friends took care to strongly emphasize to the parties this date as a deadline. We insisted that the arrival of the new Secretary-General with a different agenda and being not familiar with the issue would most probably relegate the negotiations to a lesser priority. Reasons for this were manifold: the parties were procrastinating on reaching an agreement; Boutros Boutros-Ghali's (the incoming Secretary-General) priorities certainly did not include El Salvador; the process might continue to be negotiated by the UN staff but without the personal involvement of the Secretary-General, since he would have to get acclimated to his new job. Finally, dark clouds could be seen gathering over Yugoslavia, which would soon take over the spotlight.

We repeatedly stressed to the parties the importance of the personal intervention of the Secretary-General, which most probably would not be the case with the new one. The fact that Pérez de Cuéllar was a Latin American had, no doubt, influenced him in increasingly engaging himself, especially when he saw a window of opportunity for success opening during the last three months of 1991. This was, after all, a great opportunity for him to achieve a grand finale as he completed his last term in office.

Pérez de Cuéllar and the Four Friends at the presidential level convinced both parties to continue the proximity negotiations in New York, where de Soto and his team shuttled between them and met constantly with the Friends. The new venue, New York City, gave great impetus to the process as the parties had the opportunity to meet constantly with the UN negotiators (de Soto and others on the UN team), the ambassadors to the UN of the Four Plus One, and the Secretary-General. During the last three months of the negotiations the role of the Friends changed from supporters of the process to active participants as negotiators whenever the situation demanded such a role. This issue will be explained further below. Their close proximity in New York allowed all the parties involved to gain quick reactions to their proposals and counterproposals and for the Friends to be closely engaged. Both parties operated from offices in the UN Secretariat building but on different floors. De Soto and his team operated like a pendulum, swinging back and forth between them.

In September, the issue of the creation of a mechanism to oversee the implementation of all the political agreements achieved by the parties reached a stalemate. The mechanism was to be called the "Comisión para la Consolidación de la Paz" (COPAZ). The FMLN was rejecting some of its provisions. The four ambassadors, Cepeda (Colombia), Montaño (Mexico), Yañez (Spain), and myself, went to JFK airport to meet with President Pérez of Venezuela who was on his way to visit Canadian Prime Minister Brian Mulroney in Ottawa. At our request, Pérez called Schafik Handal, who was commander of the FMLN and secretary general of the communist party of El Salvador and, with Joaquín Villalobos, the most influential member of the FMLN delegation. Pérez spoke to Handal in our presence and got him to accept the proposal that the UN team had prepared, allowing the process to continue.

Several additional factors contributed to the success of the negotiations. First, the fact that the president of El Salvador came twice to New York during that period to meet with the Secretary-General, de Soto and his team, and the Four Plus One greatly enhanced the environment of the negotiations. This was not only useful for Cristiani, but also for the UN negotiators who had the chance to deal personally with him and not only with his negotiating team, which was very ably led by his Minister of the Presidency Oscar SantaMaría.

Second, the radically changed U.S. position helped considerably. From being part of the problem, it became a substantial part of the solution. President Bush recognized the limitations of the United States to act independently and valued the cooperation available from the presidents of Colombia, Mexico, Venezuela, and Spain. Actually, a level of trust had developed among the Four, with Bush becoming a determining factor in accelerating the process. The full engagement of Assistant Secretary for Inter-American Affairs Aronson and Ambassador Pickering was invaluable.

And third, I should emphasize again the significance of the end of the cold war for the negotiations. After 74 years of communist rule, the Soviet

Union collapsed and the Russian Federation was born on December 25, 1991. On Christmas Eve, the Four Friends were meeting with Secretary-General Pérez de Cuéllar in his residence. He was also holding meetings with both parties in other rooms. At one point Pérez de Cuéllar had to leave the room to meet with Soviet Ambassador Vorontsov, who was the president of the Security Council during the month of December and had requested an urgent meeting with the Secretary-General. About fifteen minutes later the Secretary-General returned to the room, looked at us, and said, "Ambassador Vorontsov has officially informed me that as of today the Soviet Union has ceased to exist. In its place the Russian Federation has been created and will take the seat of the Soviet Union in the Security Council." The impact of such news on Christmas Eve for all of us is difficult to describe in all its intensity. History-in-the-making was before our eyes. The Soviet Union had been helping the FMLN financially and militarily. This cooperation was definitely now over. The Four Friends did not have to elaborate on the significance of this issue to the FMLN representatives who understood its impact on their movement.

The meeting at the Secretary-General's residence went on late into the night on Christmas Eve and into the early morning hours. The negotiations were still at a critical juncture when the parties had to leave the residence. At that point, according to Ambassador Montaño, he took three members of the FMLN team (including the key leader, Joaquín Villalobos) and two members of the U.S. delegation to the Mexican residence. There, they kept working well into Christmas Day for about eight hours. Montaño explains that this meeting was critical to be able to move ahead, for that one time, without the intermediaries. The Four Friends' representatives at the UN had agreed, previous to this episode, to share information and not to meet unilaterally with the parties without informing the others. This agreement was only broken on that one occasion and only came to light recently in Ambassador Montaño's account documented by the Yale Oral History Project. This news came as a surprise to the rest of the Group of Friends, who were not informed at the time.

The next day, the Friends discussed with the Salvadoran government representatives the achievements gained with the guerrillas during the Christmas discussions. The Friends met for about ten or twelve hours the day after Christmas with both sides at the Mexican Mission to the UN, and then moved across the street to the UN building. Cristiani was in New York but not directly involved in the negotiations. His delegation had to consult with him on all the agreements. This put him in the ultimate decision-making position. President Cristiani was staying at the Helmsley Hotel on 42nd Street in New York, accompanied by his wife, Margarita, who would take notes on her laptop computer of our conversations. She was evidently the only person he trusted to keep all those conversations confidential. He did not meet directly with the Friends in order not to weaken his side of the negotiation process. If he had had direct contact with us, it would have created serious problems for him with the groups that supported him at home. Among those on the negotiating team for his government were Oscar SantaMaría, military advisor General Mauricio Vargas, and a poet, David Escobar Galindo. Anything taken to Cristiani would also be known by his negotiating team. At that point in New York, the key political negotiator for the Salvadoran government side was Armando Calderon Sol, who later succeeded Cristiani as president; for the FMLN side it was Schafik Handal. The two hated each other. Both parties were situated in offices in the UN Secretariat but in different areas of the building so as to avoid contact.

During the last weeks of December 1991 the meetings at the UN lasted far into the early morning hours, even until 4:00 or 6:00 A.M. Concern about the success of the process increased, however, when de Soto and other members of his team informed us that it would not be possible to reach an agreement before December 31, when Pérez de Cuéllar would be leaving office. Some friction had developed between de Soto and the Four Friends. Because the Secretary-General was not involved directly, his information on the progress of the talks was coming only from de Soto. By not hearing directly from either the Cristiani team nor the FMLN, the Friends were concerned that Pérez de Cuéllar was not getting the complete picture. The Friends were also concerned that the UN might be putting too much pressure on the Cristiani government, which had to deal with its own military and the political realities of the country. We had the impression that the UN was trying to impose on El Salvador an ideal model of a democratic state that did not take into account these realities, and we were afraid that excessive pressure on Cristiani might derail the process. For these reasons, the Friends decided that the Secretary-General had to be more involved. However, de Soto was very protective of his own role and did not welcome intervention by the Friends in this instance. The presence of the Friends' permanent representatives with personal connections to Pérez de Cuéllar was, again, crucial in circumventing these objections and leveraging the involvement of the Secretary-General when the process faltered.

A few days later, on December 28 or 29, the negotiations began to break down once again and the Four Friends decided that the situation had reached a state of crisis. They went to the Secretary-General's office (without an appointment) to convince him to intervene personally to get things back on track. Neither Goulding nor de Soto was going to be able to break the stalemate without the intervention of the Secretary-General. The security guards did not want to let us in to see the Secretary-General without an appointment but we were adamant and proceeded down the corridor to his office.

Fortunately, Pérez de Cuéllar received us and we expressed the urgency for him to become personally involved. The Secretary-General, who was leaving office in a few days, was not eager to do this. The Friends told him that he had a major responsibility in resolving this process and if it collapsed because he would not get directly involved, we would have to hold an international press conference to explain the situation. It was obviously not a pleasant meeting, but the Friends took advantage of their personal relationship with the Secretary-General to describe the situation in very clear and candid terms. This prompted him to change his position. The four ambassadors had previously contacted Bernard Aronson on the way to the UN to tell him that they might be calling for a press conference of the Four Plus One if the Secretary-General did not agree to become directly involved, to which Aronson was in agreement.[13] The outcome of the encounter was key to boosting the negotiations. There was now no need for a press conference, but it was a useful tool as leverage. The Secretary-General said that he was "going to impose my white hair on the parties," referring to himself as an "elder statesman" and playing a paternal role, in the Latin American style.

Personal pressure was continually brought to bear on the parties as leverage at critical points. During the last days of the negotiations when the process appeared to break down, I said to the comandantes:

> In two days Pérez de Cuéllar will leave the UN. An Egyptian will take his place. He will have very different priorities. You will become priority 15th or 25th, depending on how lucky you get. Today and tomorrow you are the number 1 priority of the UN and of the Secretary-General. Don't forget that he is a Latin American who wants to clinch this deal. The next one will not have the same interest.

After that I called President Pérez and asked him to speak to Schafik Handal of the FMLN and tell him to seize the opportunity now and stop bickering, because it was a good agreement. Using the prestige of his personal relationship, President Pérez did so.

We realized that the arrival of a new Secretary-General, an Egyptian, might mean that the issue of El Salvador could change priorities in his agenda. However, we also knew that this was not necessarily the case. Most likely, Secretary-General Boutros-Ghali would have continued the agenda to clinch the deal, but we used that as leverage to pressure the parties. The Friends were afraid that the UN Secretariat might delay the process, wanting to get a better agreement and as such might be willing to "wait it out." This was a risk that the Four Friends Plus One would not want to take. The Secretary-General was already showing fatigue in the negotiations. Maybe it was his style to appear disinterested, but he was actually ready to leave the airport at 7:00 P.M. on December 31 before the agreement was signed. A full account of that last day is worth relating here.

December 31, 1991, New Year's Eve, was the next critical moment when it looked like everything was going to collapse again. Many of the issues had been resolved, but the ones that remained were the issues of agrarian or land reform and the national police. At around 2:30 in the afternoon on that day, Ambassador Montaño made a very important call to Bernard Aronson, who was in the U.S. Mission to the UN across the street with Ambassador Pickering. Montaño warned Aronson that the Friends had been informed that Pérez de Cuéllar had made plans to leave the UN building at 6:00 P.M. because he believed the negotiations were not going to conclude before his mandate was over.

The Secretary-General, accompanied by de Soto and Goulding, received Bernard Aronson and Ambassadors Thomas Pickering, Fernando Cepeda of Colombia, Jorge Montaño of Mexico, Juan Antonio Yañez of Spain, and myself after we had requested an urgent meeting. We said: "We understand you want to leave." He replied: "I don't want to leave, *I am going to leave*. I have a plane already waiting for me. I'm going to Miami and the plane is leaving at seven o'clock." Jorge Montaño recalls that Aronson sent him a note saying that he thought that the United States could have the Federal Aviation Administration stop the plane from taking off, which turned out not to be necessary.

All those present told Pérez de Cuéllar in no uncertain terms that if he did not stay to conclude the agreement, the future of El Salvador would be uncertain and the war would continue. On hearing this, Pérez de Cuéllar turned to de Soto and asked him that if he were to stay, would the agreement be signed? De Soto responded, "Mr. Secretary-General, you have already given your time and best efforts for this agreement to be signed, but I don't believe that this agreement could be signed, even if you stay." The Secretary-General then asked the same question of Goulding, who responded: "Mr. Secretary-General, yes, there is a chance." Then Pérez de Cuéllar asked Aronson if he could arrange for his flight to be changed and announced he would stay if the two sides would give him assurances that the end was in sight. Why de Soto would risk not having concluded the deal before the end of the 31st is still a mystery to me, as well as to the other members of the group. He may have thought that delay would result in a better agreement. Still, it is a fact that if the Friends had not presented themselves and pressured the Secretary-General not to abandon this last effort, the agreement would not have been signed on that occasion and the conflict would have continued.

Then the Friends went to pressure the two sides to reach an agreement before the Secretary-General's term was officially expired at midnight. They agreed and asked the UN team for support in order to put together some ideas on the issues that were pending. At around 10:30 P.M., de Soto read a draft of the final agreement to the Four Friends Plus One in the presence of the Secretary-General. I remember vividly that Ambassador Pickering immediately raised two or three objections and asked Pérez de Cuéllar to convey them to his team of negotiators as the Secretary-General's recommendations. These were taken into consideration. The agreement was finally settled at midnight, although truthfully it may have been a few minutes after twelve. We talked about "stopping the clock," but of course that was just an expression. By the time everything was signed, Pérez de Cuéllar left the building sometime around one o'clock on the morning of January 1. Secretary-General Pérez de Cuéllar became the longest serving Secretary-General of the United Nations: his two terms, plus one hour after his term was over. The agreement was actually signed on January 1, 1992 at around 0:45 A.M. The clock had been diplomatically stopped by the Secretary-General in order to complete the deal. Boutros-Ghali lost one hour of his term!

In summary, the UN was responsible for the orchestration and conduct of the peace process, but the final agreement could not have been reached without the active final support of the Four Friends plus the United States. The role of the four governments of the Friends cannot be underestimated; the UN could not have reached a solution without them. And the Four Plus One could not have done it without the UN's participation and the intervention of the Secretary-General himself at critical moments.

The Signing of the Peace Agreement in Mexico on January 16, 1992

The following introductory statement by President Alfredo Cristiani at the signing of the Peace Agreement represents the unquestionable historic record, recognizing the role played by both the Group of Friends and the United Nations:

> To be able to reach this day we have needed in the process the support and the understanding of the friends of those countries that integrated the "Group of Friends" of the Secretary-General of the United Nations: Mexico, Colombia, Spain, and Venezuela, and in particular, their presidents, their foreign ministers, and their representatives before the world's premier forum. They deserve the recognition and the gratitude of all the Salvadoran people, for their dedication, commitment, and solidarity in the search for peace in El Salvador. The Secretary-General Javier Pérez de Cuéllar and his personal representatives, Alvaro de Soto and Marrack Goulding, have had a good and significant part in the success of the whole negotiation.

CONCLUSION

At the time, I thought that the UN negotiators—principally de Soto—were leaning too heavily on the Salvadoran government and that they gave the impression that they were favoring the guerrillas. With hindsight, that perception does not seem to be so accurate. Had that not been the case, the government would probably not have accepted the terms during that time. Cristiani was suffering from the legitimate prejudice that the UN and most governments—excluding the United States—had toward Salvadoran government policies and especially the Salvadoran military. Further, without pressuring the government, the military forces could have conceivably refused to carry out their commitments. In recognition of the difficult position of the Salvadoran government, one senior diplomat said to me, "I hope that our country never finds itself in such a situation." I never saw a man suffer so much as Cristiani did during those days. He had to assume the full burden of the commitments he had agreed to and take responsibility for previous government offenses in which he himself was not involved. In fact, some of the military officers surrounding him would be listed as perpetrators of human-rights crimes in the final report of the Truth Commission and would certainly face some kind of retribution.

In summary, I believe that more pressure was placed on the government than the FMLN, but there were no alternatives to that. This was difficult to accept at the time. These perceptions were not only held by the UN negotiators, but to a certain extent also by the four countries. The brutality of the Salvadoran armed forces had to be reckoned with. This explained the hard line that was taken at times with the government during the negotiations. Nevertheless, Cristiani was our best hope for a transition from the brutality of some members of the previous administrations to a fuller democracy, and we could not risk alienating him. The prejudices towards the government because of its past diminished during the process after the UN and the Friends had the chance to witness Cristiani in action as a good man, and hence the discussions became more balanced.

Pérez de Cuéllar's Memoirs

In Javier Pérez de Cuéllar's memoirs, *Pilgrimage for Peace: A Secretary-General's Memoir*, the former Secretary-General barely mentions the Group of Friends and thus leaves the impression that the UN was trying to underplay the role of the governments involved. In fact, the presidents represented in the Group of Friends (Cesar Gaviria, Carlos Salinas de Gortari, Felipe González, and Carlos Andrés Pérez) supported his efforts in the process as explained in this chapter. Both the government of El Salvador as well as the FMLN publicly underlined and recognized the major role played by the Friends. The Security Council of the UN in its resolution on El Salvador equally noted the significance of the Friends' support. It is an an example of a successful modality of cooperation that was afterwards utilized by the UN in several other cases.

The principal UN negotiator, Alvaro de Soto, similarly emphasized the crucial role of the Group of Friends. In his chapter in the book by Crocker et al. titled *Herding Cats*, he explains that Pérez de Cuéllar kept a healthy distance from the mediation and left himself in charge. The Secretary-General would use the power of his office to invite the parties to New York for the mediation process but left the day-to-day work to de Soto and his colleagues. De Soto expresses his gratitude to the Friends in this way:

> I pay tribute to the [F]riends, especially to the ambassadors at the United Nations of Colombia [Fernando Cepeda], Mexico [Jorge Montaño], Spain [Juan Antonio Yañez], and Venezuela [Diego Arria], for their solidarity, support, and intellectual contribution. They were fully caught up in the mystique of the effort. They had a profound awareness of what was at stake. . . . The parties, in a curious reversal of roles, took to lobbying the friends so that they would bring influence to bear on the Secretary-General. The friends had been chosen deliberately among countries that did not have a strategic stake in the outcome of the conflict. . . . The solidarity, even complicity, that developed between us survived . . . the transition to the formalization of the friends as a group, which occurred during the first Ibero-American Summit in Guadalajara, Mexico, in July 1991. . . . The photos taken at the initialing of the accords, around midnight on December 31st, 1991, with the four ambassadors standing above Pérez de Cuéllar and me, bear testimony to our complicitous relationship, which was to continue throughout the years of implementation of the agreements.[14]

To this day, the role of the UN mediation continues to be controversial. Some U.S. and Salvadoran officials remain convinced that the lead UN negotiator, Alvaro de Soto, was overprotective of the FMLN arguments and positions. The criticisms stem from the belief that the UN team was not fully aware of how governments work and the limitations they are faced with. Nevertheless, there is agreement among the Friends that the friction that existed with the UN negotiating team at the time should not detract from the overall positive impact of its involvement. Probably the best defense for the UN mediators is that El Salvador is today a peaceful country.

A key lesson from the Salvadoran case is the importance for all participating parties to stay fully engaged in the developments of the mediation process in order to apply leverage at the exact time when it is needed. They have to be aware of every window of opportunity when leverage is needed and use the specific tool of leverage that will work in each instance and with what party. They also must work closely with the mediator, as they did with de Soto, so that everyone is fundamentally working in the same direction. Full engagement is a fundamental obligation of the "friends" in the process. To corroborate this assessment, it is useful to recall that after the peace treaties were signed at Chapultepec, Mexico, in January 1992, Secretary of State Baker wrote a letter to the four presidents of the Friends asking for their cooperation in continuing to remain engaged in the process in order to ensure the proper implementation of the agreements.

In conclusion, it was the leverage of the Four Plus One, the intermediation of the United Nations, the fact that Cuba and the Soviet Union/Russia supported the peace process, the democratic transition in Nicaragua and the cessation of military support to the FMLN, and finally the commitment and goodwill of President Alfredo Cristiani that brought about the successful achievement of peace in El Salvador. Many years after the agreements were signed in 1992 and after experiencing a number of successful democratic elections, El Salvador today is a very different country. This is thanks to the work of the UN, the Friends, the cooperation of the Salvadoran government and the FMLN, and the vision and courage of Alfredo Cristiani who, with such determination, had to face strong political resistance to change. Having come face-to-face with such change and its radical implications for their daily lives, the Salvadoran people are, of course, the true heroes of the Salvadoran peace process.

NOTES

1. A former under-secretary of state told me: "The intent of the letter to Somoza was not to 'congratulate' Somoza but to pressure him to open the system further. Somoza deliberately misrepresented the letter to Pérez and never showed him the actual text of the letter. Pérez only saw the letter when it was later leaked and published in the *Washington Post.* The initiative to send the letter to General Somoza and its main drafting came from the White House. There was some questioning in the State Department as to the desirability of a letter for fear it might be misinterpreted. According to Robert Pastor in his book, *Condemned to Repetition,* the U.S. concern was to persuade Somoza to give up power and allow a democratic government to take over as the best way to prevent an extremist Sandinista regime. See Robert Pastor, *Condemned to Repetition* (Princeton, NJ: Princeton University Press, 1987), 66–71.

2. In the chapter titled "Slow Intelligence" in Anthony Lake's book, he relates that a CIA brief in June 1979 concluded that the "final offensive" by the Sandanistas would not be powerful enough to defeat Somoza. Even a week later, as fighting intensified, Lieutenant General Dennis McAuliffe, commander-in-chief of the U.S. Southern Command in Panama, told a Congressional committee that the Sandinistas' "hit-and-run" attacks "were not very significant." Somoza's forces "are reacting, in my judgement, adequately to the situation and are able to regain control in the contested areas fairly quickly." See Anthony Lake, *Somoza Falling* (New York: Houghton Mifflin, 1989), 211–12.

3. Ibid.

4. Yale UN Oral History Interview with Beatrice Rangel on September 16, 1997, in New York City, 6–8.

5. Yale UN Oral History Interview with Jorge Montaño on October 1, 1999, in Mexico City, Mexico, 11.

6. Javier Pérez de Cuéllar, *Pilgrimage for Peace: A Secretary-General's Memoir* (New York: St. Martin's Press, 1997), 418.

7. In the case of Haiti, the Four Friends were Canada, France, the United States, and Venezuela. The same formula would apply again in the case of the Friends of Guatemala, where Colombia, Mexico, Spain, and Venezuela were once more united to work together for the peace process.

8. The Salvadoran government would say that these death squads were made up of rogue soldiers taking advantage of the situation; others would agree that the death squads were a part of the military's defense strategy of intimidation.

9. Montaño interview, 15.

10. Ibid., 16.
11. Ibid., 18.
12. Ibid.
13. Ibid., 24–26.
14. Alvaro de Soto, "Ending Violent Conflict in El Salvador," in *Herding Cats: Multiparty Mediation in a Complex World*, ed. Chester Crocker, Fen Osler Hampson, and Pamela Aall (Washington, DC: U.S. Institute of Peace Press, 1999), 366–69.

CHAPTER FOUR

Probing the Successful Application of Leverage in Support of Mozambique's Quest for Peace

DIRK SALOMONS

WHAT LESSONS CAN BE LEARNED from ONUMOZ, the relatively successful peacekeeping mission that within two years, from 1992 to 1994, halted a civil war in Mozambique? What types of leverage shaped the ability of the key players to bring the parties to the table, and keep them there? Was it sheer good fortune? Did the military presence make a difference?

Mozambique is a colonial construct, not a nation in any historical sense. When independence from Portugal came in 1975, a Marxist party with a southern constituency, Frelimo (Front for the Liberation of Mozambique), assumed a leadership role that was never fully accepted by the people living in the center of the country. This gave Rhodesia, and later South Africa, leverage that it used to destabilize the Marxist regime and set off a destructive civil war in which a million people died.

Renamo (Resistencia Nacional Mozambicana), the rebel movement created by Ian Smith and Roelof Botha, took on a life of its own. Arms poured into Mozambique from both sides: the Soviet Union and its allies supported Frelimo, South Africa (and some Western right-wing groups) backed Renamo. Leverage rested with the warlords. Between 1980 and 1989 Mozambique's budding social and economic infrastructure, carefully created by Frelimo in its first five years, was pulverized by Renamo and its foreign backers.

When the Soviet Union imploded, the "great African game" lost its charm and a complex system of patronage unraveled. Frelimo and Re-

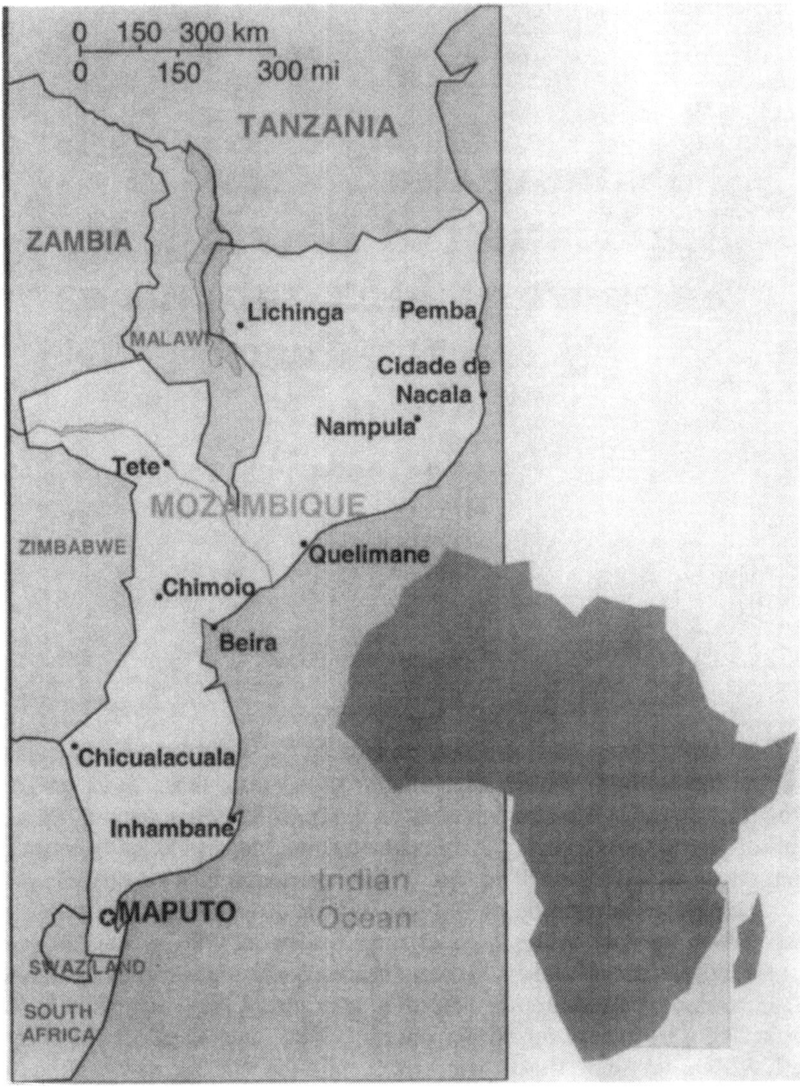

namo both lost their material support for the war, and the former, moreover, began to lose its faith in Marxism. Poverty drove it into the arms of the IMF and the World Bank; the United Nations agencies and nongovernmental organizations (NGOs) came in with food aid and technical assistance to alleviate the suffering (or to re-colonize the country, as some Frelimo hard-liners thought). Leverage had moved to the donor community, which used it to draw Mozambique into the Western camp.

Frelimo and Renamo both sought negotiations, each on its own terms. Where traditional diplomacy failed, a Roman Catholic lay community, Sant'Egidio, managed to bring the parties together. The Italian government provided the means and good advice. For over two years the parties struggled with the issues, and in doing so, each subtly reshaped the other's perception of reality. Common principles were elaborated and adopted. Now the leverage rested with those people in Renamo and Frelimo who had placed their hopes and trust in peace. They exerted pressure on the more militant factions within their ranks, but knew they only had a short time to demonstrate that peace could lift all boats.

A complex peace agreement was crafted as more players and advisers came on board. The donor community saw an opportunity to convert its humanitarian investments into sustainable development—through peace. The United Nations took on a role of guarantor for the implementation of the peace process. The international community pledged to foot the bill. Leverage worked in two ways: the international community had gained the trust of both parties through its persistent and impartial support and thus had some goodwill to trade in, while the belligerents had tied the international community down as guarantors and financiers of the process. They thus put pressure on the donors for ever-more-generous funding, threatening a breakdown of the process if adequate resources for demobilization, the formation of political parties, and elections were withheld.

Once the United Nations Security Council, in December 1992, had approved a complex, multifaceted peacekeeping mission, with political, military, humanitarian, and electoral components against a backdrop of large commitments for concurrent economic and social aid, it was hard to see who had leverage over whom. All players had invested heavily: the only way was forward.

An overtaxed, politically divided, and pathologically over-regulated United Nations Secretariat nearly managed to destroy the momentum of the peace process; the lack of troop-contributing countries did not help either. Six months into the peacekeeping mission, there was nothing on the ground that even vaguely resembled the blueprint set out in the peace agreement. Those groups within both Frelimo and Renamo that never had much to gain from the peace process, particularly the staunch ideologists and the military leaders, gained leverage with their cynicism and subtle sabotage. A military coup was only just averted. The calendar for the peace process was abandoned.

The arrival of five battalions and large numbers of military observers in April 1993 reversed this picture. Suddenly, the nearly moribund demobilization process took on new life, as Renamo felt protected against stabs in the back. The officers in Frelimo's army who contemplated a coup saw that the point of no return had been passed. The forceful presence of the foreign contingents, strategically placed along the major transportation corridors, gave everyone a much safer feeling, and the economy picked up. Leverage now rested with the peacekeeping troops whose presence sent a message that there was no way back, and that continued violence was out of the question. Politics became the new game.

With a financial shot in the arm from the donors of some $70 million, the electoral process was a big success. Was this type of expenditure proportional to Mozambique's ability to sustain democratic election over time? Voter turnout in October 1994 was impressive: Frelimo won in the south, Renamo won in the center, Mr. Chissano won the presidency with a 54 percent majority, and a now-legitimate Frelimo continued to govern as Renamo took on the role of loyal opposition. ONUMOZ closed down, the donors and the aid agencies stayed. Control of Mozambique had largely returned to the Mozambicans.

LEVERAGE, FATE, OR SERENDIPITY?

Should governments attempt to employ military forces in coordination with political, diplomatic, economic, and humanitarian measures to contain crises that threaten regional peace? This question is at the core of the research agenda of the three sponsors who have commissioned this chapter. And specifically, the question has been raised whether there are lessons to be learned in this respect from ONUMOZ, the relatively successful United Nations peacekeeping operation in Mozambique. Within two years, from late 1992 to late 1994, a civil war was halted and a democratically elected government took power in a rejuvenated country. What types of leverage made this possible?

The sponsors' research agenda is open to interpretation: the employment of military forces is not the same as the use of military force. While military deployment played an important role in the ONUMOZ operation, no force was ever used, nor were any threats ever made to use force. But the military presence itself represented a commitment of the international community, and it was an important component of a long-standing and consistent effort by Mozambique's friends to overcome the impasse of a long and destructive civil war. What does that tell us?

Whether there are lessons to be learned from the revival of Mozambique remains a matter of opinion. In many ways, the process was unique and was helped along by massive good fortune at nearly every crossroads. The shifting geopolitics in Africa after the cold war created a sudden opportunity. Influential donors had made long-term investments in Mozambique's future—many years before peace became a possibility. A small lay community in Rome, known for its soup kitchens in Trastevere, brought adversaries together who would have shunned traditional diplomacy. The rains returned in December 1992 after years of drought. The mishaps in Angola made the Security Council unusually mindful of the need to match mandates and resources. A Special Representative of the Secretary-General, who had been picked in great haste—purely on basis of his nationality—as an "interim" to hold the fort, proved to be a charismatic, forceful leader with uncanny diplomatic skills.

None of these elements of good fortune can ever be reproduced, and luck cannot be learned. And yet each of these opportunities could have been wasted, and there are lessons implicit in the ways many players made sure that they were not. In this chapter I shall try to identify those "moments of truth" where sound judgment and persistence made these opportunities into landmarks of progress, and where leverage of some kind was used to amplify and enforce these serendipitous openings.

The story of ONUMOZ begins, in fact, at least a decade before the operation was launched, and the international community's involvement in those early years has to be described in order to explain how trust could be built on its foundations. It is equally important to examine the genesis of the peace accord that set the framework for ONUMOZ, as some important lessons emerge about the use of time and internalization as tools for leverage.

One section is dedicated to the dynamics of the Secretariat and the Security Council's deliberations that led to the resolution creating ONUMOZ, and to analyze the elements in this resolution that made ONUMOZ a truly multifunctional mission, embedded in a broader UN, common system presence. The chapter further probes the rather inauspicious beginnings of ONUMOZ, against a backdrop of sometimes Byzantine Secretariat politics. It looks at the process whereby a military force was mobilized and deployed and describes the impact of this venture on the peace process. Above all, this chapter "sings the praise" of the international community that stood by Mozambique through thick and thin, and of the remarkable individuals on all sides of the issue who were willing to take vast risks so that the opportunities for peace would not slip away.

To some extent this is also a tale of personal discovery. Being a part of this unusual cabal of believers, intent on bringing the peace accord to life, was an exhilarating experience. Often, we were struggling not only with the adversarial parties, but also with our own masters in the capitals. This makes it hard to remain dispassionate, but where strong opinions surface, I hope they are well-supported by facts and arguments.

Background: Sacrifice of the Pawns, or the Leverage of Dependency

The Republic of Mozambique stretches along some 1,500 miles of Africa's eastern shoreline; across the ocean lies Madagascar. Some 17 million people live in its vast savannas, tropical forest, and coastal cities. The shape of Mozambique and its immense ethnic and linguistic diversity are clearly not the outcome of conscious political choices made by its inhabitants but rather the result of a long and convoluted history. Rarely did the inhabitants of the region have any say in their destiny—rarely, also, did they have a peaceful moment.

Soon after the year 1000 Arab traders settled on the Mozambican coast, close to the current site of Sofala. This led to trade contacts with other coastal cities, in what nowadays constitutes Kenya and Tanzania, and to the emergence of a mixed Arab–Bantu population, the Swahili. Nearby, the powerful empire of Greater Zimbabwe made its strengths felt. And as this regime disintegrated at the end of the fifteenth century, a new African imperium rose up: that of Monomatapa, stretching from the Zambezi River to the Limlopo and from the Kalahari desert to the Indian Ocean.

In 1498, Vasco da Gama first set foot in Mozambique, and soon way-stations were constructed to provision Portuguese ships on their route to Asia. Portuguese traders managed to push out the Arabs, military garrisons protected the traders, and the Portuguese Crown started to hand-out large tracts of land, *prazos*, to adventurers and former members of the military. These *prazos* expanded into autonomous small fiefdoms, using slave labor. As the slave trade became a major economic force in the seventeenth century (to supply the Portuguese plantations in Brazil), Mozambique became a key source, and as some tribes were decimated by deportations, other tribes, such as the Yao in the north, developed into fierce hunters of slaves.[1]

The Portuguese state as such, however, had only minimal control over the area now known as Mozambique until late in the nineteenth century. Earlier, South African warlords had conquered the Tsonga leaders in southern Mozambique and created the Gaza empire. The real colonial occupation began only after the Portuguese were given control of the area at the Conference of Berlin (1884–1885). The Gaza empire, as well as other autonomous coastal mini-states and cities, were soon taken by the Portuguese army. In the north, the Makonde offered fierce resistance. It took until 1920 before the Portuguese fully controlled the entire country, and even then, pockets of resistance remained. Since the government did not have sufficient resources, it granted concessions to large private companies that developed the mines and plantations producing sugar, coconuts, sisal, and rice. Portugal allowed South African companies to recruit labor in Mozambique and received fees in return. Railways were built from Johannesburg to Lourenço Marques (1894), and from Beira to Rhodesia (1899) and Nyasaland (1922).

When Antonio de Salazar came to power in 1932, following Mussolini's example in creating his *Estado Novo*, he wrested control of Mozambique's economic resources away from the trading companies and convinced poor Portuguese farmers to settle in the Mozambican countryside. A system of forced labor was formalized whereby all Mozambican men had to work six months a year for the state or its designated private contractors. Women were forced to meet production quotas of agricultural commodities. Poverty increased dramatically, and only by using violence were the Portuguese able to retain control. Not even basic education or health-care services were provided.

The Rise of Frelimo

Even during the 1950s and 1960s when other colonial powers began to sense that changes were imminent, Portugal continued to settle its poor in

Mozambique so that by 1970 there were some 250,000 Portuguese within the country. Small groups of Mozambican exiles began to organize systematic resistance against the colonial regime, and in 1962, with support from Julius Nyerere in Tanzania, Frelimo was created. In 1969, its first leader, Eduardo Mondlane, was killed by a letter bomb in his office in Dar es Salaam. After some internal struggles, Frelimo chose Samora Machel, a Marxist from the south, to succeed him. Intensive guerrilla warfare against the Portuguese continued unabated from the day in 1960 when 600 Makonde farmers were killed in an uprising until April 1974, when Caetano's fascist regime in Portugal was toppled by an army revolt. During those years Frelimo had developed into an effective fighting force, supported with weaponry by several Eastern European states and capable of shooting down Portuguese aircraft with surface-to-air missiles.

When Caetano's dictatorship came to an end, Portugal had some 60,000 soldiers in Mozambique. In addition, the colonists were all heavily armed. PDI, the secret service, had developed a vast network of informants to ferret out dissent and to play tribal leaders off against one another. Over a million farmers and peasants were relocated forcibly to *aldeamentos*, alleged safe havens under Portuguese control. When Mozambique finally became independent in 1975, with Samora Machel as its president, it was impoverished, uprooted, deprived of social, human, and economic capital, and left to fend for itself. Nearly all the Portuguese settlers returned home. Mozambique's only friends came from the Soviet bloc and from a few leftist parties in Western Europe.

Samora Machel's Marxist convictions set the tone for Frelimo's beginnings as the regime came to power. He felt that the Mozambicans had not really participated in the struggle for their liberation and thus did not understand the principles of socialism. So *grupos dinamizadores* were established in every factory, plantation, village, neighborhood, and school to explain Frelimo's goals, advocate collective labor, and squash all dissent. For collaborators with the Portuguese colonial administration (including a great number of *regulos*, village elders), re-education camps were established in the outer reaches of Niassa, known as "the Siberia of Mozambique." At the third party congress in 1977, Frelimo formally defined itself as a Marxist-Leninist vanguard party. The political and social model of the Soviet Union had great charm for Africa in those days: it inspired SWAPO, the Namibian liberation movement, South Africa's ANC, and the governments of countries such as Guinea, Ethiopia, Congo, and Benin. It was the only model that seemed untainted by colonialism.

Party membership in Frelimo became the preserve of those with impeccable peasant or laborer credentials. The few industrial enterprises that existed were nationalized; large-scale agricultural ventures followed the Soviet model and crowded out existing villages. Whereas the Portuguese administration had co-opted the local village chiefs, or *regulos*, into its administration, Frelimo replaced the local chiefs with party enthusiasts from the cities. The fact that most Frelimo party officials came from the south, and that tribes from the center were marginalized in the political process, did not help. Where under the Portuguese the local healers, or *curandeiros*, were left in peace to ply their trade, Frelimo introduced the concepts of modern medicine, excluding these powerful community "health experts." This further exacerbated the gap between the party leadership and the rural population.

At the same time, Frelimo should be given credit. It began to build a nation where none existed. It believed in the humanitarian and egalitarian tenets of an ideology that held a lot of promise for young Africans who had grown up in a culture of extended families and sharing. Its administration managed to create an effective network of primary schools within a matter of years, and it brought real health care to the countryside. Its young cadres worked with immense dedication and corruption was virtually unheard of. Everyone, to the very top of the party, lived austerely. The ideological grip of their Eastern European mentors, moreover, especially Cuba, East Germany, and Bulgaria, was firm and convincing. Capitalist society seemed decadent and exploitative. Scholarships, training, and so on all came with the Marxist seal of approval.

After the death (in a still mysterious plane crash)[2] of President Machel in 1986, however, the party line began to show cracks and the firm convictions of Frelimo's most dogmatic leaders began to waver as they were exposed to other models of society (such as the Nordic alternative). While hindsight now exposes how these zealous efforts polarized the country, one should not forget that some of the best brains in the West, in those years, believed equally fervently that human nature could be bent and that the dream of equality under the leadership of the proletariat was within reach.

How Mozambique's socialist experiment would have ended if it had not been sabotaged by South Africa and Rhodesia still remains a point of debate. It might have matured, and it might have found a social model more in line with Africa's traditions, or it might have failed anyway. The fact is that by 1980 the destabilization orchestrated by Mozambique's two unreconstructed racist neighbors made life impossible. The Rhodesians resented Mozambique's support for ZANU, Robert Mugabe's Zimbabwe African National Union (which operated from bases within Mozambique). South Africa dreaded the thought of a successful authentic African state on its borders, since this would undermine the myth that Africans "were not ready" for autonomy. Mozambique's willingness to give shelter to the ANC reinforced South Africa's aggressive stance. A vast program was launched to destabilize Mozambique. The result was horrific: more than a million dead and more than $18 billion in damages.[3]

The Emergence of Renamo and the Beginnings of the Civil War

The genesis of Renamo can only be explained against this backdrop. It has often been described as the brainchild of Ken Flowers, head of the

Rhodesian secret service, and to some extent that is true, but its was grafted onto roots of ethnic conflict that went deep into the past. Flowers wanted a rightist Mozambican resistance group to stir up things on the long border between Rhodesia and Mozambique in order to frustrate ZANU. For this purpose, he recruited former Mozambican soldiers who had fought in the Portuguese army (and thus were social pariahs). Some dissident former Frelimo fighters also joined their ranks. Initially, Renamo was led by a former soldier who had fled a Frelimo re-education camp: Andre Matsangaissa. After his death in battle, in 1979, his closest collaborator, Afonso Dhlakama, took over. Dhlakama is the son of a Ndau chief, a subgroup of the Shona, the largest ethnic group in Zimbabwe. He went to a Catholic primary school and considers himself a Catholic.

By the time ZANU came to power in Zimbabwe (1980) after Ian Smith was forced to negotiate, Renamo had developed a strong base. It controlled the road from Maputo to the north so that only military convoys could pass through. Even these convoys were often attacked. With Rhodesian patronage suddenly vanishing, the South Africans took over. This led to a new phase in the resistance against Frelimo. South African military intelligence provided Renamo with large amounts of modern weapons, communications equipment, and a new destabilization strategy. Civilians became the target of choice. Villages were raided, all innovations introduced by Frelimo such as schools and health clinics were leveled, and teachers as well as health workers were systematically killed and dismembered (many Mozambicans believe that a mutilated body will not have access to an afterlife). Renamo became a tightly knit terrorist movement, with strong internal discipline. It would kidnap young children, sometimes forcing them to kill their parents, and induct them into the service: first as carriers, later as full-fledged fighters. Renamo expanded throughout the country, with particular prominence in the central provinces. It lived off the land. At the same time, it attracted some supporters overseas, including the Heritage Foundation and various members of the U.S. Congress. In 1986, Jesse Helms blocked Melissa Wells's appointment as U.S. ambassador to Mozambique for ten months because she opposed Renamo and accused it of "widespread atrocities." It took the State Department's Gersony Report (1988), which documented Renamo's brutal war of terror, to defeat attempts in Congress to recognize Renamo.[4]

Those, however, who saw Renamo only as a puppet of South Africa and an international network of right-wing fanatics underestimated its popular support.[5] In the 1994 elections, Renamo carried Sofala, Manica, Tete, Zambezia, and Nampula with an overwhelming majority (97 out of 147 seats). In the rest of the country, it barely ran. This meant that tribal and regional issues played a far larger role than Frelimo was willing to acknowledge during the years of the civil war.

In dealing with the international community, Renamo always presented itself as driven by a free-market, liberal ideology as opposed to the

Marxist convictions of its opponents (if it made any effort at all to explain itself). Locally, it played the ethnic card, as we discovered early in 1993 when the U.S. embassy kindly shared with ONUMOZ the translated transcripts of radio broadcasts disseminated by small Renamo stations, demonstrating the awesome power of Langley (Virginia, home of the U.S. Central Intelligence Agency [CIA]) to capture and transcribe weak signals in obscure local languages and have them on the ambassador's desk by the next morning. These Renamo broadcasts stressed the tribal background of President Joachim Chissano and his cabinet members, recalled which tribe had done what during the years of the slave trade, what the composition of the army was, and so on and so forth.

This touched on some real problems that directly affect Mozambique's long-term prospects of becoming a unified state. President Chissano is from the south and belongs to the Tsonga tribe. Tsongas, especially from the Gaza province, have largely dominated Frelimo and have ruled Mozambique in an alliance with the Makondes from the north who were prominent in the military. Tribes from the central and central-north were excluded from this alliance, especially the Sena and the Ndau, who provided the base of Renamo's support.

The Role of the International Community during the Civil War

As the Rhodesian and South African destabilization campaign increased in intensity, Mozambique's friends mounted their own campaign in the country's support. The Soviet Union sent jet planes, tanks, and other heavy equipment to the Mozambican army, which was composed of some 35,000 ground troops, plus a very small navy and air force. The Soviet satellite states sent vast amounts of small arms, and militias were created in every village under Frelimo's control to keep Renamo at bay. The Europeans brought humanitarian assistance and development aid. The United States kept its distance. In 1983, Mozambique made its first appeal for food aid, as a drought and interrupted lines of transportation began to bring the country to its knees. Zimbabwe sent in troops to protect the so-called "Beira Corridor," the vital road, railway, and oil pipeline linking the port of Beira to Zimbabwe.

Nearly bankrupt, Mozambique swallowed its pride and in 1984 applied for membership in the IMF and the World Bank in order to qualify for loans. Military expenditures became an ever-increasing component of the Mozambican budget and in time absorbed nearly half of the government's yearly income. In desperation, Mozambique proposed to drop its support for the ANC if South Africa would halt its destabilization campaign. Pretoria and Maputo signed an accord to this effect in Nkomati, a small border town, in 1984. Mozambique honored its side of the agreement, but South Africa, more covertly, continued its subversive actions.

When U.S. Senator John Danforth toured famine zones in Africa early in 1984 he was shocked at what he saw. He asked for an urgent meeting with his friend President Ronald Reagan and showed him pictures of the starving children in Gaza province.[6] Reagan asked USAID to do something. The time was ripe. The State Department had already been arguing for a new policy towards Mozambique, given its turn to the West, its opening towards South Africa, and its help in pushing Angola into talks. U.S. Assistant Secretary of State Chester A. Crocker, who had been instrumental in negotiating Namibia's independence, managed to convince Congress that Mozambique was no longer the enemy. Mozambique quickly became the largest recipient of U.S. aid in southern Africa.

Aid agencies, governmental and nongovernmental, became a major presence throughout the country. The aggregate of foreign-aid disbursements increased from little more than $200 million in 1986 to almost $900 million by 1988. The United Nations specialized agencies became important and trusted advisers to the government. Frelimo, at its 1989 Fifth Congress, dropped the word "People" from the state's official designation, so that it became the "Republic of Mozambique." The claim to be a Marxist-Leninist party was quietly rescinded.

At the end of the decade, as the implosion of the Soviet Union drew near, an overall accord to end the cold-war-by-proxy in Africa was reached, whereby South Africa agreed to elections in Namibia, and Cuba agreed to withdraw its troops from Angola. In 1988, President Chissano, who had succeeded Samora Machel in 1986, met with South African President Botha and obtained his commitment—finally—to honor the Nkomati Accord. South Africa's material support for Renamo suddenly was reduced to a trickle, as the apartheid regime started talks with Nelson Mandela. President Reagan met with President Machel (1985) and later on (1987) with President Chissano. The U.S.S.R. had stopped its arms shipments to Frelimo, and the Eastern bloc, already marginalized in its influence, lost its last remnants of a voice in Mozambican affairs.

At this stage, a network of relationships had been built (and broken) that defined both Frelimo's and Renamo's external worlds: whom they knew, whom they trusted, whom they feared, and whom they owed. Clearly, the civil war was running out of steam. The pawns on the geopolitical playing field had lost their importance and the game itself came to an end. The players moved on. For Frelimo and Renamo, it was time to negotiate. For the friends of Mozambique, the time had come to use some of their leverage as donors to bring the parties together.

THE PEACE ACCORD AND THE INVISIBLE HAND, OR THE LEVERAGE OF INTERNALIZATION

The civil war had reached a stalemate, and both parties realized that they could drag out hostilities but could not win a decisive advantage. Carefully, they started to explore their options and to approach potential intermediaries. In the summer of 1988, Dhlakama met in Germany with

Kenya's foreign minister and from that day on, Kenya supplied Renamo with passports, travel arrangements, and foreign currency. That same year, President Chissano met with Kenya's President Daniel arap Moi and Zimbabwe's President Mugabe. Moi then sent an envoy to meet Dhlakama in Gorongosa, Renamo's jungle hideout. South African Foreign Minister "Pik" Botha suggested to Chissano that Mozambique should ask the United States to mediate an end to the war.

None of these initiatives was conclusive, and Renamo's leaders remained reluctant to accept the good offices of any foreign government, as they were distrustful of any unknown entity. Church leaders in Mozambique made a major effort to create a dialogue and bridge the abyss of distrust. Ultimately, it was a small Roman Catholic lay organization, the Community of Sant'Egidio, best known for its soup kitchens in the Roman neighborhood of Trastevere, which managed to penetrate Renamo's psychological armor. The community had long been associated with Don Jaime Gonçalves, a Mozambican priest from the central region who had become Archbishop of Beira in 1977. In 1982, members of Sant'Egidio had helped to negotiate the release of priests and nuns held by Renamo, and it facilitated negotiations between the Vatican and Frelimo in 1985, when religious freedom was restored in Mozambique.[7]

For two years the search continued for an acceptable formula that would allow the two parties to meet face-to-face. Renamo favored mediation by Kenya or Portugal; Frelimo preferred Zimbabwe or Kenya. Frelimo approached the Vatican. A round of talks to be hosted by Malawi foundered. Finally, in June 1990, the Community of Sant'Egidio proposed that it would host discussions in Rome and both sides promptly accepted the offer. The Government of Italy promised its support. The first direct meeting between delegations from Frelimo and Renamo took place from 8 to 10 July 1990 at the Convent of Sant'Egidio.[8]

Both sides formally stated their intent to search for an end to the war and agreed on four individual mediators: Mario Raffaeli (Italian government), Professor Andrea Riccardi and Don Matteo Zuppi (Community of Sant'Egidio), and Archbishop Jaime Gonçalves (Mozambique's Episcopal Conference). A U.S. team of military advisers gave technical support, and Kenyan, Botswanan, and Zimbabwean diplomats worked behind the scenes to influence the proceedings. A partial cease-fire was agreed to on 1 December 1990. Under its terms, Renamo would halt all attacks on the Beira and Limpopo transport corridors, while the Zimbabwean troops would strictly confine their operations to these routes and not pursue Renamo fighters. This guarantee of access, in turn, greatly facilitated the movement of food relief, particularly by the World Food Programme, in response to the debilitating drought that affected southern Africa in 1991 and 1992. A Joint Verification Commission, consisting of the Congo, France, Kenya, Portugal, the U.S.S.R., the United Kingdom, the United States, and Zambia, would formally observe the parties' compliance with the agreement and hear complaints.

Negotiations initially ran into difficulties during the following year, as Renamo did not want to recognize Frelimo's authority as the government of Mozambique. Renamo, in fact, envisaged a federal type of state whereby it could gain control of the central provinces. Frelimo rapidly preempted this argument by picking up on another demand made by Renamo, namely, the introduction of a multiparty democracy, and started a process of constitutional reform. The mediators, however, remained persistent and managed to keep the parties talking so that an agenda for full peace negotiations was ultimately agreed upon in May 1991, covering six areas: the law on political parties, the electoral system, military issues, guarantees, a cease-fire, and a donors' conference. Further disagreements over the issue of legitimacy held up the talks over the summer, but at the eighth round of talks, in October 1991, agreement was reached on the so-called "Basic Principles" of the peace accord.

These basic principles resolved two important issues: legitimacy and supervision. Renamo agreed to respect the authority and institutions of the government, to renounce the use of force, and "to conduct its political struggle in conformity with the laws in force" after a cease-fire became effective (Protocol I, point 2). The government agreed to delay legislation on any issue under discussion until after multiparty elections. The parties also agreed on the supervisory mechanisms for the peace process: a commission "composed of representatives of the government, Renamo, the United Nations, and other organizations or governments to be agreed upon between the parties" (Protocol I, point 5).

The development of these basic principles also represented a breakthrough in the negotiations: the parties had found common ground after a lengthy, frustrating, sometimes infuriatingly slow back-and-forth, with endless consultations on all sides, steps forward and backward—but the end result was ownership of the process, an internalization of the results achieved that shaped them into common values, beyond the level of "winners and losers." Each party had fundamentally changed the other's perception of reality. The investments in patience and nonjudgmental support on the part of the mediators had also paid off by creating a climate of trust in their impartiality. This then allowed them to provide guidance in some of the complex technical discussions that followed, as these principles were converted into concrete, detailed arrangements.

Over the next twelve months the parties, the mediators, and increasingly also the governments of Italy and the United States worked on the formulation of the full peace agreement.[9] In November 1991, Protocol II was signed, which set out "criteria and arrangements for the formation and recognition of political parties." This protocol defined the rights of parties, their duties, the registration process, and the implementation of its provisions, specifically establishing Renamo as a political party as of the date the peace agreement would be signed. Interestingly, the protocol specifically excluded from the political process any "associations whose primary purpose is to promote local or sectoral interest or the exclusive interests of a given social group or class of citizens" (point 1[b]). This somewhat cryptic clause addressed the fear that political parties might be set up along purely ethnic lines rather than on a substantive, ideological basis.

Protocol III, on "principles that should guide the drafting of the Electoral Act," dealt with freedom of the press, freedom of association, liberty of movement, the right of return for Mozambican refugees and displaced persons, procedures of elections, their financing, and the role of international observers in the process (a principle that became an important design element for the ONUMOZ mission).

Protocol IV dealt with military questions, first and foremost the formation of the Mozambican Defense Force. It defined the functions of the new army and described how it should be staffed in conjunction with the demobilization process, as both the government and Renamo would contribute units. The total strength of the new army would be 24,000, with an air force of 4,000, and a navy of 2,000. A detailed command structure was defined, the withdrawal of foreign troops was linked to the entry-in-force of the cease-fire (an agreement that caused great problems later on as the United Nations was unable initially to fill the security vacuum), and the State Information and Security Service was allowed to continue under direct supervision of the president (a clause that subsequently made Renamo very uneasy). Next, it dealt with the depolitization of the police force and the establishment of COMPOL, an independent, bipartisan oversight body. Finally, it addressed the reintegration of demobilized soldiers, providing a detailed and ambitious timetable, and referring to the planned donors' conference as the source of funding for the economic and social reintegration of the troops. This clause, again, created great expectations, which the international community would find difficult to live up to.

Protocol V gave a timetable for the electoral process ("one year after the date of signature of the General Peace Agreement"); it set out the composition and functions of the Supervisory and Monitoring Commission (to be chaired by the United Nations); it gave guarantees to Renamo for its security; and allowed it to continue administering the areas under its control. Protocol VI picked up where IV left off and in some respect overlapped by expanding on the cease-fire process, its oversight (by a Cease-fire Commission, CCF, with the United Nations again in the chair). This protocol also provided further details about the demobilization process and introduced the concept of 49 "assembly and billeting points" to which all demobilizing troops would withdraw (a selection that represented strategic choices by the parties, but caused the greatest logistic difficulties).

In Protocol VII, finally, the parties asked the Italian government to convene a donors' conference, and they agreed that "an appropriate share should be placed at the disposal of political parties to finance their activities" (another time bomb). It included a joint declaration by the parties on the guiding principles for humanitarian assistance (respecting the freedom of agencies as well as recipients and establishing yet another committee under the United Nations presidency). The entire General Peace Agreement, including all these protocols, was signed by President Chissano and Renamo leader Dhlakama in Rome on 4 October 1992, and transmitted to the United Nations Security Council through James Jonah, Under-Secretary-General for Political Affairs, who attended the signing ceremony.

At this stage, leverage began to work in two directions. The international community had gained the trust of the parties, and had provided moral and material support during the period of negotiations that had helped both parties. This would allow them to call in some of their chips in the following months, as the implementation of the peace agreement called for flexibility and cooperation on both sides. The potential resources forthcoming from a donors' conference meant that both parties had a material stake in success.

But the parties had also gained considerable leverage. They had tied the international community down, partly by specifying a large and potentially costly role for the United Nations in the agreement, partly by giving individual countries a special role in the oversight of the agreement's implementation, and partly by making the outcome of the donors' conference the linchpin for key parts of the process such as demobilization, the establishment of political parties, and the conduct of elections.

Genesis of the Security Council's Mandate, or the Leverage of the Visible Hand

When peace came to Mozambique at the end of 1992, the United Nations seemed to be caught by surprise. The UN Department of Political Affairs had participated in the later stages of the negotiations. In the plans for implementation of the peace accord, the UN had been given a pivotal role. Yet, when the peace accord was signed in Rome on October 4, 1992, no Special Representative of the Secretary-General (SRSG) had been identified. No Status of Forces Agreement had been discussed with the government. A mission to assess the logistic requirements for the UN's multifaceted tasks only departed in early September, less than four weeks before President Chissano formally requested the United Nations to oversee the implementation of the peace accord.

During the negotiations leading up to the peace accord, the United Nations had undertaken to orchestrate a most ambitious and complex set of interrelated activities: to verify the parties' adherence to a cease-fire; to supervise the withdrawal of foreign troops; to arrange for the demobilization of the combatants and to support their return to civil society; to monitor compliance with the political aspects of the accord; to prepare the ground for an electoral process; to facilitate the establishment and registration of political parties; and to coordinate the activities of the many UN system actors involved in the delivery of humanitarian aid as well as post-conflict recovery assistance, while ensuring their impartiality.

Only on the day the peace accord was signed did the search begin for an SRSG. Given the important role that Italy had played in the peace process, nationality became the dominant criterion for selection, and thus Aldo Ajello, then director of external relations at the United Nations Development Programme (UNDP) and an unknown quantity for the Secretariat, was summoned that same day to the Secretary-General's office, enlisted to serve as "interim" SRSG, and told to report to Maputo by October 15. This somewhat random selection process fortunately led to outstanding results, as Ajello's strong political and improvisational skills happened to match perfectly the requirements of the mission.

These skills were immediately put to the test, not only when the ceasefire was violated upon his arrival in Maputo, but also when it came to the preparation of a coherent design for the mission for consideration by the Security Council. Ajello met with Jonah in the Department of Political Affairs (DPA), as well as with Marrack Goulding, the Under-Secretary-General heading the Department for Peacekeeping Operations (DPKO). Both were already heavily taxed by the simultaneous demands made on their departments by missions in Cambodia, the Western Sahara, Angola, El Salvador, and Somalia. Many of their senior staff were in the field, as the United Nations traditionally cannibalizes on its regular staff to fill peacekeeping operations. Having seen the debacle of the UN's underfunded and understaffed mission in Angola, Ajello argued that the scope of the UN's role under the peace accord called for a large contingent of troops, a solid civilian component, and a large number of observers for the electoral process. His views prevailed within the Secretariat, and he managed to convince officials at the U.S. State Department and the Pentagon (whose support for a positive U.S. response in the Security Council was critical) that the Council could ill-afford another Angola, and that the incoming U.S. administration would end up with the bill.

On 22 October 1992 the Secretary-General reported to the General Assembly in some detail on the special programs of economic and humanitarian assistance to Mozambique that were required to remedy the combined impact of conflict and drought.[10] He cited FAO/WFP findings that some 3.1 million people in the country needed food aid to survive, and stressed the enormous strain the delivery of emergency supplies placed on the Department for the Prevention and Combat of National Disasters, the government agency responsible. Security constraints compounded the difficulties: in most districts, armed escorts were required to let convoys get through. He described what United Nations system agencies were doing to support the health sector, assist in the rehabilitation and construction of water supply and sanitation systems, and asked that 3.5 million hand-tool sets be donated at short notice in order to give farmers a fighting chance. The prospect of large returnee populations also required preparations and resources. At the same time, much was being done. A complete inventory of existing aid programs–identifying donors–painted a picture of a heavily involved and wide-ranging community effort (including donors such as Brazil, Saudi Arabia, and Turkey).

Against this backdrop of a humanitarian, social, and economic crisis, the scramble started within the United Nations to come up with a coherent mission plan for the Security Council's review and approval. A principal officer in DPKO, Dmitry Titov, was asked to prepare a draft report for the Security Council, and I was asked to work with him, after Ajello had convinced me to serve as his executive director in the mission. Titov and I quickly found common ground, and, armed with the General Peace Agreement and the report of the September logistics assessment, we set to work.

In the meantime, Ajello rushed to Rome carrying a letter from the Secretary-General to Prime Minister Amato in order to ask for the deployment of Italian troops to Mozambique.[11] This was particularly urgent because all foreign troops—that is, troops from Malawi and Zimbabwe—were to withdraw from the Beira and Nacala corridors within a month after the peace accord was signed—and now it was mid-November and they still had not left. The Secretary-General said that it was his intention to obtain authorization from the Security Council to deploy armed UN contingents, but "if normal procedures are followed, it will take some three-to-four months before such troops can be in the theatre and operational." Ajello convinced the Italian government that any delay in the departure of the Zimbabwean and Malawian troops would destroy Renamo's confidence in the process, but that a lack of security in these corridors due to a vacuum would attract all kinds of rabble and endanger the delivery of food to Mozambique's neighbors. Italy immediately made one logistically self-sufficient infantry battalion available, as well as an engineer battalion (to repair roads and bridges and to clear mines). These troops flew in within a few weeks after the Security Council approved the mission, and provided an element of credibility that shored up an otherwise sagging initial venture.

Meanwhile, negotiations within the Secretariat and among the members of the Security Council intensified. Various drafts of a mission plan circulated; we sent texts up to the Under-Secretaries-General, and they conducted the political consultations. The draft set out three basic assumptions. First of all, the trust placed in the United Nations by the parties required that it provide an effective, impartial structure to help them break the vicious cycle of violence. Second, this had to be a fully integrated mission with participation by the entire international community, especially the United Nations programs and specialized agencies, bilateral entities, intergovernmental agencies, and nongovernmental organizations. Third, attention should be paid to Mozambique's considerable size, its poor infrastructure, its persistent food shortage, the abundance of small arms in civilian hands, the banditry, and the millions of refugees and displaced people. All this had to be taken into account in assessing the human and material resources that ONUMOZ would require. Moreover, the United Nations would have to take full responsibility for the security in the key corridors that linked Mozambique's landlocked neighbors to the ocean. In other words, if we did not make a serious effort to do this well, the venture would be doomed from the outset.

This argument went over well with most Member States, the more so since some key players in the Security Council, including the United States, had already invested considerable quantities of money and effort in humanitarian and development assistance. In fact, each year from 1990 through 1995, the aggregate sum of all aid to Mozambique was close to $1 billion.[12] Meanwhile, Ajello kept pointing at the failure of the international community in Angola, where it had mounted a minimal response and harvested a disaster.

Given the structure of the peace accord, the Secretariat proposed a mandate for ONUMOZ with four components: political, military, electoral, and humanitarian. The operational concept of ONUMOZ was based on the strong interrelationships among these components:

> Without sufficient humanitarian aid, and especially food supplies, the security situation in the country may deteriorate and the demobilization process might stall. Without adequate military protection, the humanitarian aid would not reach its destination. Without sufficient progress in the political area, the confidence required for the disarmament and rehabilitation process would not exist. The electoral process, in turn, requires prompt demobilization and formation of the new armed forces, without which the conditions would not exist for successful elections.[13]

A detailed operational plan followed, setting out what needed to be done in each of these four areas, what resources were required, and what structures were envisaged. It specified the need for five logistically independent infantry battalions, plus three autonomous engineering battalions, supported by mine-clearing and engineering contractors. In addition, the Secretary-General asked for a military police platoon, a communications unit, an aviation unit with up to 24 fixed-wing and rotary aircraft (with an option to lease extra cargo capacity), a military medical unit with a field hospital, three logistic companies, and a movement-control company. A large part of these troops would be tied down in guarding the various corridors; others would provide security for the humanitarian efforts. To our great surprise, these "optimal" requests were not swept off the table in the first round of discussions, as we had feared. The U.S. military gave its tacit support to these estimates when Ajello visited the Pentagon, and while U.S. ground troops were ruled out from the beginning, logistic support was promised. Once the Pentagon, and then the State Department, had given the green light, other members of the Security Council rapidly followed suit.

One proposal was opposed vehemently by the government of Mozambique: the introduction of a United Nations civilian-police component. The peace accord had not provided for such a presence, and the government viewed this proposal as an infringement on its sovereignty and an expression of doubt that it could protect civil liberties, human rights, and political freedom within its own borders. In the document that the Secretary-General ultimately sent to the Security Council he reiterated that such a component would be useful and asked that the matter be reopened with the parties.[14] This finally happened, and after over a year of negotiations the police component was included.

The document was especially detailed in the area of the electoral process. Here the United Nations had considerable experience, and in seeking technical as well as material support from the UN, the parties had de facto agreed to accept its technical guidance in resolving disputes. ONUMOZ would need an Electoral Division with up to 148 international electoral officers, plus "an appropriate number" of volunteers and support staff. The Secretary-General further specified the need for some 1,200 international observers during the actual polling period. This large number represented a victory for the "political" faction among the Secretariat staff, who argued that only large numbers of highly visible observers could instill confidence among the voters and accompany every step of the polling process.

The electoral specialists themselves argued that a far smaller number of observers would be sufficient to do the independent sampling required to verify the outcome of the vote. The political faction recalled that in Angola, Jonas Savimbi had managed to stir-up doubt about the validity of the elections by arguing that there had been observers in the polling stations, but that later on, when trucks transported the ballots to the capital for the final count, government representatives had piled large numbers of ballot boxes onto these trucks when they were not supervised. There were no international observers on these trucks, so it became Savimbi's word against that of President José Eduardo Dos Santos. The United Nations concluded, on the basis of samples taken, that the outcome was free and fair and that Dos Santos had won, but the harm was done. Ajello accepted this line of reasoning, so the political needs-assessment prevailed.

Hindsight reveals one major flaw in the design of the mission: that is the inclusion of a United Nations Office for the Coordination of Humanitarian Assistance (UNOHAC) as an integrated component of ONUMOZ. This would replace the existing Office of the United Nations Special Coordinator for Emergency Relief Operations (UNSCERO, operated by UNDP). UNOHAC, to be managed by the Secretariat's Department for Humanitarian Assistance (DHA), would also oversee the provision of food to soldiers in the assembly areas, through a technical unit, and plan the reintegration of demobilized troops. Trying to give ONUMOZ total control backfired: the UNDP Resident Representative and his staff, who had done an excellent job in running UNSCERO and who had very good relations with the Mozambican government agencies involved as well as with the donor community, basically washed their hands of the whole matter; if DHA wanted to take over—let them. Some UNDP staff were transferred to UNOHAC, but the harm was done. Conceptually as well, this was an error. UNDP represented the continued presence of the United Nations system in Mozambique: it had been there since independence, and as of today, it is still very much there. Humanitarian aid as well had existed well before ONUMOZ and it is still flowing in, five years after ONUMOZ has closed down. Having taken this ongoing function of aid coordination out of its context, it became extremely difficult to restore it when ONUMOZ left. UNDP no longer had the resources to reabsorb the unit. One could, moreover, ask whether as a matter of principle, aid coordination should not be the domain of the recipient government. It is not surprising that many Mozambican government officials viewed ONUMOZ as a threat to national sovereignty.

On 3 December 1992 the final plan was presented to the Security Council.[15] At the end of the report came a cost estimate: nearly $332 million. This sum included the entire military component, civilian police, civilian staff costs, premises, vehicle operations, air operations, communications, supplies, and the development of assembly areas for demobilization. We all believed, or pretended to believe, that the timetable of the peace agreement could be implemented, and that we could be closing down ONUMOZ after one year as planned. The Security Council pretended to believe this too, and, in Resolution 797 (dated 16 December), it approved the Secretary-General's report "and the recommendations contained therein." It recognized that the sum requested from the peacekeeping account did not nearly reflect the total cost of the integrated operation. Thus it encouraged Member States "to contribute voluntarily to the United Nations activities in support of the Agreement," and it requested the United Nations programs and agencies "to provide appropriate assistance and support for the implementation of the major tasks arising from the Agreement."

This formula points to an essential weakness of the Security Council: its mandate is so narrow that it can only raise funds, through assessed peacekeeping contributions, for a small part of an integrated mission. It can compel the international community to foot the bill for military and political/administrative costs directly related to the peace process, but it has no control over the resources needed for economic and social reconstruction. Yet all these military and political efforts are wasted if a broader reconstruction-and-development program is not competently and promptly integrated into the peacekeeping operation per se. Resolution 797 shows only too clearly that the Security Council was well aware of this dilemma.

Fortunately, Member States and agencies responded generously. On the same day that the Security Council approved the launch of ONUMOZ, a donors' conference met in Rome. Ajello made a strong plea that the parties to the conflict be given the prospect of hope in order to encourage them to take the risk of peace, and pointed at the various elements of the General Peace Agreement that hinged on donor support: programs for the reintegration of refugees, displaced persons, and demobilized soldiers, and programs for the setting up of an electoral process. Officials of the government and Renamo had prepared a joint needs-assessment for these activities, a gesture that went over extremely well with the donors. The government and UNDP also presented their "Emergency Programme 1993–1994 towards Reconstruction," a well-argued paper showing the major investments that the government itself had planned, as well as the needs that were left to be met. In the end, donors pledged $402 million for the implementation of the General Peace Agreement, including food aid.[16] This was more that the entire estimated cost of ONUMOZ! Simultaneously, a World Bank consultative group, meeting in Paris, raised $760 million in credits, grants, and additional food aid (although there may have been some overlaps).

As 1992 came to an end it was difficult to see who had leverage over whom. All players had made major investments in the peace process. The parties to the conflict had few alternatives to peace left, and saw better times ahead as the donors held out impressive bunches of carrots. The Security Council smelled an opportunity for success and had gambled on a full-scale operation, no holds barred. Mozambique's neighbors all had their own good reasons to support the process: food supplies and security were at the top of their list. The donor community looked at the vast sums it had sunk into Mozambique thus far, at the country's appalling poverty, and at the tremendous potential human cost of a failed peace: it was worth going for broke. No one could afford failure anymore. Only fear could block the road to peace.

The Bureaucracy: Stumbling Forward, or the Leverage of Mutually Supportive Inadequacies

The first months of ONUMOZ's presence in Maputo combined elements of surrealistic theater with flashes from a ghastly nightmare. The United Nations' own rules and regulations nearly strangled its young. To begin with, ONUMOZ needed money. The $332 million approved by the Security Council had no monetary value. The Budget Division of the Bureau of Administration and Finance had to draw up a detailed budget according to the United Nations' standard format, detailing every post, every vehicle, every trash can. This had to go for review to the Advisory Committee on Administrative and Budgetary Questions (ACABQ), which would conduct hearings requiring the presence of key officials, before sending its comments to the Fifth Committee of the General Assembly (responsible for finance and administration). The Fifth Committee would allow the speakers' list to exhaust itself before sending a draft resolution to the General Assembly, which then had to adopt this resolution. This finally happened in March 1993. In the meantime, the Secretariat had no authority to spend money on ONUMOZ. Small allocations, however, were made from some hidden reserve to allow a few of us to fly into Maputo and set-up shop.

The Secretariat was facing immense pressure. It had to staff and equip several missions simultaneously: Cambodia alone required 7,000 civilians, and then there were El Salvador, Angola, Western Sahara, and Somalia, plus all the ongoing relics such as Cyprus and the various entities in the Middle East. The same countries that in the Security Council scolded the United Nations for its inadequacies spoke movingly in the Fifth Committee about bloated bureaucracies and refused to provide the resources to empower the Field Operations Division. The procurement officers who went out of their way to deliver were met by medieval and hostile auditors who questioned their every move.[17] The combination of financial rules and regulations designed for a static bureaucracy and an overburdened and often hounded staff proved to be as serious a threat to the mission as any violation by the parties to the conflict.[18]

Office space in Maputo was hard to find. UNDP had no extra room in its premises. We finally identified a hotel, the Rovuma, that was willing to upgrade its decrepit rooms, install elevators, bring electricity and running water to all floors, and give us the keys. To do so, however, the hotel's owners wanted us to sign a rental contract for one year. New York patiently explained that we could not enter into any long-term commitment until the General Assembly had approved funding. The interim Special Representative of the Secretary-General therefore ended up in a fourth-floor walk-up suite of three rooms in a seedy neighborhood. Porters were hired to carry up the water needed to flush the toilets. There was one phone. The Mozambican fears that their sovereignty was in danger faded.

ONUMOZ desperately needed vehicles. None had been ordered. It would take three months from the date that the order had been placed until cars could be delivered. But the order could not be placed until the spending authority had been received. Thus we rented whatever could be found in the region, depleting the Avis and Hertz stocks in Zimbabwe. Rentals from South Africa were not permitted because of the apartheid boycott; instead, our suppliers in Zimbabwe went to South Africa. By the time our United Nations vehicles finally arrived in July 1993 we had spent the full cost of a new vehicle on each-and-every rental. The Mozambicans and the diplomatic community in Maputo watched all this with increasing amazement.

By the end of January there were no more than a handful of international ONUMOZ staff in Maputo. The various bodies created under the peace agreement had started meeting, and staff had a hard time to provide proper secretariat services. Ajello personally chaired virtually every meeting. We found JPOs from various agencies and spouses of diplomats to help prepare agendas and minutes in Portuguese. The translators envisaged in the staffing tables would only become available months later. Computers and printers were in such short supply that we drove them from venue to venue, and then back to the office. Yet the job got done.

On the military side, however, things were bleak. Of the 350 military observers scheduled to arrive, fewer than forty were in the country. No country other than Italy had volunteered to provide any of the 5,500 troops needed to protect the mission. On 7 January 1993 Dhlakama wrote an irate letter to the Secretary-General, complaining that the United Nations did not live up to its responsibilities under the peace agreement:

> Three months have gone by unmonitored and that in itself could constitute the beginning of a new war. . . . The police force is being reinforced without any supervision and could act from a strengthened pseudo-military position. Until now, Renamo has patiently awaited the UN's intervention but these provocations cannot go unnoticed much longer especially because they are being further compounded by incoming millions of dollars from Western Governments and there is no surveillance of how these funds are being utilized.[19]

He asked that elections be postponed. He refused to come to Maputo.

In New York, support for ONUMOZ was hostage to Secretariat politics. There was considerable speculation why Ajello had been appointed as "interim" SRSG. Initially, people assumed that he was an unknown entity, brought in at short notice, and that a decision on his future would be made based on his performance. But then the Secretariat held-up all appointments for key civilian ONUMOZ positions, and rumors started that James Jonah, the Under-Secretary-General for Political Affairs, was waiting for a decision whether his own contract would be extended at the end of February. Mozambique was his fall-back position, and he intended to staff ONUMOZ with is own choices, should he be forced out of his current job.[20]

Confidence Makes Way for Cynicism

ONUMOZ's administrative and political weakness fed straight into the resistance within both the government and Renamo against the peace process. While the leadership in both parties was committed to peace, not all of their followers were. The big losers in the process, on both sides, were the military. They had not played much of a role in the peace negotiations; in fact, one could argue that the Frelimo civilian leadership, in framing the scope of the peace accord, had managed not only to eliminate Renamo's threat but also the crushing burden of its own military.

On the part of the government, there was allegedly an army of up to 92,000 (the real number remained mysterious until the end of the demobilization process), which was going to be slashed down to 15,000, integrating some 15,000 Renamo soldiers for a total of 30,000 personnel in the new Mozambican Defense Force. This was the end of a lucrative industry. The government handed over some $240 million each year to the military in one large lump sum, and the military was not accountable to anyone for the way this money was spent. When we saw the dilapidated barracks, the equipment rusting away in the rain, and the lack of preparedness of the Mozambican troops, we wondered where this money had gone—certainly not into any military infrastructure. When we heard the soldiers' laments about the many months they had not been paid, we realized that the money had not gone into payroll either. The Ministry of Finance confirmed that the army had never submitted a payroll, and that the estimates of the number of soldiers under arms had never been audited. Contractors for mine-clearing operations spoke of kickbacks. Clearly, the demilitarization of Mozambique was going to cramp the style of some of the military leaders.

On Renamo's side, the fighters were not happy either with the peace accord. The prospect of Renamo's transformation into a political party frightened them. Literacy, advocacy skills, and winning personalities were not their strong suit, and they saw most of the spoils of peace going to a group of young upstarts who had grabbed the opportunity to side with Renamo as the political process picked-up steam. The generous payoff that Dhlakama had promised them was stuck in inscrutable administrative and political delays. First and foremost, they were afraid of betrayal. If they demobilized, and if the government demobilized, there would be no soldiers left on either side. But the government would still have its police—a paramilitary force that was rapidly growing in size—and it would still have its security forces. Renamo would be left defenseless. And the foreign protection forces failed to materialize.

Around Easter of 1993 there was talk in Maputo of an impending military coup. Mediafax, the local source of independent, reliable news (distributed by fax only to "hoi polloi" of Maputo), cited detailed plans and named the generals who had taken the lead. Clearly, their trust in the peace dividend had evaporated. Immediately, the diplomatic community in Maputo sprang into action, with Townsend Friedman, the U.S. ambassador, approaching the military through informal channels. He reminded them that the only source of their income was development assistance, since this allowed the government to free-up funds for the army. He assured them that a coup would throw Mozambique back into the Stone Age, as all aid would cease. They would be the pariahs of Africa. On the other hand, the international community understood that the delays in the demobilization process, and the lack of a rewarding payoff for the top brass, were creating tensions. The international community would see to it that attention was paid. The message got through and the coup was quietly canceled.

At the end of March Ajello had reached the limits of his patience with New York. He felt that his status as "interim" SRSG weakened his position with the parties, and that the inadequacies of the United Nations operational capacities, combined with the political gamesmanship, put the success of the mission at risk. He knew he had the full support of the diplomatic community in Maputo, and he knew that the donor capitals were becoming impatient with the United Nations as well. He wanted decisive action—or he wanted out. We spent our weekend crafting a nine-page memorandum to the Secretary-General, copied to Jonah and Kofi Annan (who had replaced Goulding in DPKO). I found a copy of this fax among my files, and there are many quotable passages that will convey the spirit of the times better than any reconstruction:[21]

> The purpose of this report is to assess the situation as we are waiting for the Security Council to meet. After a positive start, the peace process has slowed down progressively since last February, due to tensions that became apparent between the government and Renamo. . . . For two weeks now, the peace process has been completely blocked. We cannot speak of a crisis, but we are in a deadlock, the most serious one since the beginning of the process.
>
> Both parties seem to get used to the idea of protracted periods of inertia, the more so since the notorious Rome calendar offers them the possibility to shift the responsibility for the delays to the United Nations. . . . The reasons for which Renamo takes its time are obvious. As I have already explained in my previous reports, Dhlakama knows that his leverage vis-à-vis the government is closely linked to the credibility of his military option. As long as Dhlakama holds his troops in their bases and controls the Renamo areas, he will be able to negotiate from a position of strength. The day he agrees to demobilization and therefore loses control over his territory, he will be completely at the mercy of the government. His only insurance policy is the presence of the United Nations.
>
> Recently, the belief that this policy can be effective has been weakened. Once more, the symbolism of objects and events has played a decisive role. Dhlakama, like everyone else in Mozambique, was expecting a spectacle of drive and efficiency from the United Nations equal to the architectural boldness of its headquarters. Instead, they encountered a straggling group of pilgrims who have been going around for months in dubiously trustworthy rented cars, which are not even marked.
>
> When, after several months, the first ONUMOZ means of transportation started to arrive, Skylink helicopters appeared which look more like Second World War leftovers than the modern, safe and efficient machines everybody was expecting.[22] These helicopters are in such precarious conditions that our people are understandably afraid to fly them. On top of that, the first group of pilots spoke only Russian, and they could not communicate with either the passengers or the control towers. Due to these problems in the communications system (and I hope you appreciate the euphemism), a helicopter landed in the playground of a school. The government complained. The people laughed. Skylink has since put in a pilot who babbles some English into each helicopter. Our main passenger plane, the Beechcraft, fared even better. Recently, soon after takeoff, it lost its left engine cover; they had to return to screw it on properly. Frankly, we do not make a very martial impression.
>
> The only image of efficiency is being offered by the Italian battalion which has set up, in only a few days, a totally self-sufficient structure,

> with a perfect communications system and an operations room which would not seem out of place in a science-fiction production. But they are in Beira, and the impact of their image is therefore quite relative. Even I, after six months in Maputo, have not been able to get a telephone that goes through a secretary, and I have to personally answer all calls. Most employees, including department heads, still do not have a telephone, and they have to queue before the offices of the few lucky ones who do.
>
> Our procurement system may be transparent and possibly save us money, but its impact in terms of efficiency, and above all in terms of our public image, is absolutely devastating. Dhlakama naturally has noticed this and has begun to take us less seriously. He has come to think more and more that he has to rely on his forces, rather than on our protection. I do not think that he will agree at this stage to any level of demobilization before he has obtained all he wants. And in the meantime, he will keep us immobilized. . . . He could then even question the mandate itself of the United Nations contingents, demanding that they undertake to use force against any government effort to enter Renamo territory.
>
> In the meantime he will discover that the presence of militias and irregular troops represents a menace and he will demand that they are demobilized before the demobilization of the regular troops can begin. Lastly, he could ask that even the weapons in the hands of common citizens be collected first. There is enough to keep us immobilized for years.

This devastating analysis of the impact of poor management support on the political process did shake-up the Secretariat to some extent. Things began to move: Jonah's contract extension had been confirmed; Ajello was quietly elevated to SRSG (no formal announcement was ever made); the General Assembly finally approved the budget and released the funds; and slowly staff and resources trickled in. But the harm had been done. The process had lost momentum, the United Nations had lost credibility in Mozambique and in the capitals, the timetable for the peace process was set back by a year (as elections could only be held in the dry season), costs would go up, and staff were demoralized.

By the end of March 1993 the United Nations had lost most of its clout, the voices for peace within the conflicting parties were drowned out by the cynics, the donors kept a low profile and wondered whether this was yet one more promising venture that had come to naught. The people of Mozambique were the only remaining believers, as roads opened, the rains came, the food situation improved, and entrepreneurs began to test the waters. Shops and eateries opened up in Maputo, old trucks began irregular bus services, and street markets flourished.

THE MILITARY: THE LEVERAGE OF A FORCEFUL PRESENCE

Suddenly, in April, the troops came. The Italians had already taken-up positions along the road, rail, and pipeline corridor between Beira and Zimbabwe. Now a battalion from Bangladesh guarded the transport corridor along the Nacala–Malawi railway line. Botswana's battalion served along the Tete road corridor between Malawi and Zimbabwe. Uruguay covered the south–north Route 1—the national highway between Maputo and Beira—and Zambia protected the Limpopo Valley railway line connecting Maputo and Zimbabwe. Italy also provided logistic equipment, a medical team (with a complete field hospital), and an air wing. India made logistics available and brought in an engineering company, Portugal sent a small signals battalion, and Argentina sent a medical unit. By 15 April, Zimbabwe had withdrawn all its troops from Mozambican territory, and the Malawian troops left Nacala a few weeks later. The balance of power had shifted dramatically.[23]

Unarmed military observers also increased in numbers, and by April 1993 there were some 300 observers in the country, coming from a dozen countries. Their work was indispensable: they verified complaints of cease-fire violations and reported to the Cease-fire Commission on their findings, and, above all, they supervised the demobilization process, keeping tabs on personnel and arms registered, overseeing the destruction of the weapons turned in (if they were not stored for the New Mozambican Army), and generally displaying standards of professionalism that made others shape-up.

Now all discussions of a coup had become moot. Now Renamo could no longer argue that it was unsafe to begin demobilization. Now the convoys with humanitarian relief felt a lot more confident. The Italian government sponsored a special trust fund to allow Renamo officials to settle in Maputo, and a first check of $65,000 was delivered in April to cover March's expenses. This was over and above the resources promised to all political parties in order to jump-start the political process. By the end of August the total number of troops had reached 6,000. Refugees began to return in large numbers. The international aid agencies stepped-up their delivery. Mine-clearing programs, again long-snagged by UN bureaucracy, finally began to operate. The Dutch government decided to sponsor a Mozambican mine-clearing school and sent trainers as well as a check for $11 million.

Clearly, the presence of a robust military force served a strong deterrent to combatants on both sides, as well as to irregular militias looking for spoils. Over time, the contingents' mandates shifted. The Italians withdrew from the Beira corridor in April 1994 (having completed one year), and they were replaced with two companies from Botswana and one from Bangladesh—a considerable reduction in force. Nearly all of the Indian contingent was withdrawn in August 1994. This coincided with increasing banditry on Mozambique's roads, often caused by unruly demobilized soldiers, and thus the United Nations troops were spread out more flexibly, and with greater coverage, to provide security not only to humanitarian convoys and traffic in key corridors but also to the traveling public at large.[24]

While the presence of these 6,000 soldiers was essential for the success of the peace process, it also caused serious problems. First of all, there was AIDS, or the threat of it. While AIDS had largely bypassed Mozambique during the 1980s, since there was virtually no mobility, it found its way in as roads opened, trucks plied the country, prostitution began to flourish, and the virus began to travel. The United Nations Standard Operating Procedures in those days had no provisions to deal with AIDS.[25] We were worried about the soldiers, given the rapid spread of AIDS in the country, and we were worried about the population, given the relatively large number of soldiers who were AIDS-positive (as we learned from the physicians in the field hospital, until they were told to stop involuntary testing). The World Health Organization (WHO) immediately flew in a large supply of condoms for distribution, but some contingents refused to accept this offer. The force commander did not consider this a serious issue, no ground rules were set, and no curfew or off-limits zones were introduced. Prostitution around the military camps thrived. Allegations of soldiers seeking out child prostitutes hit the Mozambican press and soured the mood. After a year, the force commander was replaced. The decision of the Italian troops to leave after one year may well have been linked to these allegations also.

Since then, the United Nations has to a large extent taken charge and issued clear, no-nonsense regulations for all troops under its control. A working group on AIDS in the military has been established. To their credit, many of the soldiers of the battalions in the transport corridors, who did not see much action and thus led fairly boring lives, made themselves useful in community-improvement projects and gained the respect of the people whom they served. But the initial lack of cooperation from some of the troop-contributing countries in stemming the threat of AIDS demonstrates that the "peacekeeping culture" is not innate; it must be learned.

Demobilization

In October 1993, the Secretary-General visited Maputo, met with all the parties, and reached agreement on a new timetable, extending the process by one year. Preparations for demobilization began in earnest. Assembly sites were inspected, and the number was initially reduced from 49 to 35. Food, cooking equipment, tarps, blankets, medicines, water, and civilian clothing were distributed to the sites selected. Building materials and tools were brought in so that the soldiers could construct their own housing. According to the plans, each soldier would receive a severance payment, subsidies, and assistance with transportation to his home. Soldiers with families could bring their dependents. A mainly Swiss civilian "technical unit" was responsible for all the preparations; the International Organization of Migration was contracted to coordinate the transportation. Computerized tagging-and-tracking systems were developed. Personal documents were issued to the soldiers. Upon their return, they were received by provincial and district authorities and helped in their resettlement efforts.

Initially, the level of severance payments was so low that it reinforced the factions within both the government army and Renamo who felt betrayed by the peace process, and it was only after the international community provided matching funds, thus doubling the pay-out, that soldiers from both sides began to trickle into the assembly areas.

By mid-August 1994 all assembly areas were officially closed to new entrants, and the final demobilization tally amounted to 57,540 government and 20,538 Renamo soldiers, a total of 78,078. In addition, some 13,000 government soldiers had been demobilized before the signature of the General Peace Agreement, but the total was still considerably less that the initial estimates. The demobilization process was at times traumatic, and a few conclusions can now be drawn. First of all, early coordination is essential. Demobilization is a political process, involving a large cast: the military, the government, the rebels, NGOs, international organizations, donors, and the private sector. The process, moreover, has to be dovetailed with national reconstruction programs, since returning soldiers have a major economic and social impact, not to mention security.

The military is not a homogeneous, faceless entity. While the conscripts are often happy to go home, the officer class has often served for many years and has lost touch with the civilian world. It is also the group that has the most to lose (status, legal, and illegal income), and therefore the officers should be given viable and attractive options. It is still surprising that a coup in Mozambique was avoided; if the donor community had not dramatically increased the final pay-outs for the officers, major unrest would have been unavoidable.

It is crucial to conduct surveys of the number of combatants, their educational and skills level, their employment history and aspirations, disabilities, family composition, and transportation needs *prior* to demobilization. Considerable lead time is required for the planning, funding, and delivery of programs. In ONUMOZ, we did such surveys only as the soldiers passed through the assembly areas, and we were not able to deliver effective training or reintegration programs. Moreover, programs targeted only at ex-combatants and their families may create resentment among other groups affected by conflicts: refugees, displaced persons, and local inhabitants whose lives were negatively affected by strife. Demobilization and rehabilitation programs, therefore, should be dovetailed, to the extent possible, with other humanitarian and economic recovery programs in the area. This argument was repeatedly made by UNHCR staff in the region, who saw the impact of the soldiers returning with their bounty. The effect on veterans should also be considered. In Mozambique, there were riots triggered by AMODEG, the association of former combatants, who were left out of the peace accord.

Disarming ex-combatants in a setting where arms are freely available among civilians and private militias is ineffective. Broader arms-control measures should be introduced simultaneously with the demobilization process (e.g., buy-back schemes, police enforcement of gun laws). In Mozambique, there were (and are still) tens of thousands of small arms in circulation, mainly Soviet-bloc AK-47s distributed to villagers during the civil war. Former soldiers can easily get their hands on weapons and thus public security will suffer. This also happened in Mozambique, where common banditry became a major scourge, both in the cities and the countryside.

It turned out that there are also some inherent problems in giving a parting settlement to soldiers. Cash is easily squandered. Differentials in payment between officers and soldiers or between members of opposing parties (six-months' final Renamo pay was not the same as six-months' final government pay) can cloud the demobilization process. It is probably best to disperse payments in such a manner that they are made over time, in the soldier's elective place of residence and in the context of a community-rehabilitation plan. This is what we aimed at in Mozambique, but failed to deliver.

The leverage given to the international community by this massive display of military force was considerable: once the United Nations contingents were deployed, neither party could revert to the military option without running serious risks. Or could they? The United Nations troops in Mozambique were never challenged to move from peacekeeping to peace enforcement, and in authorizing their deployment, the Security Council assumed that the government and Renamo shared a genuine commitment to peace. But what if the militant wing in either group had come to power? It was the use of economic threats, in conjunction with a robust military pressure, that kept the stalwarts in line. The incentives initially linked to demobilization under the peace accord lacked sufficient appeal to ensure the soldiers' compliance with the withdrawal process. Once again, the donors were pressed to provide additional financial incentives to salvage the peace.

FROM ELECTIONS TO THE EXIT: THE LEVERAGE OF MOMENTUM

Once demobilization was completed the game was essentially over, and the outcome of the peace process was no longer in doubt. This was no sham demobilization as it had been in Angola—neither party had a fighting force left. The focus was now on the political process. The international community began to concentrate on the establishment of political parties, on the elaboration of electoral laws, on preparations for the electoral process, and on the sustainability of Mozambique after the departure of ONUMOZ.

The General Peace Agreement stipulated that a National Election Commission should be established by the government, with one-third of its members nominated by Renamo. It also stated that the elections would be funded with resources to be pledged at the December 1992 donors' conference. The initial estimate presented to the donors amounted to $76.9

million. UNDP set-up a technical-assistance project, a Mozambican Technical Secretariat was created, and an "Aid for Democracy" donor group convened regularly to define needs and obtain support for the elections. A separate trust fund, as foreseen in the peace accord, channeled money to a wide array of newly created political parties who wanted to compete in the elections. UN volunteers were stationed at each of the 128 electoral-district offices, and a costly hi-tech photo ID system was introduced to produce electoral cards. Once again, the promise of external funding did a lot to shape the political phase of the peace process: political parties mushroomed—politics became rewarding. Several dozen newly established parties registered, possibly out of conviction, possibly in order to claim their share of the trust fund.

Elections are costly even if expenses are kept at a minimum: any budget will include equipment, salaries, transport, civic education, training, telecommunications, data-processing, setting-up locations, and support for the electoral process itself such as per diems for officials. At the same time, one can wonder whether a model of such complexity and cost truly helps a country like Mozambique to get started on the road to democracy. The advice given by the United Nations and the donor community produced state-of-the-art elections, but at a cost that does not seem sustainable. Will the international community have to fund every round of elections for the foreseeable future? And will there be no elections if donor support cannot be found?

Voter registration went well despite the difficult circumstances given the country's size and poor infrastructure. The Mozambican government made a tremendous effort, mobilizing no less that 52,000 election officials for the registration-and-voting process. The elections were held over a three-day period, starting on October 27. At the very last moment Dhlakama panicked and threatened to boycott the vote. A flurry of telephone calls from heads of state around the world quickly made him reconsider. On 2 November, the Special Representative of the Secretary-General made a statement that the elections had been free-and-fair. The turnout was tremendous: 88 percent of the electorate cast its vote. For many voters, this meant an arduous trek on foot through difficult terrain to the polls. The results favored Frelimo in the south, and Renamo in the central provinces. Chissano received 53 percent of the votes for the presidency, and Mr. Dhlakama obtained 34 percent. Renamo took up its role of opposition in parliament, and the government went back to governing.

There was widespread euphoria in the donor community, and in January 1995 the Security Council held a final session on the "Situation in Mozambique" that came close to a celebration, as speaker after speaker sang the praise of the Mozambicans, ONUMOZ, and the Security Council itself. Immediately after the elections, ONUMOZ began its withdrawal, and the unsung hero of this venture, Aldo Ajello, closed the doors behind him on December 13, 1994, as the ONUMOZ mandate expired.

EPILOGUE: OF HINDSIGHT AND PERSONALITY

Historians still argue whether individuals shape events, or whether there are dynamic and unstoppable historic forces that shepherd humanity from here to there, no matter what individuals do. The case of ONUMOZ could be brought up on both sides of the debate. The general détente after the cold war had reached southern Africa and there were more incentives for peace and commerce than for a continuation of the war. At the same time, many serious prospects for peace in history have collapsed, or stumbled, because of individual foolhardiness.

Without Ajello's ingenuity, honed by a Sicilian upbringing and a life in Italian politics, ONUMOZ might well have failed. Before making a move, he would make sure that it had the backing of everyone who counted. Every time ONUMOZ took a position, it had been cleared with all the major players on the Security Council. Once or twice a week he would strategize with the ambassadors of the countries on the Supervision and Control Commission (CSC). He met regularly with all the major donors. There were no surprises, and neither the government nor Renamo ever found an opening to divide the allies. Ajello had the uncanny ability to figure out the hidden agenda of even the most poker-faced players (such as Dhlakama) and to develop scenarios whereby everyone got what they most wanted. His astute use of flexible trust funds is a case in point: everyone has his price, and often that price is affordable. At the end of ONUMOZ, Renamo had a new future as a political party with a steady income from the donor community. Frelimo had gained legitimacy as a government and had unburdened itself of a crippling military budget. The Security Council had a success story to compensate for its many failed attempts. The United Nations Secretariat had a peacekeeping mission to be proud of, and the people of Mozambique had room to breathe.

There were other forceful players. First and foremost the U.S. ambassador, Townsend Friedman. Friedman's reports shaped the position that the United States took in the Security Council, and he supported ONUMOZ and Ajello at every twist and turn. His deputy, Chris Dell, functioned as his alter ego and proved to be exceptionally adept at shaping the meetings of the CSC due to his excellent Portuguese as well as his shrewd insight into the issues. The ambassador of the United Kingdom, Richard Edis, was an equally effective ally, particularly in pushing the combatants over the brink of demobilization by offering the most enticing training courses for the newly integrated Mozambican Defense Force. The Italian ambassador, Manfredo Incisa di Camerana, repeatedly found essential money for things that auditors would not approve of, but that were crucial to keeping Renamo happy.

John Sunde, the South African "trade representative" (an apartheid euphemism) managed, at crucial moments, to find people who could lean on Dhlakama, such as "Pik" Botha. When one of Dhlakama's key negotiators, Raul Domingos, developed problems with his eyes, Sunde knew how to spirit him away to a top-notch South African hospital, where surgery took place courtesy of the government. The president of Mozambique, Chissano, personally approved the issuance of a Mozambican passport to Domingos for the occasion. Chissano, a master strategist, knew exactly how to stay in the background for all but the most momentous occasions, thereby always leaving a door open in negotiations for a policy reversal at the highest level. The capacity of all these strong personalities to work together was remarkable, and again, one had the sense that serendipity had brought these people together.

Ajello, during the final months leading up to the elections, made a forceful case for power-sharing with Renamo. In informal discussions with friends in the government, he argued that the concept of a loyal opposition would simply not work in Mozambique. He pointed at the success of power-sharing in Namibia, Zimbabwe, and South Africa, and at the lack of power-sharing in Angola, with its dismal results. This thought should, I believe, still be pursued. In a country already destroyed by war and polarized by ethnic divides (as again became clear in the 1999 presidential elections), a government of national unity and reconciliation would help to heal wounds, and it would make the best use of the skills and leadership available within the pool of talent on both sides.

It is remarkable, in retrospect, how well the Mozambican people have been able to forgive their adversaries. Certainly among the soldiers, relief was the dominant mood after the cease-fire. The many civilians who had been caught between the cogs of conflict seemed more than ready to move on with their lives. No demands for war-crimes tribunals or historical commissions were heard. Was it purely fatigue, or do the Mozambicans have an innate generosity, a penchant for living, that allows them to accept the past, if not to forget?

While the war is over and ONUMOZ is gone the international community has not turned its back on Mozambique. Aid remains at a level close to $1 billion a year, and the World Bank, the IMF, and the United Nations development programs and agencies are doing what they can to help Mozambique lift itself out of poverty. Private investors are flooding the hotels of Maputo. Mozambique's ranking in UNDP's human-development report has gone up a few notches. Let's hope that the forces of history are unstoppable.

Notes

1. Wim Bossema, *Mozambique* (The Hague: NOVIB, 1995), 8.

2. See Milton Leitenberg's letter in the Woodrow Wilson International Center for Scholars' *Cold War International History Project Bulletin*, issue 5 (spring 1995): 158ff.

3. Joseph Hanlon, *Mozambique, Who Calls the Shots* (Bloomington: Indiana University Press, 1991), 2.

4. Ibid., 47.

5. See also Christian Geffray, *A causa das armas: antropologia da guerra contemporãnea em Moçambique* (Porto: Edições Afrontamento, 1991), 9–26.

6. Hanlon, 43.

7. *The United Nations and Mozambique*, United Nations Department of Information, 1995.

8. A detailed account of the delicate process leading to direct negotiations can be found in Cameron Hume's excellent *Ending the Mozambique War: The Role of Mediation and Good Offices* (Washington, DC: U.S. Institute of Peace Press, 1994). Hume represented the United States as an observer during the final rounds of negotiations.

9. The complete text can be found as Document 12 in *The United Nations and Mozambique*, 105ff.

10. United Nations document A/47/539.

11. *The United Nations and Mozambique*, 147.

12. Nicole Ball and Sam Barnes, *Mozambique*, a country study presented at the November 1998 conference on "Investing in Peace: Donor Support for Post-conflict Reconstruction and Transition," sponsored by the Center on International Cooperation, New York University. The study appeared in a publication prepared by the Center on International Cooperation: Shepard Forman and Stewart Patrick, *Good Intentions: Pledges of Aid for Post-Conflict Recovery* (Boulder, CO: Lynne Rienner Publishers, 2000).

13. UN Security Council document S/24892 of 3 December, 1992, section III, paragraph 19.

14. Ibid., section V.

15. Ibid., and S/24892/Add.1, 9 December 1992.

16. S/25044, 4 January 1993.

17. Readers interested in the poisonous audit climate that nearly paralyzed the United Nations operational capacity during the height of the peacekeeping "boom" are invited to study the so-called "Skylink" case, where the Administrative Tribunal severely criticized the United Nations administration for its inquisitorial and unprofessional audit practices at the time.

18. In December of 1994, after similar problems had stymied other peacekeeping missions as well, the United Nations General Assembly, through Resolution A/RES/49/233, adopted a comprehensive set of reforms to simplify the budgetary process for peacekeeping operations. It established a $150 million reserve, gave the Secretary-General the authority to disburse up to $50 million per mission pending approval of a budget, streamlined the budget cycle, standardized the budget process and format, and generally empowered the Secretariat to work more efficiently.

19. *The United Nations and Mozambique*, document 29, 170.

20. This rumor was later confirmed by Richard Synge, who conducted extensive interviews with senior Secretariat staff in preparation for his outstanding book on ONUMOZ, *Mozambique: UN Peacekeeping in Action, 1992–94* (Washington, DC: U.S. Institute of Peace Press, 1997).

21. Code Cable/Fax dated 29 March 1993, Subject: Assessment of Peace Process Prior to Security Council Meeting.

22. Skylink, a Canadian broker, was the lowest bidder for every air contract and procured its equipment from privatized military units in the former Soviet Union. The pilots were mainly survivors from the Afghanistan conflict.

Serbs. In May, and subsequently in August, the newly formed Croatian army regained possession of Western Slavonia and the Krajina and began to turn its attention to Eastern Slavonia as the last piece of Croatian territory to be recovered.

The dramatic events in Bosnia in the spring and summer of 1995 progressively demonstrated the totally untenable position that the UN Protection Force (UNPROFOR) had been placed in by the Security Council. Unequipped for enforcement action and given confusing, and sometimes contradictory, mandates, UNPROFOR was unable to respond adequately to the worsening situation on the ground and was rapidly becoming an embarrassing and demoralized presence rather than a military force capable of establishing and maintaining peace. Matters came to a head with the fall of the "safe-area" Srebrenica in July 1995—the overrunning of the hopelessly outgunned and unsupported Dutch battalion of some 450 soldiers by several thousand Serb troops and the subsequent massacre of Bosnian Muslims trapped in Srebrenica.

At the London Conference in August 1995, governments determined that significantly more military muscle should be applied as soon as an appropriate opportunity arose, which it did at the end of that month following the deadly Serb mortar attack in Sarajevo. This led to NATO's major air campaign, the negotiations at Dayton led by Richard Holbrooke, the Dayton Accord, and the subsequent replacement of UNPROFOR by the heavily armed combat troops of the Implementation Force (IFOR).

The Erdut Agreement for Eastern Slavonia

The ethnic cleansing of the Krajina by Croat troops in July and August 1995 resulted in large numbers of Serb refugees arriving in Eastern Slavonia (officially termed as "displaced persons" as they were in fact fleeing from one part of Croatia to another). Their arrival and the news of what appeared to be an endless reversal of Serb fortunes created significantly heightened tensions in Eastern Slavonia. The Serbs were fearful, just as the Croats were exultant at their victories, and many in Zagreb voiced eagerness to finish the task by one final military action. The prospect loomed of yet another bloodbath and ethnic cleansing, this time of Serbs fleeing Eastern Slavonia.

In September and October, U.S. Ambassador to Croatia Peter W. Galbraith and UN Mediator Thorvald Stoltenberg worked hard locally with the Serbs and Croats to negotiate an agreement. But it needed the authoritative acceptance of Presidents Milosevic and Tudjman, both of whom were involved in a much bigger poker game at Dayton by early November,[3] from which the UN had been deliberately excluded.

The main lines of the agreement for a "transitional administration" were in place but the principal point of contention was the length of time of that administration before the territory would be returned to Croatian authority. Finally, prodded by Holbrooke at Dayton, the two presidents, at a private meeting on 11 November, accepted language that could be presented differently for home consumption in Croatia and in Serbia. It provided for "a transitional period of twelve months which may be extended at most to another period of the same duration if so requested by one of the parties." No definition was given to the word "may" nor was it specified whose authority was needed to authorize such an extension.

The oral agreement between the two presidents was conveyed to the two delegations negotiating the agreement and it was signed in the village of Erdut in Eastern Slavonia on 12 November 1995. Contrary to the hundreds of pages and maps that finally constituted the Dayton Accord for Bosnia, the Erdut Agreement consisted of only fourteen paragraphs. These became the basis for the subsequent Security Council resolution and the whole UNTAES operation.

The Erdut Agreement (see Addendum—it became known as the "Basic Agreement") was communicated to the Security Council by Croatia on 15 November.[4] On 30 November the Council requested the Secretary-General to submit for its consideration "at the earliest date and no later than 14 December a report on all aspects of the establishment by the Council of an operation consisting of a transitional administration and a transitional peacekeeping force to implement the relevant provisions of the basic agreement."[5]

The Mandate

The birth of UNTAES was not an easy one: at UN Headquarters in New York this period was not one that allowed unalloyed concentration on a single issue. Overshadowing by far the situation in Eastern Slavonia was the outcome of the Dayton negotiations leading up the formal signing of the agreement in Paris on 14 December. There continued to be large numbers of UN personnel, military and civilian, in Bosnia, Croatia, and the former Yugoslav Republic of Macedonia. The end of UNPROFOR was now in sight, but there had to be major plans made for a hand-over—but what? to whom? when? and how? In addition, there were other missions elsewhere in the world that demanded daily attention, and the General Assembly, with its extensive agenda, was still in session.

Perhaps more importantly, morale at UN headquarters was at its lowest ebb. There was a widespread feeling of being heavily bruised by events and unfairly criticized by Member States for what were often their *own* failings. Certainly UNPROFOR had fallen into increasing disarray, but it had never been equipped and supported for the enforcement tasks that had become necessary and for which traditional UN peacekeeping was signally inappropriate. Moreover, as already mentioned, the UN had been bluntly excluded from Dayton by the United States and therefore was not party to, or even aware of, the inner thinking and actions at Dayton that led to the Dayton Accord or the Basic Agreement on Eastern Slavonia. Accordingly, with much thought being given to the implementation of the civil side of the agreement, it seemed obvious that the military aspect should be carded out by an extension of the IFOR that was about to be deployed in Bosnia. In support of this view, it was noted that the Basic Agreement called for "an international force," rather than a UN force.

It was therefore with considerable surprise that it was learned in the Secretariat that this was not the answer that some influential members of the Council wanted to hear: what they wanted from the Secretary-General was a proposal for a UN peacekeeping force.[6] With the experiences of being left in the lurch in Somalia in 1993, blind-sided in Bosnia and Croatia, and given an impossible task in the "safe areas" as illustrated in Srebrenica in July 1995, this created little less than amazement. There was a feeling that UN peacekeepers would once again be sent into an untenable situation, and this time with a strong likelihood that a nod and a wink would then be given to the Croats to go ahead and finish the job.[7] The outcome would be further ignominy for the UN. A yet more critical view was that of Boutros-Ghali as expressed in the quotation given at the opening of this chapter.

Separately, it had been determined in the UN Department of Peace-Keeping Operations (DPKO) that never again should troops be asked to enter a likely combat situation in the former Yugoslavia without the proper military resources to defend themselves and hit back hard. The military adviser (a major-general from the Netherlands and therefore acutely sensitive on this point) and his military staff proposed a "mechanized division of two brigades, with combat capability, air support, and a strong mobile, armoured reserve"—about 9,300 combat troops and about 2,000 logistic troops.

These were the thoughts and considerations that lay behind the observations and recommendations of the Secretary-General contained in his report to the Security Council on 13 December.[8] He recommended that the force should be under a Chapter VII mandate and that it "would best be entrusted to a coalition of Member States rather than to the United Nations . . . for command and logistic purposes, it should be attached to the implementation force to be deployed in Bosnia and Herzegovina" (paragraph 23). As a response to the preferred alternative being pressed by the United States and others, he added, "Nevertheless, a second option would be for the Security Council to entrust the operation described above to a United Nations force" (paragraph 24).

Much of the Secretary-General's report addressed the civilian and police aspects of the task, suggesting the structure and form of the civilian administration that would be needed. These suggestions were largely accepted and, as the end of December approached, the forthcoming draft resolution began to take shape in the hands of the governments belonging to the Contact Group, with the Secretariat being brought into the discussion as needed on specific points.

Apparently, early in the drafting process the United States made it clear that not only should it be a UN peacekeeping force, but it should not be any larger than 5,000 troops. With congressional fights on budget issues ever-present, and the U.S. share of a UN peacekeeping operation being over 30 percent, there was a strong domestic need to keep costs down. This ceiling served only to arouse further concern within the UN Secretariat—but suddenly some of the cloud was lifted when Washington made it clear that it was prepared to offer a candidate to lead the operation as "transitional administrator." As a pointer to that candidacy, the United States dispatched Jacques Paul Klein, a senior Foreign Service official (and also a major-general in the U.S. Air Force Reserve), to Zagreb and Belgrade for discussions with Presidents Tudjman and Milosevic. On his return, he reported that the two leaders had given him their personal assurances of support for the implementation of the agreement, and his own opinion that it could be carried out within a ceiling of 5,000 troops.

This positive, and previously absent sign of real commitment by the United States to the success of the new operation, made a significant difference within the Secretariat. There would be political and resource support from the right quarters, and the UN force, albeit smaller, would be appropriately and robustly armed. Perhaps most important, it was clear that behind the scenes a restraining hand had been placed on Croatian ambition. Spirits began to lift. As the draft resolution emerged in the early days of January 1996, it became clear that China was having difficulty with the Chapter VII provision. Eventually this was resolved only by adroit drafting of the relevant preambular paragraph[9] and the resolution was adopted as 1037 (1996) on 15 January 1996.

The mandate given to UNTAES has generally been regarded as a good one. In its authority to use force—and at the time of voting all members of the Council were aware that UNTAES would have much more firepower available to it than any previous UN peacekeeping force of its size: the spirit of the mandate was clear yet the wording left the operational interpretation to the transitional administrator. In its civil and police aspects, the mandate given to the transitional administrator was unusually extensive. The Basic Agreement had called upon the Security Council to establish a "transitional administration" to "govern" the region, and the Council specifically gave the power to exercise that authority to the transitional administrator. In that regard, the brevity of the Basic Agreement turned out to be an advantage, as its economy of provisions permitted the transitional administrator wide latitude in the exercise of his powers, a latitude that, backed by the availability of force, he did not hesitate to use when occasion demanded. Together, these provided tools of leverage that proved to be highly valuable: always there was a general awareness among the local Serb population and also in the respective government authorities in Zagreb and Belgrade that UNTAES had military options not hitherto available to UN forces in the Balkan theater and a readiness to use them within the terms of its mandate. From time to time they were used to good effect and, to use an old adage, "they were wonderfully good for sharpening the mind."

The Central Question of Military Force

Already present in Eastern Slavonia in 1995, as part of the UN Confidence Restoration Operation in Croatia (UNCRO) to whom the region was known as Sector East, were some 1,600 Belgian and Russian soldiers. When consideration was given to the composition of UNTAES, their continued involvement was one starting point; another was that not only would there be no U.S. troops, but there would not be any British or French contingents either. Those two countries had already had troops on the ground in the Balkans since the early days of UN military activities and were not inclined to provide further troops for Eastern Slavonia. Other troop contributors willing to provide competent and appropriately equipped contingents had to be found. If force proved necessary, UNTAES must not be found wanting. Jordanian and Pakistani mechanized battalions were identified to supplement the Belgian and Russian troops already in the area, buttressed by a Ukrainian helicopter squadron.

For a UN operation, the arrival and deployment of its forces were done with unusual speed. In the absence of any standing army or ready-reserve units, and with the need to pursue cumbersome negotiations with each potential troop contributor as well as making the necessary transport arrangements to move the troops and their equipment to the region, UN contingents can take many months to assemble. In the case of UNTAES, arrangements were made for the Pakistani and Jordanian battalions to travel on the same chartered ship. Unloading at the Croatian port of Rijeka, their heavy equipment was transported by road across Croatia to Eastern Slavonia where they began to deploy by late April 1996, only three months after the adoption of the resolution establishing the mission.

Another unusual aspect was the relationship with IFOR and NATO. Not only for operational reasons such as intelligence but as a source of military backup and/or extraction if needed, it was necessary for UNTAES to have links with the new operation in Bosnia. Moreover, exercise of overflights by NATO fixed-wing aircraft would keep all concerned (including Belgrade and Zagreb) aware of NATO/IFOR support without spelling it out in specific terms. Links were established with NATO's Fifth Allied Tactical Air Force in Italy to ensure the speedy provision of close air support in times of crisis, and UNTAES tactical air-control parties conducted regular training courses with NATO aircraft operating over the region. It turned out that such support was minimal and never needed. The overflights, when eventually established, usually took place at such a height that they were scarcely visible from the ground, although doubtless with their detection by JNA radar across the Danube they did not pass unnoticed.

In the early days, before UNTAES was fully deployed, much was made of the fact that IFOR supply lines from Hungary to Bosnia passed through Croatia very close to Eastern Slavonia and in themselves would discourage any temptation to adventure by Croat forces. In practice, however, this was a temporary phenomenon and one that looked more significant on paper than in the field. Nevertheless, much of the value of deterrence lies, like beauty, in the eye of the beholder. The knowledge that IFOR/NATO assets were over the horizon, together with the knowledge that UNTAES itself was robustly armed, probably gave cause for thought in the quarters that might have entertained any ideas of military adventure against UNTAES.

The combat-capable units of UNTAES, once deployed under a Belgian force commander and a Russian deputy force commander, were as follows:

Belgian battalion—668 personnel:

- 44 M113/AIFV armored personnel carriers
- 21 Scimitar reconnaissance tanks

Pakistani battalion—981 personnel:

- 14 T95 tanks
- 34 M113 armored personnel carriers
- 6 130mm howitzers

Russian battalion—842 personnel:

- 63 BTR-80 armored personnel carriers

Jordanian battalion—863 personnel:

- 14 M60A3 tanks
- 39 M113 armored personnel carriers
- 6 M109 155mm self-propelled howitzers

Ukrainian helicopter squadron—221 personnel:

- 6 Mil Mi-24 assault helicopters
- 6 Mil Mi-6 transport helicopters

In addition, there were an Argentine reconnaissance company, a Czech field surgical team, a Slovak engineer battalion, an Indonesian medical company, a Ukrainian light-infantry company, and a Polish special-police group.

In general, the policy was to keep the tanks and howitzers in the background; the remaining forces were used in patrols and other operations deliberately designed to be seen by the local population. The assault helicopters exercised frequently over open fields, but again in such a way as to be publicly visible. From time to time, on occasions of tension, the availability of force on the ground and in the air was openly demonstrated.

Specific efforts were made to ensure that such demonstrations were not perceived by the local Serbs as to be threatening to them, but rather as a readiness and willingness by UNTAES to maintain security from external threat and in support of internal law and order.

The highest level of the use of force occurred during the summer of 1996 when UNTAES took over the Djeletovci oilfield in the southern part of the region. Following the Serb victory in 1991, the product of the oilfield, which came from some 70 wells, had been taken to Serbia in exchange for financial subventions to the local Serb government in the region. Oil transfers ceased in late May 1996, and with the disarmament of the local Serb army in June, the Djeletovci oilfield passed into the hands of a Serb paramilitary group calling itself the "Scorpions." After some weeks, the transitional administrator decided that its continued occupation of the oilfield and thereby its denial of UNTAES's entry to the property constituted a serious undermining of UNTAES authority. Although the Scorpions were not using the oilfield as a base for guerrilla activities, if UNTAES continued to do nothing about such a blatant challenge to the transitional administrator's authority to "govern" the region, UNTAES would be perceived as being little more than a "paper tiger." On the grounds that UNTAES's freedom of movement was being prevented, the transitional administrator determined that action under the Chapter VII clause of his mandate was appropriate. In taking that action, the risks of casualties had to be taken into account, and also the danger that the Scorpions might lay explosives to destroy the wellheads.

Djeletovci lay in the area under the control of the Jordanian battalion. On the morning of 14 May 1996, the force commander sent his chief of staff (a Belgian colonel) to Djeletovci to inform the head of the Scorpions that the transitional administrator had instructed UNTAES to take possession of the oilfield. The paramilitaries were invited to leave peacefully by mid-afternoon, in which case they would be escorted by UNTAES to the border with Serbia. The alternative offered was that UNTAES would take possession by force. In support of this ultimatum, tanks, artillery, and other elements of the Jordanian battalion were deployed around the oilfield and the Scorpions' positions. To press the point further, UNTAES assault helicopters arrived overhead and thereafter maintained a constant (and noisy) vigilance.

This action by UNTAES clearly caused consternation among the paramilitaries who could see that they were outgunned and who were left in no doubt about the resolve of UNTAES to carry out the declared intention. As the day passed, the head of the Scorpions requested more time; this request was carefully weighed then granted when it appeared to be more likely to lead to a peaceful result. Early in the evening, the paramilitary group departed in a convoy and was escorted southward to the border, leaving the oilfield in the hands of UNTAES without a shot being fired.

It transpired, however, that some of the paramilitaries had either vanished into the local countryside before the convoy departed or perhaps returned across the open border. On the nights after the takeover, the Jordanian battalion found itself under sporadic fire by rifle and, at times, by heavy machine gun. Instructions were given to return fire by heavier caliber, escalating as necessary to the full extent of the Jordanian battalion's firepower. This response had the desired effect of silencing the attackers, who ceased their activities altogether after two or three weeks.

The message that lay behind this and other measured demonstrations of force was unequivocal: UNTAES was not to be regarded as UNPROFOR or UNCRO with a different name. UNTAES had greater force options and would certainly use them, if necessary, in pursuit of its mandate. In taking this posture of calculated deterrence, however, care was taken not to overplay UNTAES's capabilities. A cardinal rule of successful peacekeeping should always be borne in mind: *Never make promises that one cannot keep, or threats that one cannot carry out.*

NONMILITARY LEVERAGE FOR IMPLEMENTATION

It is often said, and worth repeating, that no two peacekeeping operations are alike. What may work in one situation may not be successful or even applicable in another. Nonmilitary leverage may therefore take a wide range of forms, and this was certainly so in UNTAES.

In the early months of 1996 much of UNTAES's effort was put into getting itself organized. In several respects UNTAES was fortunate, in that UN assets such as communications, transport, logistics, containers, and other equipment were already in the general theater. As UNPROFOR ran down, some of these assets were obtained and transferred to Eastern Slavonia. A site was found for UNTAES headquarters in Vukovar and premises were constructed and in operation by mid-April with the collocation of civil, military, and police command.

In April and May UNTAES troop strength was building, although it took considerable administrative effort to create for them acceptable accommodation, feeding, and sanitation facilities.[10] These efforts drew resources away from attending to the demands of the civilian and police aspects of the UNTAES task, whose personnel were also seeking to establish themselves and their contacts with the local population. From the start it was recognized that the challenge of reaching out to the local population could not wait for the UNTAES military to become operational. Contacts were developed at a number of levels, from the transitional administrator with the region's political and religious leaders, to meetings with local groups and individuals through civil-affairs offices established on a district basis. Winning the trust and confidence of the local Serb population was accorded high priority in order to construct leverage for use in the future.

This was often a difficult task. The local Serbs were war-weary, fearful, and very doubtful—indeed, suspicious—about yet another international-community mission in their midst. Many did not understand why the Serb cause had turned sour so suddenly, and it soon became apparent that the Basic Agreement of Erdut had been negotiated entirely above their heads and that their leaders had not informed them of its content and implications for their future. UNTAES introduced a series of town and village meetings throughout the region at which the role of UNTAES was explained and the people assured that as long as it was present, they would be safe from external attack by the Croats.

This was at first often greeted with disbelief and some derision—"The UN didn't protect us from the Croats in the Krajina, so how can we trust you now?" On several occasions the meetings would become highly energized and even dangerous when it had to be made clear to the crowd that UNTAES's mandated tasks included demilitarizing the local Serb army and delivering the region—demilitarized, stable, and secure—into the hands of the Croatian government. Aggressive and highly emotional Serbs would express astonishment that there had been an agreement to this effect signed by their own political leadership. It quickly became a challenge to win hearts and minds. The UNTAES mantra became: "We can do nothing about the past, but together we can help to build a future." The glimmerings of hope for a better life had been created.

A wide range of activities was pursued. At Catholic Easter 1996 the transitional administrator, Jacques Klein, supported by many UNTAES personnel, attended Mass at the Catholic church at Ilok, one of the few left standing by the Serbs, and the bells rang for the first time in five years. Two weeks later, at Serbian Orthodox Easter, the scene was repeated by attendance at the Patriarch Bishop's Church at Dalj. Thereafter, the transitional administrator made regular Sunday visits to attend Serbian Orthodox church services throughout the region to make contact with community priests and elders.[11]

The town meetings became a frequent feature of UNTAES activity, presided over by either the deputy transitional administrator, the head of civil affairs, or by the members of the UNTAES civil-affairs offices. Arrangements were made, with the help of the World Health Organization (WHO) and the Croats, to carry-out aerial antimosquito spraying (which had not been done for some five years). Seed, fertilizers, and herbicides were obtained for the farmers. Heating oil was delivered to the hospitals. Temporarily, UNTAES fuel was supplied to the local police so that their vehicles could operate. Mail exchanges were arranged across the no-man's land to other parts of Croatia (taking care that no postage stamps were used, as they carried nationalist symbols unacceptable to each side). Meetings were arranged between Croat and Serb doctors, lawyers, teachers, and others with mutual practical issues to be resolved. NGOs were also active, as in the erection by the International Committee of the Red Cross (ICRC) of large tents at UN-controlled crossing points and family meetings arranged, bringing together relatives and friends who had been separated by five years of hostilities.

In August 1996 a new venture was introduced. At the initiative of UNTAES, a Saturday market was permitted in the no-man's land at Klisa, almost within sight of the Croat town of Osijek. With the cooperation of the Croatian authorities and with security provided by UNTAES, people from both sides were allowed to meet and mingle for several hours. This arrangement quickly became very popular, with market stalls being set up by entrepreneurs and people exchanging gifts and clothing. Despite efforts by Croat nationalists to stop the event (for example, by claiming that the market was allowing foot-and-mouth disease to pass from Serbia to Croatia, or that it was unhealthy because UNTAES had not provided proper sanitation facilities), the market proved to be very successful, with as many as 11,000 people being counted at its highest attendance. In these and many unrecorded ways, UNTAES personnel worked to engender trust and confidence and thereby created leverage for implementation of the mandate. UNTAES was not unique in these practices: they are standard and common fare, in one way or another, throughout all UN peacekeeping operations.

Complementing these efforts was a major media campaign. UNTAES created a newspaper, printed on one side in Serb Cyrillic script and on the other in Croat Latin script. Published every ten or fourteen days and actively distributed free throughout the region, it was one of the vehicles used for announcements, reports on what UNTAES was doing, information and contact numbers for assistance, and for NGO activities. For example, when a weapons buy-back program was introduced, details of the scheme and prices being offered for weapons were published in the UNTAES newspaper.

Another aspect of the media campaign was use of the radio. Within the region there were local Serb radio stations, while in the nearby Croat towns of Osijek and Vincovci there were Croat stations. Each was given to airing rabidly nationalist songs and propaganda. Within Eastern Slavonia, where UNTAES could assert control, the local Serb stations were instructed to halt broadcasting provocative material. UNTAES call-in programs were introduced to answer questions, correct rumors, and announce new arrangements such as how pensions could be obtained or where to go to register for new identification documents. On the Croat radio, senior UNTAES personnel made themselves available for interviews and took steps to counter the stream of anti-Serb abuse and propaganda.

In retrospect, UNTAES should have instituted its own television channel early in its administration. Unlike many parts of the world in which the UN operates, the standards of living in Eastern Slavonia before the war were quite high and television was in almost every household. Moreover, as an agricultural area, once the harvest was in and winter began, there was little for people to do in the evenings other than watch television. In addition to a local station in the Baranja, the region was open to Serbian television from Belgrade, which was watched by most local Serbs. The region was also well within the range of Croatian television, which almost nightly replayed video clips of the successful Croat military actions and victories that had evicted Serbs from Western Slavonia and the Krajina. The constant tone of gloating triumphalism and Croatian martial music undermined UNTAES's efforts to encourage the start of a positive attitude among the local Serbs. But television is highly material- and resource-intensive. There was no provision in the UNTAES budget for such a venture, and the cumbersome nature of UN financing would scarcely have approved it before the expiration of the UNTAES mandate. In future operations, where applicable, the potential of television and Internet access should be given more attention at the outset.

One of the aspects in which UNTAES was let-down by the international community was in the availability of funds. There was no provision in the UNTAES budget for a contingency fund for use by the transitional administrator.[12] An authorization for the transitional administrator to spend at his discretion up to one or two percent of the six-month budget, amounting to some 1.5 to 3 million dollars and subject to finding savings from within the established budget, would have been of very great value. It would not have cost the international community any extra money, but would have given UNTAES the ability to pump immediate lifeblood into much-needed projects such as clearing rubble and basic reconstruction. In turn, such projects would have provided work for jobless, demilitarized young men from the local Serb army and injected money into the local economy.

Separately, promised financial assistance from the European Community and other sources was more often than not slow to arrive. Thus at town meetings UNTAES endeavored to encourage confidence by saying that financial assistance from the international community was on its way, only to be followed later by excuses and explanations that it had not yet been received. This was particularly galling, since it seemed that money was being poured into Mostar and other projects in Bosnia. The financial grants often seemed to bypass UNTAES and rarely benefited Eastern Slavonia.

In the absence of financial resources it was difficult to retrain former soldiers to pursue more productive activities. Some were taken into the Transitional Police Force while others were reformed and given training as a demining company that made its services available commercially to the Croatian government to clear Serb mines. There was also the factor that the Croatian government was not interested in encouraging a revival in the economy of the region until it could do so on its own terms. On the contrary, as perceived in Zagreb, a continuation of the more than 70 percent unemployment would probably lead to Serbs leaving the region of their own accord that, from a Croat point of view, would be the preferred result.

In order to improve cooperation and coordination among the various international and indigenous actors several actions were taken. At UNTAES headquarters in Vukovar, daily morning staff meetings were held, to which, in addition to the heads of civil, military, and police sections, representatives of such actors as the UN High Commissioner for Refugees (UNHCR), Office of the High Commissioner on Human Rights (OHCHR), and NATO liaison were always welcome. Meetings were held with international and national NGOs working in the region on issues and problems of mutual interest and sometimes they were also present at these staff meetings. Ambassadors and others from embassies of interested countries in Zagreb were encouraged to visit the region and were given full briefings on UNTAES operations. In addition, approximately monthly a senior member of UNTAES would visit Zagreb and hold a briefing for a wider circle of diplomatic and other representatives.

In addition to visiting New York for consultations with the Secretary-General, the Secretariat, and briefings to the Security Council, Klein specifically made visits to the centers of regional organizations such as the European Union (EU), the Council of Europe, Organization for Security and Cooperation in Europe (OSCE), and NATO, and to capitals such as Moscow, Brussels, Bonn, London, Paris, Rome, Budapest, and Washington to address relevant bodies and give personal briefings. Contacts with Presidents Tudjman and Milosevic and others in their respective governments were particularly frequent. This "nursing" of interested constituencies was an important part Klein's responsibilities as transitional administrator in order to keep the UNTAES operation within the attention span of appropriate actors—not always easy to achieve when there was a much larger operation taking place in Bosnia. Striking a suitable balance between focusing on internal matters by remaining in the region and keeping external authorities and actors properly informed by visits outside the region is one of the difficult juggling acts that a Special Representative of the Secretary-General (SRSG) has constantly to manage in order to keep his or her bag of leverage tools in good condition.

Let me make a final comment on the interaction between the UN operation's personnel and the local population. While armed military contingents are accommodated as military units, it is standard practice for UN civil personnel, police, and UN military observers (who are unarmed) to be paid a per-diem allowance and find their own accommodation within the local community. This has several benefits that usually outweigh the disadvantages: perhaps most important is that by this practice UN personnel are not shut off from the local population. They may share a house with a local family or rent the house or apartment and live separately, but in either case they are seen as living in the community. Despite language difficulties personal relationships are formed, trust is more easily developed, and barriers to interaction are broken down. By living with the local population UN personnel are viewed as suffering similar privations of weather, electricity, and other inconveniences. They are also seen as being prepared to take certain risks of personal security: being in the UN is of necessity being exposed, being vulnerable.

In some operations the local situation is so insecure that UN personnel have to live together in a guarded compound. But this is the exception rather than the rule. In UNTAES, over a thousand international civilian staff, UN police, and UN military observers lived within the local community. Some probably had little or no personal contacts with the local Serbs, but many developed valuable acquaintances and friendships and, at times, were able to offer assistance on a person-to-person basis. All this contributed positively to the achievement of mission objectives. In any UN operation, senior management must constantly and carefully watch the internal security situation; a security plan is developed to offer greater protection to UN staff during times of tension. Such was the case in UNTAES and only occasionally was it necessary to take special precautions against the threat of personal attack by grenades or other armed violence.

Personalities and Other Factors

As all such situations involve human action and reaction, personalities play a very important role in UN peacekeeping operations. The ideal SRSG must be able to "walk on water, swim with the piranha fish, and fly with the angels." These and the other qualities needed occur together only very rarely, and even when they do it may be discovered that it is the angels that have sharper teeth than the piranha.

In connection with the UNTAES operation there were some powerful personalities and large egos. Presidents Tudjman and Milosevic possessed both and it was therefore fortunate that in Jacques Paul Klein there were similar attributes that enabled him to deal with both leaders very capably. Strength of personality, fortitude, and pugnacity were present in abundance. He also possessed the right *nationality*. In general at the UN, it is *personality* that counts, not *nationality*. There are times in UN operations when the right nationality is of little importance but there are others when it is crucial. The UNTAES operation was of the latter kind. In the circumstances, it was probably only an American who could have established the necessary relationships with the two leaders in such a forthright and unflinching manner as Klein did and not be tossed out on his ear.

It is the view of this writer that there are basically two ways that an SRSG can regard his or her mandate: either it is a ceiling, under which the operation may be developed fully up to its legislated roof, or it is a floor upon which the operation may be imaginatively constructed without any limit as to the height that may be attained. In both cases, however, great care must be taken so as not to build any part of the operation on the unsure and shifting sands that lie outside the solid foundation set down by the Security Council. In UNTAES, the mandate was taken as being the floor. The attitude was not, "Is it in the mandate? If not, we can't do it," but rather, "If the mandate does not provide for it, is there any reason why we shouldn't do it?" Led by Transitional Administrator Klein, UNTAES staff personnel were encouraged to think imaginatively and act with vigor.

Another aspect to consider is the national character and personality of the local population. In Eastern Slavonia there was a distinct perception among the Serb population that political decisions had little to do with them; they were decided by those Serbs in authority and the role of the majority was, by and large, to do as told. The effect was that it was difficult to get Serbs to think independently. It was also difficult to identify and encourage alternative leadership.

Yet another factor was the noticeable tendency of the Serbs to view themselves as martyrs. While it was true that, probably with rare exceptions, those who committed atrocities in 1991 were long gone from the region, leaving behind the ordinary people to suffer the consequences when the Croats returned, there seemed to be a widespread feeling that it was the Serbs themselves who had been, were being, and would be wronged by the world at large. No town meeting would last less than two hours and UNTAES personnel were repeatedly faced with hearing the long tale of woe as perceived by Serbs since 1389 with their loss of the Battle of Kosovo against the Turks. How was it that Europeans did not see that it had been Serbia's sacrifice that had saved Europeans from Moslem domination throughout the centuries? The triumphant nationalism of the Croats did nothing to ease matters. To the Serbs, their attitudes and the postures struck by Tudjman and his political party reminded them only too vividly of the Croat concentration camp at Jasenovac during the Second World War in which, according to the Serbs, the Croats had slaughtered 600,000 or more Serbs, Jews, and Romanies.

One of the major tasks of UNTAES was to organize and assist in the conduct of elections. In order to be able to vote, the local Serb population had to have *domovnica*, a Croatian government–issued document certifying Croatian citizenship. Possession of *domovnica* was also necessary in order to apply for other important Croatian government documents such as a passport. Approximately half of the 130,000 Serbs in the region were displaced from elsewhere in Croatia, and virtually all the Serb population detested the thought of holding documents carrying Croatian nationalist symbols. The preparations for elections, difficult in themselves, were further complicated by these factors. Despite opening document centers throughout the region for the issuance of *domovnica* and later offices for registration for voting, many Serbs were for a long time very reluctant to step forward. It was clear within UNTAES that if Serbs did not apply for and obtain *domovnica* and subsequently take part in the elections, they would find themselves without any voice in the democratic process and probably be stateless. The end result would not be a multiethnic society in any way similar to the one present in the region before the war—a result that would not be unpalatable to Zagreb but one that would entirely negate much of what UNTAES was trying so hard to achieve.

Rather than remaining neutral on this issue, UNTAES energetically encouraged the Serbs to obtain their documents, register to vote, organize themselves for the elections, and ensure that they turned out on election day. In taking so clear a position, the personality of Transitional Administrator Klein and other senior members of the UNTAES staff was of major significance. By the date of the elections (April 1997), confidence and trust in UNTAES had largely been established; therefore, when UNTAES called upon Serbs to remain in the region and take part in the democratic process as Croatian citizens, it was a call that was accorded serious attention.

In sum, the authoritative personality of the transitional administrator set the tone for the entire mission. In the circumstances obtaining in the region and in relations with Zagreb and Belgrade it was successful and entirely appropriate. It also enabled the members of the UNTAES staff, at all levels, to feel that there was firm and dynamic leadership that undoubtedly led them to take similar, clear-cut positions in carrying out their own tasks. This tone did not always lead to comfortable relationships within UNTAES, but if dynamic tension is recognized as a valid management style in multinational and multicultural relations, then it was certainly at work in Eastern Slavonia. In other circumstances in different parts of the world this style may not have worked, but in Eastern Slavonia and the Balkans generally it did.

The Integration of Leverage

An important advantage for UNTAES was that the geographical area was small. Stretching for some 160 kilometers from north to south, and some 60 kilometers west to east (wider in some places and narrower in others), it was a region of controllable size. The northern part—the Baranja—could be reached by road only by passing through Croatian-controlled territory. While this presented no problems to UNTAES, it meant that physical contacts between Serbs in the north and those in the south required crossing the bridges over the Danube and traveling through Serbia, a much longer journey. This geography contributed to easier integration of leverage for UNTAES. From Vukovar, almost any part of the region could be reached by car within two hours, and even quicker by helicopter. Zagreb and Belgrade, in opposite directions, could be reached by road in three hours or so.

The collocation of the civil, military, and police leadership at UNTAES headquarters in Vukovar, together with the other headquarters elements, also contributed greatly to the integration of leverage. Separately, a joint civil–military logistic and administrative organization was established at Klisa, the former airport serving Osijek but in Serb-held territory since 1991 and used by UNTAES as its major helicopter and logistic base.

These arrangements, together with the daily joint staff meetings at UNTAES headquarters, helped considerably to ensure good command-and-control of the operation. A constant effort was made from headquarters to keep the outlying offices informed, but even so there were many occasions when UNTAES staff that was away from headquarters felt that it was not being kept fully informed. This is a feature of virtually every field operation; all that can be said is that in UNTAES, the information chain was probably better than most others.

In these circumstances, integration of leverage worked comparatively well. If some incident or situation demanded a specific response, be it military, police, or civilian, it was usually possible to provide it reasonably promptly. As necessary, military patrols could be dispatched, the state of military alert raised, and/or police presence increased, and all supplemented by overhead helicopter surveillance when appropriate. For example, in an instance when Croatian special-police units were detected operating inside the no-man's land in contravention of the agreement that it was a closed zone, it was possible to apprehend and disarm them quickly and then escort them back to their side of the zone. This action was immediately accompanied by a strong protest lodged with the authorities in Zagreb by Klein.[13]

On the civil side, assistance to and leverage on the local Serb administration was achieved by establishing a UNTAES liaison office in the offices of the Serb administrative leadership. The UNTAES civil-affairs officers in this office, which was situated literally less than fifteen feet from the Serb leader's own office, spoke Serbian and were often—but not always—invited to attend meetings of the Serb council. These links helped to avoid misunderstandings and were a valuable conduit for two-way information and one-way instructions.

On occasion, the application of integrated leverage could be quite dramatic. In late 1996, Klein invited President Tudjman to make an unannounced visit to Vukovar. Such a visit carried high personal and political risks, as UNTAES would be responsible for the president's safety from assassination attack. Arrangements were made with utmost secrecy for him to arrive at UNTAES headquarters by UN helicopter and then be taken for a quick tour by road of Vukovar before meeting local Serb leaders face-to-face in the UNTAES conference room. The latter were invited to UNTAES headquarters to discuss some major outstanding issues but without being informed that President Tudjman would shortly be in their presence. The visit took place safely and precisely as planned and without any incidents that were unforeseen. The Serbs' facial expressions when President Tudjman entered the conference room accompanied by the transitional administrator will be long remembered by this writer.

The leverage resulting from this visit was itself considerable. It was of high domestic political value to Tudjman and could not have been achieved without UNTAES. For UNTAES, it demonstrated that it had complete control of the region and could organize and implement such a visit without any breach of security. For the Serbs, it served as a stark reminder that there would soon be a time when UNTAES would depart and Croatian authority would be complete; therefore they should make full use of the assistance of UNTAES while it was still available.

Inevitably, with the benefit of hindsight, occasions can be identified when leverage might have been used more successfully than it was. Early in the UNTAES period, and continuing for several months, it became apparent that valuable trees were being cut down for their timber and driven across the open border to the south into Serbia. Various steps were taken to halt the theft such as placing obstructions on the side roads leading to the border and instituting a permit arrangement whereby permits had to be stamped by the local Serb authority and by UNTAES border monitors. The thieves, however, always found ways of circumventing these arrangements.

As UNTAES civil police had no executive authority, perhaps it would have been better to have taken a stronger line and used UNTAES troops to greater effect. But it would have required a disproportionate number of troops to close all side roads and rural tracks across the border, to the detriment of mandated tasks such as achieving the demilitarization of the local Serb army. As those who were stealing the timber were probably no more than common thieves seeing an opportunity to take advantage of UNTAES and probably with the complicity of local Serb police, there was little to be gained by trying to apply pressure on the Serbian government authorities. Moreover, if the situation had escalated to shooting incidents and casualties, there was no basis in the mandate for UNTAES troops to lose their lives to prevent theft of property and hence there would probably have been no support forthcoming from the Security Council. This is an illustration of the kind of incident that can often arise in UN peacekeeping operations and where there is no practical leverage available, whether by use of force or political means.

Peace-building Issues

As the remarks of Secretary-General Annan at the head of this chapter indicate, the UNTAES operation is widely regarded as a good example of a modern, multifaceted UN peacekeeping operation. It was achieved at the cost of only one UN soldier's life lost in action (regrettably, other military and civilian lives were lost through unrelated causes) and the region, now made demilitarized and secure, was transferred to Croatian authority when UNTAES's mandate ended on 15 January 1998. Since the departure of UNTAES the region has remained at peace. No residual capacity for international force was left behind, since residual monitoring responsibilities were handed over to a police and civil presence run by OSCE (Organization for Security and Cooperation in Europe).

Whether the UNTAES operation was a success depends on how one measures success. In the short term, the introduction of UNTAES effectively stopped the risk of further war in late 1995 or early 1996 that would certainly have resulted in yet more destruction and probably many more dead Serbs floating down the Danube. In the medium term, the local Serb army was demilitarized in accordance with the mandate, a transitional police force was established, respect for human rights and fundamental freedoms was promoted, democratic elections were held and observed to be free and fair, the region was handed over to Croatian sovereign control, and the UNTAES operation ended. In all these respects UNTAES can be regarded as being successful.

In the long term, however, there are some questions. Although UNTAES strongly urged the Serbs, whether those indigenous to the region or displaced from elsewhere in Croatia, to remain and become Serb citizens of Croatia, many thousands have left since the departure of UNTAES. In the latter months of the UNTAES presence, a Serb comment made with increasing frequency was: "We are safe while UNTAES is here, but who will look after us when you are gone?" While this was a noteworthy tribute to the extent that UNTAES had won the confidence and trust of the local population, it also indicated the deep mistrust and suspicion of their prospects being left in the hands of the Croats.

Since the departure of UNTAES the Croats have done little to confound these doubts. Houses have been rebuilt, but generally not for Serbs, and few Croats have actually returned to live in the region. The economy is still far from recovered. The hostility between Serbs and Croats remains. The provincial leader with his base in Osijek is a Croat who is widely regarded as one of the key persons responsible for the start of the hostilities and harassment of Serbs that led to conflict during the summer of 1991. The elected municipal council of Vukovar, led by a Croat, is nonfunctional in many respects. There are reports of Serbs being discriminated against in the allocation of jobs and the availability of loans. Despite the efforts of UNTAES to obtain a reliable amnesty for all combatants except those properly charged with war crimes, police persecutions of Serbs have continued. In these circumstances it is valid to ask whether a truly sustainable peace has been achieved in which a multiethnic society, similar to that present before 1991, can be reconstituted. If not, why did the international community spend well over $600 million on the UNTAES operation if it is not prepared to follow through to attain success in the long term?

This situation is not unique to Eastern Slavonia. Too often, the international community is slow to react to an impending crisis and fails to take preventive actions that might head-off the crisis or, at least, reduce its worst effects. When it does react, the international community spends money and resources to set in motion an operation that achieves valuable objectives—but then fails to maintain attention and follow through to ensure that the investment pays off. Perhaps it is one of the inevitable failings of democracy: democratically elected governments find it difficult to justify to their electorates continued expenditure of this nature or use of political pressure in circumstances that no longer command the headlines. There being no domestic political value to pursue this, attention wanders away from yesterday's investment to today's crisis elsewhere and long-term peace-building becomes little more than a vain hope. What is needed is not only a broad set of guidelines that could be recommended to governments, international organizations, and NGOs to help achieve common goals more effectively, but also suggestions on how the hard-won achievements of peacekeeping operations may be successfully maintained in the long term.

Addendum: The Situation in the Occupied Territories of Croatia[14]

Letter dated 15 November 1995 from the Permanent Representative of Croatia to the United Nations addressed to the Secretary-General

Upon instructions from my Government, and in addition to my letter dated 6 October 1995 addressed to the President of the Security Council (S/1995/843), I have the honour to enclose the text of the basic agreement on the region of Eastern Slavonia, Baranja and Western Sirmium, signed between the Government of the Republic of Croatia and the local Croatian Serb authorities in Eastern Slavonia on 12 November 1995 in Croatia.

I would kindly request your assistance in distributing this letter and its annex as a document of the General Assembly under agenda item 92, and of the Security Council.

(Signed) Mario NOBILO
Permanent Representative

Annex
Basic agreement on the region of Eastern Slavonia, Baranja, and Western Sirmium

The Parties agree as follows:

1. There will be a transitional period of 12 months which may be extended at most to another period of the same duration if so requested by one of the parties.

2. The United Nations Security Council is requested to establish a Transitional Administration, which shall govern the region during the transitional period in the interest of all persons resident in or returning to the region.

3. The United Nations Security Council is requested to authorize an international force to deploy during the transitional period to maintain peace and security in the region and otherwise to assist in implementation of this agreement. The region shall be demilitarized according to the schedule and procedures determined by the international force. This demilitarization shall be completed not later than 30 days after deployment of the international force and shall include all military forces, weapons, and police, except for the international force and for police operating under the supervision of, or with the consent of, the Transitional Administration.

4. The Transitional Administration shall ensure the possibility for the return of refugees and displaced persons to their homes of origin. All persons who have left the region or who have come to the region with previous permanent residence in Croatia shall enjoy the same rights as all other residents of the region. The Transitional Administration shall also take the steps necessary to re-establish the normal functioning of all public services in the region without delay.

5. The Transitional Administration shall help to establish and train temporary police forces, to build professionalism among the police and confidence among all ethnic communities.

6. The highest levels of internationally recognized human rights and fundamental freedoms shall be respected in the region.

7. All persons have the right to return freely to their place of residence in the region and to live there in conditions of security. All persons who have left the region or who have come to the region with previous permanent residence in Croatia have the right to live in the region.

8. All persons shall have the right to have restored to them any property that was taken from them by unlawful acts or that they were forced to abandon and to just compensation for property that cannot be restored to them.

9. The right to recover property, to receive compensation for property that cannot be returned, and to receive assistance in reconstruction of damaged property shall be equally available to all persons without regard to ethnicity.

10. Interested countries and organizations are requested to take appropriate steps to promote the accomplishment of the commitments in this agreement. After the expiration of the transition period and consistent with established practice, the international community shall monitor and report on respect for human rights in the region on a long-term basis.

11. In addition, interested countries and organizations are requested to establish a commission, which will be authorized to monitor the implementation of this agreement, particularly its human rights and civil rights provisions, to investigate all allegations of violations of this agreement, and to make appropriate recommendations.

12. Not later than 30 days before the end of the transitional period, elections for all local government bodies, including for municipalities, districts, and counties, as well as the right of the Serbian community to appoint a joint council of municipalities, shall be organized by the Transitional Administration. International organizations and institutions (e.g., the Organization for Security and Cooperation in Europe, the United Nations) and interested States are requested to oversee the elections.

13. The Government of the Republic of Croatia shall cooperate fully with the Transitional Administration and the international force. During the transitional period the Croatian Government authorizes the presence of

international monitors along the international border of the region in order to facilitate free movement of persons across existing border crossings.

14. This Agreement shall enter into force upon the adoption by the United Nations Security Council of a resolution responding affirmatively to the requests made in this agreement.

DONE this twelfth day of November 1995.

SIGNED:

Milan MILANOVIC, *Head, Serb Negotiating Delegation*
Hrvoje SARINIC, *Head, Croatian Government Delegation*

WITNESSED:

Peter W. GALBRAITH, *United States Ambassador*
Thorvald STOLTENBERG, *United Nations Mediator*

Notes

1. Boutros Boutros-Ghali, "Unvanquished—A U.S.–UN Saga," 256.

2. Kofi A. Annan, "On Peacekeeping and National Sovereignty," in *Hard Choices—Moral Dilemmas in Humanitarian Intervention*, ed. Jonathan Moore, 61.

3. The following extracts from Holbrooke's account in *To End a War* are illuminating: "Events had given [Tudjman] a central role in the peace process. . . . Tudjman could prevent a settlement in Bosnia until he got control of eastern Slavonia. Given his previous behavior, his threats to go to war again soon after Dayton if he did not get the region back peacefully had to be taken seriously. Tudjman's ability both to prevent a Bosnia agreement and to threaten another war was his primary leverage over Milosevic" (238–39).

4. A/50/757-S/1995/951.

5. Security Council Resolution 1025(1995) of 30 November 1995.

6. To the author's best knowledge, it was not known in the UN that at Dayton Tudjman had asked for some American troops and a U.S. force commander for the transition force and the request had been declined. According to Holbrooke (*To End a War*, 260) he favored a U.S. military presence, but the Pentagon and the National Security Council had a different view. To ask Congress for yet more U.S. troops would create an insurmountable problem and one that the White House wished to avoid.

7. The writer's view expressed at an internal meeting at the time was: "If it looks like bad fish, and smells like bad fish—it is probably bad fish."

8. S/1995/1028* of 13 December 1995.

9. It read as follows: "Determined to ensure the security and freedom of movement of the personnel of the United Nations peacekeeping operation in the Republic of Croatia, and to these ends, acting under Chapter VII of the Charter of the United Nations. . . ." This formulation quickly became known as "Chinese Chapter VII."

10. The time and resources taken in achieving these pedestrian but critical items of the deployment of a UN operation are too often given little attention in postoperation analysis by those who do not have military experience. The ordinary

challenges of a national contingent settling in and becoming operational are multiplied several times in a multinational deployment.

11. One of the disappointments was that it never proved possible to bring together the Serb Orthodox and Catholic churches to reconcile some of their differences and provide joint religious leadership in the region. Given the historical schism between the two churches and the nationalist feelings expressed by both, perhaps this was always too much too expect.

12. There was not even any provision in the approved budget for covering the operating costs and salaries of the Transitional Police Force that the mandate specifically called upon UNTAES to establish. The provision of neutral uniforms for the police was resolved only by selecting suitable uniforms from a commercial U.S. catalog and the costs being covered by some $500,000 from the U.S. Department of Justice. Police pay had to be covered by negotiating a subvention from the Croatian government, which left UNTAES hostage to monthly decisions and delays in Zagreb.

13. This protest was accompanied by an oral assurance (threat?) that if the incident was repeated, the Transitional Administrator would have the perpetrators arrested by UNTAES military units and would deliver them personally to the presidential residence in Zagreb. This was apparently taken seriously in Zagreb, as the incident did not happen again.

14. A UN Security Council and General Assembly document (AS): General Assembly: A/50/57; Security Council: S/1995/951. Dated 15 November 1995.

CHAPTER SIX

UN Leverage in East Timor

inducing Indonesian compliance through international law

MARK QUARTERMAN

HOW TO GET RECALCITRANT STATES to adhere to international law is a question that continues to vex policy-makers and scholars. It is a matter of both theoretical and practical interest in light of the recent proliferation of mechanisms by which states have ceded aspects of their sovereign authority to supranational institutions and regimes. The focus of this chapter is the connection between leverage emanating from United Nations' resolutions and actions and compliance by states. It attempts to discern if and how applications of leverage by the UN contribute to state compliance, and under what conditions such leverage is most effective.

This chapter examines the nexus of leverage and compliance by focusing on the case of Indonesian behavior regarding East Timor. From the Indonesian invasion and annexation of the territory in the 1970s, until 1996, the UN, through General Assembly and Security Council resolutions, never recognized Indonesia's claim to East Timor. The international body, with varying degrees of gravity over time, called for the withdrawal of Indonesian troops and the granting to the East Timorese people an act of self-determination. After decades of ignoring UN demands, in January 1999 newly appointed Indonesian President B. J. Habibie surprised most observers by announcing that the people of East Timor would be allowed to choose as to whether they wished the territory to remain under Indonesian law and be part of Indonesia or to become independent. On August 30, 1999 the East Timorese chose overwhelmingly to become independent in a UN-run referendum, also known as a "popular consultation." Immediately after the results were announced, pro-Indonesian groups supported

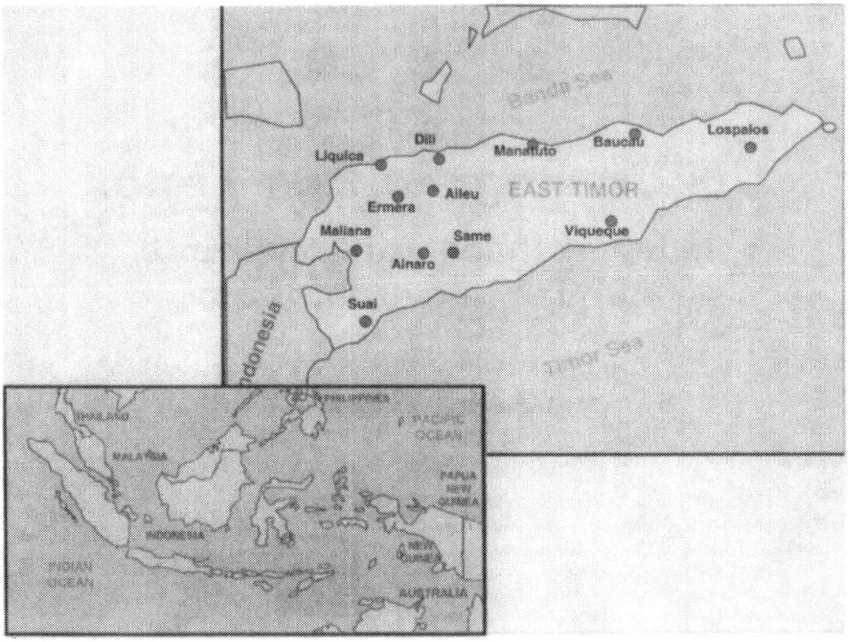

by the Indonesian military began a campaign of killing and destruction in the territory. By mid-September the Indonesian government had reluctantly agreed to the deployment of an international force to end the violence. Throughout this saga, the international community[1] acted with varying degrees of intensity to influence Indonesia's behavior. This examination attempts to determine how effectively and by what means those efforts were made.

In this case as in others, it is necessary to disaggregate how, and how well, the international community worked to affect its will. From direct observation of the East Timor case, I posit that there is a system of interlocking actors within the international community whose work in tandem, although generally not in coordination, will determine the effectiveness of UN action to achieve compliance. The effectiveness of any attempt, for example, to induce compliance with a Security Council resolution will not necessarily succeed unless multiple actors within this international system work to achieve this goal. Within this system the UN is one of a number of actors—rarely of itself the most powerful. However, within the system the UN is both a forum for such efforts at achieving compliance, or, in the terminology of international relations, a *regime*,[2] and an actor in its own right.

The actors that played a role in the case of East Timor could be found within the UN system, among transnational actors (including transnational NGOs [nongovernmental organizations] and transnational norm entrepreneurs such as East Timorese leader Jose Ramos Horta), transnational issue networks (made up of national governmental staff, staff of intergovernmental organizations, domestic NGOs, and academics, among others), individual states, the news media, and, of course, the object of the efforts at compliance—Indonesia.

In addition to the above external factors, internal factors have played a crucial role in influencing compliance with UN resolutions. Those factors can be summed up as relating to: (1) whether a state considers compliance within its interest (this often involves questions regarding the mobilization of domestic opinion); (2) a state's definition of itself internally and in relation to the international community; (3) its participation in creating and shaping the international norm at issue; and (4) whether the norm has been internalized within the state's domestic political and legal structures. These factors influence both the behavior of the target state and the states that might try to influence its compliance.

The United Nations' ability to leverage the compliance of states is dependent in part on coordination within and among the principal organs of the UN—the Security Council, the General Assembly, the Secretary-General, and the Secretariat—in part on other international and transnational actors; and in part on factors internal to the state in question discussed above. In such a process, the UN's leverage could be conceived of as falling along a continuum from relatively weak to relatively strong. The UN is at its weakest in its application of leverage when it has no strong negative action to threaten, its legislative bodies are not seized of the issue, individual Member States are not willing to apply pressure, transnational actors are not active, transnational issue networks are not mobilized, and the media is not focused on an issue. The strongest leverage occurs when either the Security Council or the General Assembly is willing to respond to noncompliance with coercive measures, Member States—especially those with influence on the noncomplying state—bring bilateral pressure to bear, transnational actors and issue networks are actively engaged, and the glare of international media attention spotlights the issue. Most cases, of course, fall along the spectrum and are neither examples of the weakest or the strongest applications of leverage. The salience of each factor, in relation to the others and in terms of its persuasive power on the state in question, varies from situation to situation and from one time period to the next within each situation.

Discerning the effectiveness of the UN's efforts to influence state behavior is an exercise fraught with difficulties. On the one hand, those who subscribe to the realist theoretical perspective that views international relations solely as a contest of power between states consider the UN to be a hollow regime that has little relevance when examining state behavior. On the other hand, supporters of the UN often too easily fall into the trap of *post hoc, ergo proper hoc*. When presented with state compliance within a reasonable period of time after UN action, such boosters will, more from the heart than the head, infer that the latter led to the former. What is necessary, therefore, is a clearer understanding through empirical studies of how the UN regime influences state behavior in a range of cases and under various circumstances.

For those who work for the world body, the problem of determining the effectiveness of one's actions makes it difficult to plan the work of the Organization to maximize influence. Often, even those involved in particular cases are unable to state with any specificity how well an action, such as a Security Council resolution or an intervention by the Secretary-General, has served the cause of compliance. In a rapidly changing situation, such as in East Timor in the period before and immediately after the popular consultation, so many acts of leverage were brought to bear on Indonesia that determining *which* was decisive is nearly impossible. As an alternative to a vain attempt to identify the decisive act, I attempt in this chapter to describe the environment in which international pressure was brought to bear on Indonesia. Such a description could lead in turn to an understanding of where the UN fits into and is the core of an international regime that can influence state behavior and bring about compliance with international law.

In the first section I will consider the academic literature on why, or whether, states comply with international law. The second section of the chapter is focused on East Timor. I set out a brief history of the question of East Timor from the end of Portuguese colonial rule to Indonesian President B. J. Habibie's offer of a popular consultation. The bulk of the section on East Timor comprises an examination of the use of leverage to influence Indonesian behavior in three key periods in the recent history of East Timor: (1) the period from the Indonesian invasion to the seemingly unilateral decision by President Habibie to allow the East Timorese to engage in an act of self-determination; (2) the period after the signing of the May 5 Agreement between Indonesia and Portugal calling for the UN to hold the referendum and the popular consultation; and (3) the deployment of an international force in response to the postballot violence. Each of those periods presents an example of how leverage was brought to bear on the Indonesian government and how that entity responded to such pressure.

I conclude that the UN's influence was probably negligible in the period leading up to President Habibie's offer; it increased in the period during which the UN deployed a mission in East Timor to carry-out the referendum; and was at its most effective, in partnership with other aspects of the international community, in persuading Indonesia to accept the deployment of an international force to quell the postreferendum violence. My focus is on United Nations' leverage because the Organization is often the means through which the international community attempts to carry-out its will.

THE LEVERAGE–COMPLIANCE NEXUS

Leverage

The tools of leverage at the disposal of the international community through the United Nations encompass three types of ways to influence the behavior of recalcitrant actors: physical force; economic and political leverage, including the carrot of assistance or the stick of sanctions; and ostracism or embarrassment.[3] Only the last tool was available to the UN during most of the period covered by this chapter, except for the postballot violence when, for the first time during the process, certain actors threatened to impose sanctions if Indonesia had not allowed an international force to be deployed in East Timor.

It is necessary, in examining how the United Nations applies leverage in the area of peace and security, to disaggregate the parts of the international community that work to influence compliance, starting with the principal organs of the international body. It is important in such a study to seek explanations that comprehend the multiplicity of international and domestic, official and unofficial actors who play a role. The Security Council, the General Assembly, the Secretary-General, and the Secretariat have separate authority and responsibilities set forth in the Charter of the United Nations. To apply leverage and achieve compliance, it is necessary that these organs work in partnership.

It should be noted that by the time the General Assembly or Security Council has adopted a resolution aimed at altering the behavior of a particular Member State, it is likely that a significant number of states consider the target state to be in substantial breach of an international legal obligation. In most cases, prior to the adoption of the resolution, a negotiated alternative, aimed at achieving compliance without the public passage of a resolution, has been tried and failed. Compliance with this category of international law differs markedly from compliance within a regime into which a state entered voluntarily with other states for mutual gain. Of course, by signing the UN Charter the state entered voluntarily into the UN's peace and security regime; its breaches of that regime are public and often notorious, and the resolutions aimed at its compliance are aimed specifically at that state.

Compliance

Louis Henkin famously declared that "almost all states observe almost all principles of international law and almost all of their obligations almost all of the time."[4] This formulation suggests that when their interests diverge from international norms, most states would not act in keeping with this maxim most of the time. Therefore, Henkin's rule appears not to leave much hope for compliance in hard cases, such as those that raise issues that impinge on territorial integrity as in Indonesia and its claim over East Timor. Scholarly consideration of why states obey, or at least comply with, international law has to a large extent tracked the theoretical divisions in international relations and international law. I should note that *compliance*, not *obedience*, is the focus of this chapter.[5] Given the Indonesian government's grudging acceptance of the popular consultation,[6] notwithstanding that the offer came from President Habibie, the best that could have been hoped for from Indonesia was compliance. Obedience would have been too much to expect.

Scholarly approaches to compliance fall into four broad areas. The first, *realist theory*, essentially asserts that compliance with international law only occurs when states believe it is in their interest to comply. That is, conforming to international norms only appears to be compliance, but can be seen at a basic level as the coincidence of norm and interest. Under this framework, international institutions play little role in affecting state behavior, and power is the only currency. International institutions are merely forums in which these power politics are played out. A threat of sanctions or other action from a more powerful state would be the only factor that could induce compliance if noncompliance is the preferred course. While realists assert that the theory describes the range of state behavior across sectors, critics claim that it best describes situations that implicate national security.[7]

Institutionalists believe that creating rules that constrain and mold state behavior through regimes will increase the possibility of cooperation and compliance. They focus on devising structures that states enter voluntarily that prevent noncompliance. The theory was developed in part in response to the perception that realism did not fully capture the cooperation among states that occurs in the regimes states create to foster compliance with international norms. However, institutionalist scholars tend to focus more on economic and environmental regimes than on security concerns.[8]

Liberal international relations and international law scholars attempt to show that *domestic regime type* determines international behavior. Liberal scholars, building on Immanuel Kant's idea of a liberal peace brought on by the expectation of peaceful interaction between liberal democratic states, have asserted that liberal states are more likely to comply with international law than are nonliberal states. They argue that liberal democratic states are more likely to abide by international agreements, especially with other liberal democratic states, because of the multilayered connections between civil societies, especially legal communities, that develop among liberal states and that serve to reinforce compliance and even obedience.[9]

The fourth approach is the *constructivist* school that views international institutions as not only being influenced by state behavior, but also influencing the shape and interests of the states that interact within them. Under this approach, behavior is induced by the existence of a norm, which influences the interests of a state, which in turn behaves according to the norm.[10] Collective understandings and shared causal perceptions develop over time under a regime and animate and shape state approaches to compliance with norms.[11]

Each of these approaches has some explanatory power in the attempt to determine why states comply, but neither separately nor collectively do they provide a full or accurate answer to the question posed by the heading of this section. This constellation of theories does not account for domestic factors, beyond those determined by regime type that influence compliance. Realists, institutionalists, and constructivists view states as unitary actors and do not take into account domestic pressures in foreign-policy decision-making.[12] Liberal theorists look largely to liberal states for their examples of behavior. Building on the transnational process school of thought, Koh suggests an approach that provides a richer explanation when added to the above theories.[13] He asserts that the internalization of an international norm within a domestic political and legal structure enhances compliance and can lead to obedience. This is through an interactive process that involves multiple international, transnational, national, and official and unofficial actors working to internalize the norm:

> It is through this transnational legal process, this repeated cycle of interaction, interpretation, and internalization, that international law acquires its "stickiness," that nation-states acquire their identity, and that nations come to "obey" international law out of perceived self-interest. In tracing the move from the external to the internal, from one-time grudging compliance with an external norm to habitual internalized obedience, the key factor is repeated participation in the transnational legal process.[14]

As an example of this shift Koh cites an incident from the Middle East peace process: the 1997 Hebron disengagement agreement. He describes how the then Israeli Likud government had run for election in opposition to the peace process and that the new prime minister, Benjamin Netanyahu, had denounced the 1993 Oslo Accords that called, *inter alia*, for the Israelis and Palestinians to reach an agreement for the withdrawal of Israeli troops from Hebron. Netanyahu had even insisted that he would never meet with Palestinian leader Yasser Arafat. Despite that opposition, Netanyahu reached an agreement with Arafat in 1997 to redeploy Israeli troops from Hebron. Koh attributes the change in Netanyahu's position to each of the factors describe above.[15]

On gaining office, Koh asserts, Netanyahu began, at least on a limited level, to see certain benefits for Israel in terms of foreign investment and an improved regional climate by engaging in the peace process. By entering into the Oslo Accords, Israel created both a set of legal obligations and a group of countries, among them the United States, that had an interest in Israel's compliance with those obligations. A domestic process in Israel, led by the legislative institutionalization of the peace process through its approval in the Knesset, but supplemented by media and non-governmental actors, made full breach costly. Finally, the Oslo Accords created mechanisms for interactions with the Palestinians, which involved each side holding the other accountable for living up to its obligations under the agreements, that created further possibilities for internalizing the process. Koh admits that these processes do not guarantee compliance, much less obedience, and that the Middle East peace process remained "shaky," but he asserts that this process of interest, identity, international society, and internalization provide a useful framework for understanding state compliance.[16]

However, realism, institutionalism, and constructivism make no provision for evaluating the impact of nongovernmental organizations or of domestic politics. And while transnational legal process addresses both nongovernmental organizations and domestic mobilization, its scope might not reach the short-term questions of compliance raised by the case of East Timor. Such a situation might not allow the necessary time for internalization to occur. None of these theories provides a "unified field theory" to explain compliance. But it is not clear that the complexity of international interactions provides an enabling environment for the development of a grand, single theoretical framework.

THE CASE OF EAST TIMOR

Background

For more than 400 years the eastern half of the island of Timor, located in the southeastern part of what became the Indonesian archipelago, just north of Australia, was a Portuguese colony. West Timor was part of the Dutch East Indies and became an original part of Indonesia when Dutch rule ended in the archipelago and most of the Dutch colony became independent Indonesia. Portuguese colonialism continued in East Timor until 1974. Portuguese grip relaxed in the aftermath of the 1974 "Carnation Revolution" that removed an authoritarian military regime in Lisbon. Although the new Portuguese government promulgated legislation to form a transitional government in East Timor as a step toward full independence by 1978, a political process was underway in the territory that overtook Lisbon's planning. Violence increased among the contending East Timorese parties, causing the Portuguese governor to flee the mainland to Atauro Island, off the coast of the territory's capital, Dili. One of the parties opposed to Portuguese rule, Fretilin, took advantage of the distraction in the metropole to declare independence on November 28, 1975. With the support of many of its members who were trained by the Portuguese army, Fretilin established control over the half island for a short time, but faced strong opposition from groups opposed to Fretilin's Marxist orientation and in favor of varying degrees of ties with Indonesia. Fretilin's attempt to rule and consequent opposition from the pro-Indonesia parties led to substantial violence.[17]

On December 7, 1975 Indonesia launched an air, sea, and land invasion of East Timor, ostensibly at the request of the pro-Indonesia parties. Jakarta was also motivated by a desire to make East Timor Indonesian in order to further unite the archipelago. Indonesia established a degree of control of the territory in relatively short order, but many Fretilin supporters fled to East Timor's mountainous interior and formed a guerrilla force, Falintil, that mounted an armed resistance to Indonesian rule. The guerrillas continued to harass Indonesian authorities until the Indonesian withdrawal in October 1999. In 1976, Indonesia incorporated East Timor, making the territory, under Indonesian law, the country's 27th province.[18]

Legal Status

East Timor's status had become an issue of international concern before Portugal's grip on the territory weakened in 1975. In 1960, the General Assembly urged Portugal to make plans for East Timor's self-determination; it added East Timor to its list of Non-Self-Governing Territories.[19]

On December 22, 1975 the United Nations Security Council deplored the Indonesian invasion, called for the withdrawal of Indonesian troops, regretted that Portugal had not discharged fully its responsibility as administering power in East Timor, and recognized the inalienable right of the East Timorese to self-determination. The Council called upon Portugal to cooperate with the UN to enable the East Timorese people to engage freely in an act of self-determination.[20] Throughout the next 24 years, the United Nations maintained that Indonesia's actions were contrary to international law and never recognized its "incorporation" of East Timor. Portugal continued its official status as the administering power of the territory, and each year in its annual report informed the UN that conditions prevailing in the territory prevented it from exercising its responsibilities.[21]

Three Crucial Turning Points

Descriptions of the application of leverage in three key periods follow. I have chosen these periods not just because they present interesting case studies of the uses of leverage and its effects on compliance, but also because they represent three crucial turning points in East Timorese history.

Period One—Indonesian Invasion to President Habibie's Decision (1975–1999): Weak Leverage. Weak leverage was all the UN had at its disposal in the period following the Indonesian invasion of East Timor, and even that leverage weakened with the passage of time. It became clear soon after the invasion that the Security Council would take no action beyond its initial resolutions. Indeed, former U.S. Permanent Representative to the UN Daniel Patrick Moynihan wrote in his memoir of his time at the UN that he was instructed to prevent any further effective action.[22]

As time passed after the Indonesian invasion, the likelihood of Indonesia bearing even the costs of ostracism or embarrassment diminished. More punitive steps, such as armed force or economic sanctions, were out of the question. The costs that Indonesia did bear, having to answer criticism in the UN Human Rights Commission, the Decolonization Committee, as well as regular protests from NGOs and the attendant bad publicity, were, for over 20 years, within the range of toleration by the Suharto government. Only the fall of President Suharto and the gradual opening of the Indonesian political system led to a change in policy regarding East Timor.

On January 27, 1999 Indonesian President B. J. Habibie suddenly, and seemingly unilaterally, announced that the people of East Timor would be allowed to vote on whether they wished to have autonomy within, or be separate from, Indonesia.[23] The act seemed even more unilateral because Habibie informed the cabinet of his decision only immediately prior to the public announcement. Most of the members of the cabinet, especially the military and the Department of Foreign Affairs, both of which had always maintained a special interest in East Timor (the former because of its role in combating a pro-independence insurgency, and the latter because of its role in defending Indonesia from international political attack), had known nothing of the decision and had had no opportunity to register their dissent before the world was informed of the policy.[24]

Habibie's offer might have seemed at the time to be unilateral, but four events in the 1990s combined to increase the previously waning international pressure on Indonesia. The 1991 Santa Cruz massacre of several hundred unarmed East Timorese protesters committed by Indonesian troops in the presence of foreign journalists refocused international attention on the issue and galvanized NGO activity. In 1996, the awarding of the Nobel Peace Prize to East Timorese Bishop Carlos Belo and independence leader Jose Ramos Horta represented a classic example of the use of the prize as international leverage.[25] The awarding of the prizes guarantees an automatic measure of international attention and helped to revive the debate about the illegal Indonesian occupation of the territory. In 1997, the newly appointed UN Secretary-General, Kofi Annan, decided to increase the UN's involvement in the matter of East Timor, in part by appointing a distinguished retired Pakistani diplomat, Jamsheed Marker, as his Special Representative for East Timor, and in part by picking-up the pace of UN-sponsored talks between Indonesia and Portugal that had begun in 1982. Finally, in December 1998, Australian Prime Minister John Howard sent a letter to President Habibie informing the latter that Australia was changing its stated policy on East Timor to support self-determination for the East Timorese.[26] This action was significant because Indonesia's neighbor, Australia, had previously been the only state that had given *de jure* recognition to Indonesia's claim to East Timor.[27]

The period of increasing pressure in the 1990s, coupled with standing General Assembly and Security Council resolutions on East Timor and the other irritants previously described, contributed to gradual compliance. None of those actions was focused on achieving immediate compliance, as would be the case during the next period. The effect of the pressures on the Indonesian government, or at least on President Habibie, could be likened to erosion. While the pressure of the 1990s was likely not the proximate cause of the offer of the vote, it is unlikely that the offer would have been made in the absence of the pressure. And, as mentioned before, it is unlikely that the government of Australia would have changed its policy in the absence of international advocacy on the issue of East Timor.

Identity, as described by liberal theorists, might have played a role as well. Habibie frequently referred to himself as a "democratizer," and if a liberal identity *does* lead to greater obedience of international law, it might have added to his motivation to allow the process of self-determination to take place. He was more outward-looking than his predecessor or many of his colleagues, possibly because he had spent most of his career overseas in Germany where he worked as an aircraft engineer. In addition, possibly because he had so thin an internal base, he seemed to focus on the benefits to Indonesia's international standing that would come from removing the albatross of East Timor from Indonesia's neck.[28]

Habibie also had practical reasons for proposing the policy change. Indonesia was recovering from the Asian economic crisis and attempting to lure foreign investment back into the country. He appeared to believe that a solution to the problem of East Timor would increase Indonesia's attractiveness to investors. Finally, Habibie only nominally headed the formidable but unpopular political machine established by President Suharto and was facing the first competitive elections in Indonesian history in June 1999. He could have seen his proposal as a bold gambit to increase his chances of winning the presidency in his own right.

Under Suharto, Indonesia had begun to play a more active regional role in the 1990s, exemplified by the activist diplomacy of Foreign Minister Ali Alatas, especially in the Southeast Asia region.[29] During 1998 Indonesia was campaigning for the presidency of the UN Economic and Social Council. Indonesia's ability to interact fully on the international stage, in a manner commensurate with its size and stature as a regionally pivotal power, was hampered, however, by its continued occupation of East Timor.[30] The issue acted as a continued irritant to the Indonesian government. Indonesia yearly had to defend itself before the UN Human Rights Commission, the General Assembly's Decolonization Committee, and against regular attacks from the highly mobilized NGO community focused on East Timor. The Indonesian Department of Foreign Affairs expended a significant amount of time and energy in Western countries challenging the pro-independence line of the NGOs. That energy, and the legitimacy that would come from resolving the issue, could have been used to engage in a more active foreign policy.

Finally, internal grumbling was developing within Indonesia during the late 1990s, especially among the political and intellectual elite, that too much attention and money were being devoted to East Timor. They argued, in the aftermath of the fall of Suharto and the regional economic crisis of

1997–98, that East Timor was a distraction that the Indonesian government could not afford to indulge and that the continued *de facto* military regime in the territory perpetuated the power of TNI (Indonesian national military) in an era when Indonesia should have been moving toward democratization. Others asserted, not necessarily accurately, that the East Timorese had been the beneficiaries of financial assistance, including educational scholarships, that had not been made available to Indonesians.

Some advocates of this view also commented on the perceived ungratefulness of the East Timorese who, after receiving the benefits of incorporation into Indonesia, continued to agitate for independence. This argument was often allied with the assertion that East Timor was more trouble for Indonesia on the international stage than it was worth. While this view was not necessarily widespread within the Indonesian polity, it was held by certain elites in government and in nongovernmental organizations in Jakarta who are believed to have influenced Habibie's thinking. Some Muslim intellectuals with close advisory relationships to Habibie welcomed the possibility of ridding Indonesia of a troublesome, overwhelmingly Catholic burden.[31] Finally, certain domestic human-rights organizations took part in efforts to change Indonesia's policy toward East Timor.

The main part of the Indonesian polity opposed to a change in Indonesian policy toward East Timor was the military, which was more inward-looking than other parts of the government and focused on the military's legitimacy as the guarantor of the country's unity. In considering the value of East Timor, some officers expressed concern that the end of Indonesian control over the territory might lead activists in other parts of the fractious archipelago to take advantage of the constant centrifugal pressures present in the country. They also cited the effort and blood expended by their comrades in the effort to keep East Timor. Other observers also cited the financial profits military leaders reputedly gained from East Timor in partnership with the Suharto family.[32]

The international community was divided on the issue of East Timor for much of the period following the Indonesian invasion. Those divisions enabled Indonesia to avoid its international obligations for over 20 years. For reasons related to the cold war and economic profit, the United States and Australia acquiesced in Indonesia's occupation of the territory. Indonesia's size and strategic location (210 million people compared to East Timor's approximately 700,000) gave it a power and importance that made it difficult for the UN to bring pressure to bear. The best the Organization was able to do during this period was keep the issue alive and take opportunities, when presented, to assist the people of East Timor engage in an act of self-determination. Only in the second period did states, especially states with close relationships with Indonesia, take up the cause of East Timor and make international pressure intense enough to have an effect on Indonesia's behavior.

Period Two—Popular Consultation. On May 5, 1999 Indonesia and Portugal signed an accord witnessed by the Secretary-General, agreeing to allow the people of East Timor to engage in a popular consultation to determine whether they wanted final-status autonomy within Indonesia or separation from Indonesia. An autonomy plan, or constitutional framework, initially drafted by the UN and negotiated by Indonesia and Portugal but unilaterally finalized by Indonesia, was attached to the agreement and was the basis of the decision to be put before the people of East Timor. The agreement called on the Secretary-General to deploy a mission, subsequently named the "United Nations Mission in East Timor" (UNAMET), to carry-out the popular consultation but left responsibility for maintaining peace and security in the territory in the hands of Indonesia.[33] It was clear during the negotiations that Indonesia would not have allowed the ballot to go forward had the other participants in the negotiations insisted on Indonesia relinquishing security control.[34]

Leverage became stronger once Indonesia signed the 5 May Agreement and entered into obligations for which it could be held responsible if it did not comply. While actions by the international community such as armed intervention or economic sanctions were no more likely to be imposed on Indonesia in the aftermath of the signing of the agreement than they were before, the possibility of ostracism and embarrassment *did* increase. The Secretary-General and his mission in the field had more leverage to apply because he had the backing of the Security Council, key Member States who could raise concerns with the Indonesian government, an aroused NGO community that mobilized to send observers to the territory for the ballot and who became more active in the capitals of interested countries, and an international media corps that realized that East Timor was a major story.

Under the terms of the agreement, if the East Timorese were to vote for autonomy, Indonesia would be required to take constitutional steps to implement the autonomy plan, and Portugal would be required to initiate steps to remove East Timor from the General Assembly's list of Non-Self-Governing Territories and delete the question of East Timor from the agendas of the Security Council and General Assembly. If the East Timorese were to reject autonomy, the government of Indonesia would be required "to terminate its links with East Timor, thus restoring under Indonesian law the status East Timor held prior to 17 July 1976." Indonesia and Portugal would then work out with the Secretary-General the modalities for "a peaceful and orderly transfer of authority in East Timor to the United Nations." Finally, the Secretary-General would be given the responsibility for assisting the East Timorese to move toward independence.[35]

The parties signed two additional agreements on May 5, 1999 on the modalities for carrying-out the popular consultation and setting forth the security arrangements for the period. The first of the supplemental agreements set August 8, 1999 as the date for the ballot.[36] The second stipulated that Indonesia was responsible for creating peaceful conditions for a free-and-fair ballot and gave that responsibility to the Indonesian police, not the Indonesian military.[37] The Indonesian military had over the years in East Timor established a reputation for brutality inside the territory. Even before May 5, 1999, evidence was coming to light that elements in the Indonesian military were providing support, training, and direction to pro-Indonesian militias.[38]

Because of the Secretary-General's concern about the security situation in East Timor, on May 4 he distributed to the parties a confidential memorandum containing conditions, which, if met, would have signified an important step toward creating an environment conducive to the peaceful holding of a free-and-fair ballot. The memorandum called, *inter alia*, for the militias to be brought under control, a ban on rallies of armed groups, the prompt arrest of those who incite or threaten to use violence, redeployment of Indonesian military forces to central bases within East Timor, and the immediate establishment of a process of the laying down of weapons by all armed groups. Within a few days the confidential memorandum was widely reported in the press, which probably inadvertently increased public pressure on Indonesia to improve its handling of security in the territory.[39]

The ballot date of August 8, 1999, as set forth in the May 5 Agreement, called for a time-line that was considerably shorter than usually necessary to hold a referendum. UNAMET ultimately succeeded in the herculean labor of conducting the popular consultation under very difficult circumstances by August 30, 1999, less than five months after the beginning of the deployment of the mission.[40]

While the logistical difficulties for the mission were numerous, the security challenge to UNAMET's ability to fulfill its mandate at times seemed insurmountable. Soon after President Habibie announced his offer of a popular consultation, East Timor experienced an upsurge in political violence directed at supporters of independence. The first few months of 1999 saw a dramatic increase in the number and size of pro-Indonesia militia groups.[41] By the spring of 1999 militias had been established in every administrative district of the territory, and the people of the western districts were living under a constant threat of violence. In April, less than a month before the signing of the May 5 Agreement, two brutal militia attacks, one in the town of Liquiça and the second in Dili, resulted in the deaths of at least 70 persons and increased the focus of the international community and the media. In Liquiça, more than 50 people were massacred in a church on April 4.[42] In Dili, on April 17, approximately 20 persons, some of them refugees from Liquiça, were murdered during a militia rampage that was witnessed by the visiting Irish foreign minister.[43] In neither case was there any evidence that the Indonesian military or police intervened to prevent these atrocities. By the time the first UNAMET personnel deployed in East Timor, initially in Dili, the independence movement had been driven underground and the militias were operating with impunity. The deployment of the mission brought a visible improvement to the security situation in the capital, but at no time did the Indonesian authorities provide a safe-and-secure environment for the popular consultation.

UNAMET had two closely related tasks: the holding of the referendum, and the securing of at least adequate security conditions for the free-and-fair conduct of the referendum. It is not an understatement to say that a substantial majority of UNAMET's interactions with the Indonesian authorities focused on the security situation and were aimed at getting Indonesia to fulfill its obligations arising from the May 5 Agreement. The interactions during this period at the most senior level involved contacts between the Secretary-General and President Habibie and Indonesian Foreign Minister Ali Alatas. The interactions also involved direct communications between the mission, represented by the Head of Mission Ian Martin, Special Representative of the Secretary-General (SRSG) for the East Timor Popular Consultation, and the Indonesian Government Task Force, an interdepartmental group sent by Jakarta to East Timor as the primary Indonesian government interface with UNAMET. In addition, Martin and the Personal Representative of the Secretary-General for East Timor, Jamsheed Marker, made periodic trips to Jakarta to meet face-to-face with senior Indonesian officials to attempt to influence official Indonesian behavior.[44]

In addition to the contacts at the highest levels, the efforts of UNAMET personnel at every level of the mission in their interactions with Indonesian officials and militia leaders were generally aimed at trying to establish an improved security environment. In their attempts to induce Indonesian compliance and persuade the militias to desist from violence and intimidation, those UNAMET personnel—from the electoral and political sections, the civilian police, and military-liaison officers—conducted a daily, constant interface with Indonesian authorities.

The Security Council maintained a direct, focused interest in the popular consultation. In its Resolution 1246 (1999), which provided the mandate for UNAMET, the Council emphasized Indonesia's responsibility for maintaining peace and security in the territory and called on the Secretary-General to report to the Council every fourteen days "on the implementation of its resolutions and of the Tripartite Agreements and on the security situation in East Timor."[45] The reporting requirement, with every other report being submitted in written form, kept the issue before the Council, ensured that the Secretariat frequently briefed the Council on the evolving situation, and provided for a monthly public, on the record, statement on the situation in East Timor by the Secretary-General. Security Council presidential statements calling on Indonesia to abide by the Agreement often followed such briefings.[46]

Other international pressures included visits of senior officials of interested Member States to Jakarta and East Timor. During the popular consultation period the Australian Foreign Minister and the U.S. Assistant Secretary of State for Asian Affairs among others made such visits. In addition, during that period, the U.S. Secretary of State, Madeleine Albright, visited Jakarta and, in addition to her meetings with Indonesian officials, met with jailed East Timorese independence leader Xanana Gusmão. During each of those trips the visitors urged the Indonesian authorities to abide by their May 5 obligations. Interested states also made their positions known to the Indonesian government through their diplomatic missions in Jakarta.

In order to assist the UN in coordinating the international response to the evolving situation in East Timor, the Secretary-General established a Group of Friends of the Secretary-General for East Timor. The Friends helped to harness the efforts of interested states, kept those states informed about the progress of the mission and the security situation, and solicited financial support for UNAMET. It was comprised of donors and other interested Member States. It met periodically during the popular-consultation period generally to receive reports about the mission and the situation in East Timor. A smaller group of interested states with potential influence over Indonesia, the Core Group—Australia, Japan, New Zealand, the United Kingdom, and the United States—was brought together by the Secretariat to meet more frequently both in New York and Jakarta. The Core Group supported the UN's efforts to carry-out the popular consultation by exerting pressure on Indonesia, leading support for UNAMET in the Security Council, and providing substantial financial and logistical assistance.

International media coverage focused the world's attention on East Timor and maintained pressure on the Indonesian government. The substantial press corps in the territory was even more blunt in its assessment of the Indonesian military's complicity with, and support for, the militias than was UNAMET.[47] Its coverage gave support to those East Timor solidarity NGOs that in turn used the increased attention to the issue to induce their governments to pressure Indonesia into compliance. UNAMET provided the media with substantial access to, and information about, its work in keeping with the transparency with which the UN wishes to conduct its field missions. That transparency, and the ability that UNAMET provided to journalists to travel safely around the territory, which they were not able to do before the mission's deployment, meant that the militias and their supporters within the Indonesian military were subjected to a degree of scrutiny beyond that which they had previous experienced. The leverage by the UN (both the Secretariat and Security Council), interested Member States, and the media was frequently deployed throughout the popular-consultation period, but leverage was used with greater intensity at particular times or in response to specific incidents.

The popular-consultation modalities agreement called for the Secretary-General to determine whether security conditions existed to enable the commencement of the operational phase of the mission. This was to be done prior to the start of voter registration based on the advice of UNAMET. In his May 22 report, the Secretary-General described the situation in the territory as one in which militias were acting with impunity, creating a situation in which holding a peaceful free-and-fair popular consultation would be extremely difficult.[48] The Secretary-General reported on June 22 that the negative security situation had persisted and that he could not certify that the necessary conditions existed for the start of registration on that date as planned. At the recommendation of UNAMET, he proposed a delay, meaning that registration would commence on July 13. While he cited logistical difficulties along with security concerns for the delay, it was clear to members of the mission and the international media that if logistical problems had not existed, the security situation alone would have prevented the Secretary-General from allowing the registration to begin.[49] The delay drew wide attention to Indonesia's noncompliance with the May 5 Agreement. In the days before the Secretary-General's report, his Personal Representative, Marker, traveled to Jakarta to discuss the security situation with Indonesian officials, including President Habibie.[50]

In the aftermath of attacks on UNAMET personnel and East Timorese on June 29 and July 4, international focus on the situation in East Timor increased. After both incidents, a combination of intense media coverage, condemnation of the violence by interested states, and strong press statements from the Secretary-General and Ian Martin followed. Martin visited Jakarta after the second incident and met with Indonesian officials, including General Wiranto (the head of the Indonesian armed forces), urging them to end the military's support for the militias and create an environment of peace and security. In response to the outcry, President Habibie sent eight government ministers to Dili to investigate the situation.[51] During that visit, Foreign Minister Alatas met with Martin and his senior staff and assured them that the Indonesian government was investigating the incidents and taking steps to bring the violence to an end. The UN's history of the popular consultation said: "This combined pressure probably ensured such acts against UNAMET were not repeated until ballot day."[52] The report points out that the degree of restraint did not imply an overall improvement of the security situation. The campaign of violence and intimidation continued unabated throughout the territory.

The Secretary-General allowed registration of voters to begin on July 16, but noted in a letter to the president of the Security Council that the security conditions still did not exist to enable the process to be carried-out in a peaceful atmosphere.[53] While the registration surprisingly proceeded without serious security incidents, and the East Timorese bravely registered early in the process in large numbers, the period between registration and the ballot day saw numerous very serious security incidents. Within the mission, there was a perception that continued delay would play into the hands of those who did not want the ballot to occur. There did exist the possibility that if the process extended beyond the selection of a new Indonesian president, expected to occur in September, it might be indefinitely postponed in the new political environment. The mission leadership was impressed by the determination to vote exhibited by the East Timorese during the registration period, and took the calculated risk of moving forward with the vote despite the security situation.

Throughout the campaign period militias carried out attacks on the staff and offices of the pro-independence umbrella group, the Council of National Timorese Resistance—the CNRT. By the ballot day, many of the CNRT offices that since June had opened around East Timor with the help of UNAMET had been closed due to violence and threats of violence, and were in many cases destroyed by militias. At no time during the campaign period did the conditions exist to allow pro-independence groups to campaign freely, despite the signing of a code of conduct by the pro-Indonesian and pro-independence parties. In contrast to the days immediately preceding it, the ballot day itself was relatively peaceful and the East Timorese people voted in large numbers. However, it ended tragically when two UNAMET local staff members were murdered after the polls closed.[54]

Habibie's initiative and Indonesia's signing of the 5 May Agreement set in motion a process that would necessarily reach its logical conclusion unless Indonesia abrogated the agreement. Short of inducing Habibie to abrogate it or overthrowing him and then abrogating the agreement, there was little the Indonesian armed forces could do but try to disrupt the process. The military *did* disrupt the process, but never took steps to stop the balloting. That degree of restraint might have been because the May 5 Agreement placed Indonesia within a skein of transnational interaction that would have created substantial costs for the country in the event of complete noncompliance. Thus, as a second-best option, the preferred outcome, for certain members of the Indonesian military, would probably have been for an intimidated population to vote for autonomy. It appeared that aspects of the Indonesian government believed that, with enough intimidation, the East Timorese would just do that.

Despite contradictory internal political pressures, Habibie appeared to be acutely aware that he came to office in part because Suharto was not able to maintain control of the Indonesian polity in the aftermath of the Asian economic crisis that saw the Indonesian rupiah plunge in value and foreign investment,[55] on which the economy depended, dry up. Those events resulted in a dramatic fall off in the standard of living of ordinary Indonesians and led to the fall of Suharto. Habibie and his advisors had as one of their central concerns increasing foreign investment. Given that foreign investors scrutinize countries to determine, among other things, whether they comply with international agreements and international law, noncompliance, or at least the appearance of noncompliance, might not have been an option for policy-makers interested in attracting foreign money.[56]

Indonesia's integration with the international community made complete rejection of the May 5 Agreement difficult. By signing the 5 May Agreement, Indonesia created for itself obligations that mobilized a formidable set of interested transnational actors, including the international community as embodied by the Security Council and the Secretary-General, individual states such as Australia, the United States, and Japan, an already-motivated NGO community, and an international press corps. Once the agreement was signed, Indonesia no longer enjoyed the relative isolation of the prepopular-consultation period necessary to undermine the agreement without incurring the ire of that transnational community.

Period Three—Postballot Violence. Almost immediately after the simultaneous announcement by the Secretary-General in New York and SRSG Martin in Dili of the result of the popular consultation, violence exploded in East Timor. Close to 80 percent (78.5 percent) of the East Timorese voted against autonomy and in favor of independence. After the vote but prior to the announcement, a rising tide of violence across the territory appeared to have been focused on closing UNAMET offices and forcing the mission to remove its staff from the outlying districts. As a result, UNAMET was progressively rendered blind across the territory. UNAMET staff had, of course, a strong perception that a wave of violence was being unleashed on the people of East Timor, but they had no way to confirm that, much less try to stop it, as they became increasingly restricted to the Dili UN headquarters. The campaign of violence also succeeded in causing most journalists and international observers to leave East Timor, restricting the ability of the international community to see and report on what was being done to the East Timorese.[57]

On September 6 SRSG Martin evacuated nonessential personnel to reduce pressure on the mission's limited resources and to safeguard those staff not required by the mission. By September 7 it was not possible for UNAMET personnel to leave the compound without an Indonesian military escort. It was not unusual during this period for the sky to be filled with smoke from burning buildings. There was also frequent gunfire outside the walls of the compound. On September 7 a militia attack on internally displaced persons (IDPs) who had sheltered in a school next to the UNAMET headquarters forced the IDPs to scramble for safety over the fence and into the UN compound, swelling the population there by 1,500–2,000 persons. Parents threw their children over the high walls and people climbed over the razor wire, heedless of the danger, because of their fear of the militias. Some UNAMET staff cut themselves on the wire to protect the IDPs.[58]

After that painful experience, the UN determined it could not rely on the Indonesian military to protect UN personnel. Also, the Indonesian military commander was unsure about his own troops, and the resources of UNAMET could not support the large number of people in the compound. Therefore, on September 8, Martin recommended to UN Headquarters in New York that the mission evacuate from East Timor. It was agreed with the Australian military that would conduct the evacuation that local UN staff, who had been special targets of the militias, would be evacuated along with international staff. After a delay, the evacuation to Darwin, Australia, which had become a remote base of operation for the mission, took place on September 10. When it appeared that the IDPs could not be taken with the UNAMET staff, many fled the compound. Eighty UN personnel, including the SRSG, volunteered to remain with the IDPs. On September 14 the remainder of the mission, except for a skeleton staff, was evacuated along with the IDPs.

Throughout the siege of the compound Martin remained in contact with the Indonesian authorities, who were reduced quickly only to the military due to evacuations, urging them in the strongest terms to restore order in East Timor. On September 5 a delegation of Indonesian government ministers was sent to Dili by President Habibie. Martin and his senior staff met with TNI head General Wiranto and Foreign Minister Alatas. Wiranto, echoing his subordinates' statements, said that the situation would be brought under control in two or three days. Fearing the violence, the ministers did not leave the Dili airport except for Wiranto.[59]

During this period the Secretary-General sharply increased his pressure on the Indonesian authorities, especially President Habibie. As the crisis developed, the Secretary-General conducted multiple telephone conversations with Habibie each day, at first urging him to bring the situation under control and later seeking his consent to allow the deployment of an international force. On September 7, Habibie declared martial law in the territory and sent in new troops. The Secretary-General gave Habibie 48 to 72 hours for the situation to improve.[60] The situation did not improve as a result of Habibie's action.

At the same time as these other events were occurring, the Security Council had decided on September 6 to send a mission to Indonesia comprised of the Permanent Representatives of Malaysia, Slovenia, the United Kingdom, the Deputy Permanent Representative of the Netherlands, and led by the Permanent Representative of Namibia to directly express to the Indonesian government the UN's concerns regarding the situation in East Timor. The Deputy Personal Representative of the Secretary-General for East Timor, Francesc Vendrell, also participated in the mission. After a series of meetings in Jakarta, including ones with President Habibie and General Wiranto and jailed East Timorese leader Xanana Gusmão, the Security Council mission decided to go to Dili to view the situation firsthand. On September 11, when the Council mission set off for Dili, the Secretary-General's 72-hour time limit was about to expire without an improvement in the security environment. While in Dili on September 11 the mission experienced a dire security situation and received no convincing assurances that TNI was capable or willing to end the violence.[61]

The intense worldwide media coverage of the events in East Timor provided fuel for protests, and organized nongovernmental-organization activity around the world put pressure on key governments to act to end the violence. Events such as a militia attack on Nobel laureate Bishop Belo, the killing of people taking refuge in his residence, and his subsequent trip to the Vatican raised the profile of the crisis and led to widespread expressions of condemnation directed at Indonesia. This focus led governments such as Portugal and Australia to exert pressure on other governments to act.[62]

This form of state-to-state peer pressure was aided by the coincidental convening of the Asia-Pacific Economic Cooperation forum in Auckland, New Zealand from September 9 to 13, 1999, at the height of international attention to the crisis. Both President Habibie and Foreign Minister Alatas canceled their participation in the APEC meeting. Foreign ministers, who were to meet from September 9 to 12, convened in a separate special informal meeting on September 9 to discuss East Timor. At that meeting, attended by almost all APEC members including Asian members and officials of such non-APEC countries as U.K. Foreign Minister Cook who was especially sent to Auckland for this purpose, the group reached a consensus, calling on Indonesia to end the violence and expressing support for international intervention. This action increased Indonesia's isolation. The country was to become much more isolated in the coming days.

The United States, which had been a staunch supporter of the Suharto regime and that had a close military relationship with Indonesia arising from the cold war, began to increase its pressure on Indonesia. Senior U.S. civilian and military officials at the highest levels called their Indonesian counterparts urging an end to the violence. Significantly, in light of the nature of the relationship between the two countries, the commander-in-chief of the U.S. Pacific Command visited Jakarta on September 9 to meet with Indonesian Defense Minister Wiranto (also head of the military) to directly urge an end to the violence. Also on September 9, President Clinton severed military-assistance links to Indonesia and called for sanctions through international financial institutions. By September 11, the United States had suspended arms sales to Indonesia.[63]

In an unprecedented step for organizations that had previously eschewed even the appearance of delving into politics, the World Bank and the International Monetary Fund (IMF) added to the pressure. At a July 1999 donors meeting for Indonesia, pledges to the country were made with explicit mention of Indonesian responsibility for security for the popular consultation, and Indonesia had assured donors of its support for the process. In September, World Bank President James Wolfensohn cited the July meeting in issuing a statement that the situation in East Timor was "of paramount concern to our shareholders."[64] The IMF issued similar statements. Wolfensohn also wrote to Habibie that the July pledges had been made with the understanding that Indonesia would provide security in the territory and urged Indonesia to take action to end the violence.[65]

As the situation in East Timor worsened, certain Member States and the Secretary-General began to explore the possibility of international military intervention. Australia expressed a readiness to lead a coalition of the willing if the Indonesian government consented to the insertion of foreign troops into East Timor. The frequent contacts between the Secretary-General and Member States and Habibie focused more and more on the issue. On September 10 the Secretary-General stated that if Indonesia did not accept offers from Australia, Malaysia, New Zealand, and the Philippines to send troops for an international force, "it cannot escape responsibility for what could amount, according to reports reaching us, to crimes against humanity."[66]

On September 11 the Security Council met in New York in public session on East Timor in which the Secretary-General led strong statements of support for military intervention. The Security Council delegation had a last meeting with Habibie on the evening of September 12. Soon after that meeting President Habibie publicly announced Indonesia's agreement to allow the deployment of an international force.[67] On September 15 the Security Council passed Resolution 1264 under Chapter VII of the UN Charter, authorizing the deployment of an international force to East Timor that was empowered to use force to restore peace and security.[68]

The UN's leverage was at its strongest when a substantial amount of the international community's attention was focused on Indonesia during the violence that followed the announcement of the results of the ballot. At that point, international interest was at its height, in part because Indonesia had egregiously breached an international agreement it had signed with some fanfare and publicity, but largely because its breach showed signs of consisting of massive human-rights abuses, including massacres and possibly genocide. The presence of members of the UN mission trapped in the UNAMET compound during the destruction of East Timor increased the international focus and the drama of the crisis. Reports from journalists also in the compound during the period were featured in news outlets around the world. As a result of perceived international inaction in Bosnia and Rwanda in the face of massive human-rights abuses, a substantial amount of attention was directed toward Indonesia's behavior. Examples of this interest include the Security Council's first field trip in its history to a conflict area. Attention was also concentrated on the issue due to the previously scheduled annual APEC summit that was meeting during this period in Auckland, New Zealand. The Secretary-General was able to make use of this increased leverage through daily, multiple telephone calls to Habibie during the crisis in an attempt to find a way out.

DID INDONESIA COMPLY?

Compliance is generally not a black or white issue, a yes or no question. According to Bilder, "foreign office officials typically will approach a dispute about international norms not as an isolated transaction, but rather as an incident in the state's continuing relationship with the other state, states, or other international actors concerned."[69] This could be how other international actors with a variety of interests with Indonesia viewed putting pressure on the country, especially in the years after the invasion. Regarding Indonesia's perception of compliance, a lax approach might have had as its core the fulfilling expectations of behavior, which might not match full compliance.[70]

It is necessary to look at the substance of cooperation and compliance. During the first period, Habibie complied by finally allowing an act of self-determination, but it quickly became clear that the military, or at least part of the military, intended to undermine Habibie's decision. The pace of the formation of militias increased, and violence and intimidation rose to levels not seen in East Timor since the Santa Cruz massacre in 1991. In the second period, while the ballot day itself was quiet and largely peaceful and the count occurred unimpeded, the Indonesian military on the ground in East Timor never lessened its violent campaign of intimidation. The authorities never complied with requests to rein-in the militias and control those elements of the military supporting the militias. In the third period, the Indonesian authorities allowed the deployment of the international force, but only after a furious campaign of destruction. It soon became clear, however, that the base of operations of the militias had moved to West Timor where tens of thousands of East Timorese refugees still live under the control of the militias with ongoing deadly consequences, an example of which we saw in early September 2000 with the murder of three UN staff.

In reviewing Indonesian government behavior during the three time periods described above, it appears that President Habibie was best able to comply when he did not need to rely on cooperation from other parts of his government. On the one hand, both the January 27 announcement and, to a lesser extent, the decision to allow the deployment of an international force in the aftermath of the postballot violence were ones that could not have been immediately and openly defied by TNI with any action short of an open, explicit confrontation that would have had the potential of leading to chaotic consequences. On the other hand, during the popular-consultation period, the military could profess support of the president while actively undermining the holding of a free-and-fair ballot.

In the case of East Timor, the state-to-state interaction contemplated by the various theories is supplemented with appearances on the world stage by the UN, other international bodies such as the World Bank and the International Monetary Fund, nongovernmental organizations, and the media as players in the drama. Furthermore, the pressure flowed not only towards Indonesia but also to other states. For example, Australia's decision to change its policy of recognizing Indonesian rule over East Timor and urging the government of Indonesia to allow the people of the territory to engage in an act of self-determination was likely influenced, at least in part, by Australia's highly mobilized East Timor nongovernmental advocacy community. During the postballot period states were confronted with a crisis that called for a response, and the UN, in this case the Secretary-General and Security Council, were faced with a looming humanitarian and human-rights catastrophe in a situation under a UN mandate that required action.

CONCLUSION

The theories regarding international interaction and state compliance by international-law and international-relations scholars, while providing some explanatory power, do not individually fully explain the complicated environment in which the UN worked on the issue of East Timor. The effective coordination of the interlocking actors in the international system described in the introduction was essential to strengthen UN leverage. When that system was not focused on the issue of East Timor, the UN Secretariat was able only to keep the issue alive during the weak leverage period of the late 1970s until the late 1990s. When the various parts of the international system were applying direct and indirect pressure on Indonesia during the postpopular-consultation violence, the UN, as the focal point of action, was able to apply greater pressure leading to Indonesia's agreeing to the deployment of an international force. While the other actors in the system played crucial roles, the presence of the UN—the Secretary-General, Security Council, and Secretariat—as the focal point of activity was central to the application of leverage.

Obviously, further work on the effectiveness of how the UN induces compliance with international norms is necessary. The multilevel, multifaceted experiences of the United Nations on the question of East Timor provide a rich array of examples of the Organization's use of leverage. Those and other experiences should be further explored to increase our understanding of how the UN can apply leverage and how that leverage works under a range of different conditions to achieve success.

NOTES

1. I use the term "international community" to describe the framework of international, transnational, national, and individual actors, official and unofficial, that worked to influence Indonesia's behavior in this case.

2. Regimes are defined as: "Governing arrangements constructed by states to coordinate their expectations and organize aspects of international behavior in various issue areas. [Regimes] thus comprise a normative element, state practice, and organizational roles." Frederick Kratochwil and John Gerard Ruggie, "International Organization: A State of the Art on an Art of the State," *International Organization 40* (1986): 753, 759.

3. This is similar to the typology developed by Jean Krasno in her chapter on Namibian in this book.

4. Louis Henkin, *How Nations Behave: Law and Foreign Policy*, 2nd ed. (New York: Columbia University Press, 1979), 47 (emphasis omitted).

5. As defined by Koh, *compliance* occurs when one acts in keeping with a rule because there would be a sanction for breaking the rule; *obedience*, when the internalization of a rule creates greater legitimization that leads to actions in keeping with the rule because one believes that the rule is just. Harold Hongju Koh, "The Frankel Lecture: Bringing International Law Home," *Houston Law Review 35* (1998): 623, 628.

6. The Indonesian Government insisted in negotiations with the United Nations and Portugal that the vote not be referred to as a "referendum" but as a "popular consultation." Official documents use the term *popular consultation*. This chapter will use *popular consultation*, *referendum*, and *ballot* interchangeably.

7. For a broader description of the realist school of thought, see, for example, John J. Mearsheimer, "The False Promise of International Institutions," *International Security 19*(3) (winter 1994–95): 5–49; Kenneth W. Abbott, "Modern International Relations Theory: A Prospectus for International Lawyers," *Yale Journal of International Law 14*(1989): 335; and Duncan Snidal, "Coordination versus Prisoners' Dilemma: Implications for International Cooperation and Regimes," *American Political Science Review 79*(1985): 923.

8. For more information on institutionalism, see, for example, Robert O. Keohane, *After Hegemony* (Princeton, NJ: Princeton University Press, 1984); Oran R. Young, *International Cooperation: Building Regimes for Natural Resources and the Environment* (Ithaca, NY: Cornell University Press, 1989); and Robert O. Keohane, "Institutional Theory and the Realist Challenge after the Cold War," in *Neorealism and Neoliberalism: The Contemporary Debate*, ed. David A. Baldwin (New York: Columbia University Press, 1993).

9. For a broader explication of the liberal theory, see, for example, Anne-Marie Burley, "Law among Liberal States: Liberal Internationalism and the Act of State Doctrine," *Columbia Law Review 92*(1992): 1907; and Andrew Moravcsik, "Liberalism and International Relations Theory," Center for International Affairs, Harvard University, Working Paper No. 92-6, 1992.

10. Key constructivist articles include: Peter J. Katzenstein, ed., *The Culture of National Security: Norms and Identity in World Politics* (New York: Columbia University Press, 1996); and John G. Ruggie, "Multilateralism: The Anatomy of an Institution," *International Organization 46*(3) (summer 1992).

11. "The principal mechanism by which such ideas are developed and disseminated is by epistemic communities: transnational networks of policy professionals who share common values and causal understandings. Members of epistemic communities will seek to introduce national measures consistent with their beliefs, and utilize the enforcement mechanisms of the bureaucratic units in which they operate." Peter M. Haas, "Choosing to Comply: Theorizing from International Relations and Comparative Politics," in *Commitment and Compliance: The Role of Non-Binding Norms in the International Legal System*, ed. Dinah Shelton (p. 63) (Oxford: Oxford University Press, 2000).

12. All four theories treat states as unitary actors on the international stage. Some realist scholars see state interaction as being akin to billiard balls of varying sizes on a billiard table. The balls are self-contained and bump against each other and it is immaterial what is inside the balls when one studies the international sys-

tem. See Mearsheimer, 48. A more nuanced view sees a role for domestic factors in analyzing state behavior: "The degree of political will necessary to comply varies according to the anticipated degree of domestic resistance, due in part to the identity, number and influence of those actors who will have to change their behavior." See Haas, 47. "None of these perspectives are deterministic: rather, they are contingent on the interplay between domestic and foreign politics, between comparative politics and international relations," Haas, 51.

13. Koh uses the term "transnational" to incorporate state, nonstate, domestic, and international actors that influence and participate in the development of international law. He defines transnational legal process as "the theory and practice of how public and private actors including nation-states, international organizations, multinational enterprises, nongovernmental organizations, and private individuals, interact in a variety of fora to make, interpret, internalize, and enforce rules of transnational law." Harold Hongju Koh, "Why Do Nations Obey International Law?" *Yale Law Journal 106*(1997): 2626–27.

14. Ibid., 2655.

15. Ibid., 2651.

16. Ibid., 2651–54.

17. *The United Nations and East Timor: Self Determination Through Popular Consultation* (New York: Department of Public Information, United Nations, 2000), 3.

18. Ibid.

19 Ibid., 62.

20. UN Security Council Resolution 384 (1975).

21. *The United Nations and East Timor,* 4.

22. Daniel Patrick Moynihan, *A Dangerous Place* (Boston: Little, Brown, 1978).

23. See, for example, Susan Sim, "East Timor Shift: The Inside Story," *Straits Times* (February 5, 1999).

24. See "Confusion over Indonesia's True Intentions Towards East Timor," *Agence-France Presse* (February 5, 1999). "The announcement took everyone by surprise, including the government's own foreign ministry." See also Hamish McDonald, "Impulsive, Habibie Ignored ABRI in Making Jan. Timor Decision," *Sydney Morning Herald* (April 20, 1999).

25. *The United Nations and East Timor*, 5.

26. Ibid., 6.

27. Australian *de jure* recognition came as the two countries negotiated over oil and natural-gas rights in the Timor Gap between Timor and Australia. See, for example, Gino Naldi, "The East Timor Case and the Role of the International Court of Justice in the Evolution of the Right of Peoples to Self-Determination," *Australian Journal of Human Rights*, regarding Portugal's action against Australia in the ICJ objecting to the Timor Gap Treaty between Australia and Indonesia as a breach of the East Timorese people's right to self-determination.

28. For an interesting discussion of why Habibie proposed the popular consultation, see Ian Martin, *Self-Determination in East Timor: The United Nations, the Ballot, and International Intervention* (Boulder, CO: Lynne Rienner Publishers, 2001), 22–23.

29. See "Alatas Looks Back on 11 Years of Indonesia's Foreign Policy," *Jakarta Post* (November 2, 1999).

30. See Jose Manuel Tesoro, "Insider-Outsider," *AsiaWeek* (December 31, 1999).

But the East Timor issue seemed not to have seriously damaged Indonesia in the Asia region, given their election of Indonesia to the Security Council in 1995–97.

31. Martin, 22.

32. See George J. Aditjondro, "ABRI, Inc.," *Sydney Morning Herald* (May 8, 1999).

33. "The Question of East Timor," Report of the Secretary-General, Annex I, S/1999/513 (5 May 1999).

34. The author participated in these negotiations. Martin asserts that "[i]t is doubtful whether any amount of pressure could have induced Habibie and Wiranto [head of the Indonesian armed forces] to accept international peacekeepers at this juncture," 33.

35. "The Question of East Timor," Annex I.

36. Ibid., Annex II.

37. Ibid., Annex III.

38. See "The Question of East Timor," Report of the Secretary-General, S/1999/595 (22 May 1999), paragraph 23. See, for example, McDonald.

39. Memorandum of the Secretary-General to Indonesia and Portugal, 4 May 1999. The UN negotiators initially attempted to deliver the memorandum to the Indonesians in the form of a letter from the Secretary-General, which the Indonesians refused to accept. It was then drafted as a memorandum and given to both parties. For a fuller discussion of the negotiation process, see Martin, *Self-Determination in East Timor*, chapter 1.

40. For a fuller discussion of the obstacles faced by UNAMET to hold the popular consultation, see Martin.

41. See, for example, "A Campaign to Liquidate the Resistance in East Timor," *Agence-France Presse* (April 19, 1999).

42. See, for example, Don Greenlees, "Soldiers Watched Timor Massacre—Australian Embassy Report," *The Australian* (April 17, 1999).

43. See, for example, "A Campaign to Liquidate the Resistance in East Timor," *Agence-France Presse.*

44. *The United Nations and East Timor*, 25. See, generally, Martin.

45. UN Security Council Resolution document number: S/Res/1246 (1999), 11 June 1999.

46. Ibid.

47. See, for example, Richard Lloyd Parry, "East Timor Counts Down to Ultimate Nightmare," *The Independent* (UK) (August 1, 1999); and Mark Riley, "How the UN Plans to Abandon a People," *Sydney Morning Herald* (August 7, 1999).

48. "The Question of East Timor," Report of the Secretary-General, S/1999/595 (22 May 1999).

49. "The Question of East Timor," Report of the Secretary General, S/1999/705 (22 June 1999).

50. *The United Nations and East Timor*, 27.

51. Ibid.

52. Ibid., 31.

53. Letter dated 14 July 1999 from the Secretary-General addressed to the President of the Security Council, S/1999/788.

54. *The United Nations and East Timor*, 37-38.

55. See, for example, Tim Healy and Jose Manuel Tesoro, "Judging Habibie," *AsiaWeek* (September 4, 1998).

56. See, for example, Tesoro, "Insider-Outsider."

57. Martin, 97–101.

58. Ibid.

59. The author attended these meetings.

60. *The United Nations and East Timor*, 49.

61. Ibid., 48–52.

62. Martin, 106.

63. Ibid., 109.

64. World Bank Statement on East Timor, Washington, D.C., September 7, 1999.

65. Martin, 107–8.

66. Secretary-General Kofi Annan, Statement on East Timor, New York, September 7, 1999.

67. UN Security Council Resolution, document number S/Res/1264 (1999), 15 September 1999.

68. Ibid., 50–53.

69. Richard B. Bilder, "Beyond Compliance: Helping Nations Cooperate," in *Commitment and Compliance*, 66.

70. Ibid., 69. According to Bilder, "officials may be willing to meet or comply with what they see as their actual commitment, but may see that commitment as only one of meeting the fair and reasonable expectation they and others had regarding how they would behave in reference to the norm." If this is the case—if officials tend to regard failure to observe the norm under such circumstances as not really breach or noncompliance at all, but rather as something tacitly understood by all the participants as part of their joint expectational framework itself—then our attempts to analyze their behavior in terms of formal notions of compliance may be unsatisfactory indeed.

Meeting at Governors Island, New York. From left: Dante Caputo, Special Representative of the Secretary-General; delegate from the French Mission to the UN; Jean-Bertrand Aristide, president of Haiti; David Malone, Deputy Permanent Representative of Canada to the UN; Diego Arria, Permanent Representative of Venezuela to the UN; and Edward Walker, U.S. ambassador at the U.S. Mission to the UN.

The Friends, September 1992. From left: Juan Antonio Yañez, Permanent Representative of Spain to the UN; Jorge Montaño, Permanent Representative of Mexico to the UN; Carlos Andrés Perez, president of Venezuela; Fernando Cepeda Ulloa, Permanent Representative of Colombia to the UN; and Diego Arria, Permanent Representative of Venezuela to the UN.

Alfredo Cristiani (left), president of El Salvador, and Ambassador Diego Arria, Venezuelan ambassador to the UN.

Midnight signature of the El Salvador Peace Accord, December 31, 1991. At the table from left: General Mauricio Vargas (El Salvador); Oscar Santa-María (El Salvador); Dr. Eduardo Torres (El Salvador); Alvaro de Soto (Special Representative of the UN Secretary-General); UN Secretary-General Javier Pérez de Cuéllar; Pedro Nikken (UN Secretariat); Eduardo Sancho (FMLN); and Francisco Jovel (FMLN). Standing from left: a Salvadoran UN Mission staff member; Armando Calderon Sol (mayor of San Salvador and later president of El Salvador); UN Ambassador Juan Luis Yañez (Spain); UN Ambassador Jorge Montaño (Mexico); UN Ambassador Diego Arria (Venezuela); UN Ambassador Fernando Cepeda Ulloa (Colombia); and three members of the FMLN.

From left: James Jonah, Under-Secretary-General for Political Affairs; Dirk Salomons, then executive director of the United Nations Mission in Mozambique (ONUMOZ); and Renamo guests on the way to a negotiating session in the rebels' Gorongosa National Park hideout, January 1993.

The United Nations negotiating team being picked up at the Gorongosa airstrip, in the heart of rebel territory, January 1993. Renamo used motorcycles to move quickly through a heavily mined maze of narrow paths through the bush, where no enemy could follow.

From left: Aldo Ajello, the Special Representative of the UN Secretary-General; James Jonah, Under-Secretary-General for Political Affairs; Afonso Dhlakama, president of Renamo; and Renamo negotiators in the rebels' hideout in the Gorongosa National Park, January 1993.

Vukovar, Eastern Slavonia, Croatia, 1996, five years after its destruction in October/ November 1991.

Vukovar, February 1996, destroyed in the Serb/Croat fighting during September through November 1991. Before the war, Vukovar had a population of over 60,000. Five years later, with almost no rebuilding, the population was still below 15,000.

Jacques Paul Klein, Transitional Administrator, and Derek Boothby, Deputy Transitional Administrator, at a donors' meeting in Zagreb, March 1997.

Over the shoulder: Derek Boothby encouraging Serbs to accept Croatian citizenship at a town meeting, January 1997.

Jacques Paul Klein, Derek Boothby, and Major-General Willy Hanset, UNTAES Force Commander, briefing visiting ambassadors at UNTAES headquarters, February 1997.

PART TWO

Crosscutting Analyses

CHAPTER SEVEN

The Group of Friends of the Secretary-General

a useful leveraging tool

JEAN KRASNO

DEFINING THE CONCEPT

What Is the "Group of Friends of the Secretary-General"?

In a 1996 article in *Foreign Affairs*,[1] Secretary-General Boutros Boutros-Ghali referred to the use of the "Group of Friends of the Secretary-General" as one of the tools available to him in carrying out his functions at the United Nations. Very little other information has been available to the public on this phenomenon and very little is recorded in United Nations documents. Yet the use of the Group of Friends concept has been growing. In preparing the research for this chapter, it was necessary to interview people within the United Nations system in order to gather the needed information.[2]

The Groups of Friends are made up of a small number of Member States, usually three-to-six members, which keep in close contact with the Secretary-General and support his efforts to find a peaceful solution to a specific crisis. Keeping the groups small is essential so that meetings can be called quickly and easily and that a consensus can be maintained. A Group of Friends is formed around a specific issue, usually a country in crisis, for example, the Group of Friends of the Secretary-General on Haiti. The countries that form the Friends give the Secretary-General the leverage he needs to bring the parties to a conflict to the negotiating table and keep them engaged throughout the process. The formation and meeting structure is ad hoc and informal. Each Group has come together under different circumstances and for different reasons, at times being called together directly by the Secretary-General and at other times through a self-selection process. Therefore each Group needs to be examined on a case-by-case basis. Nevertheless, there does seem to be a pattern to the phenomenon. In most instances there is at least one member of the Security Council in the Group and, in fact, they may all be current serving members of the Council, forming a combination of permanent and nonpermanent members. This may vary though and members not on the Council may also be an important part of the Group. Interestingly, as was pointed out by a member of the Secretariat, the Friends of the Secretary-General were originally conceived of as a counterbalance to manipulation of the Secretary-General by the permanent members of the Security Council. This is explained further below.

The initial formation of any Group appears to be dependent on the issue and which countries are already engaged in the crisis. Initially, it was the Secretary-General who formed the Groups and selected the memberships, for example, the Groups on El Salvador and Haiti. Later, Groups were formed by states who then approached the Secretary-General—a kind of self-selection process. However, once a Group of Friends is formed, it tends to remain very stable. The purpose of this chapter is to explore how the Groups of Friends are formed, how they operate, and how they are used to keep a peace process on track and prevent a breakdown and return to hostilities.

The Creation of the First Group of Friends

In December 1989, Secretary-General Javier Pérez de Cuéllar began the process to establish the "Group of Friends on El Salvador," the first such group, as a way of support for the Secretary-General's role in using his "good offices." The concept was specifically conceived by Alvaro de Soto with the help of Francesc Vendrell and supported by the Secretary-General. It was understood to be a tool specifically at the service of the Secretary-General in his efforts on the issue at hand. Thus it was intended from the outset that any action of these groups would be conducted only at the request of or under the auspices of the Secretary-General.

The idea to form a group of like-minded states supportive of the Secretary-General's effort was created to work out a negotiated political solution to the conflict in El Salvador through the support of governments who were not allied to either party to the conflict or had a stake in its outcome. The term "Group of Friends of the Secretary-General" evolved later. De Soto and Vendrell, both in the United Nations Secretariat at the time during the tenure of Secretary-General Pérez de Cuéllar, worked together to develop the idea over the first several months. At that time the UN, while it had been involved in Central America, particularly in Nicaragua, was not yet involved in El Salvador.

In the summer of 1989, the UN had been invited as an observer to meetings between the parties in which the Salvadoran Catholic Church was operating as an intermediary. But by the fall of 1989 talks between the two sides had broken down. In November, the rebel forces, the Frente Farabundo Martí para la Liberación Nacional (FMLN), had launched the largest attack of their nearly ten-year campaign, taking much of the capital, San Salvador. In reaction, the military attacked and killed several Catholic priests, an event that evoked the outrage of the international media as well as the U.S. Congress, which threatened to withhold support for the government. The Church could no longer serve as an intermediary and the UN was still not invited to take its place.

What followed was a series of contacts by both sides to explore a greater role for the UN. Salvadoran President Alfredo Cristiani, elected to office in the spring of 1989, contacted the Secretary-General to ask for his assistance. At about the same time, the FMLN through Rubén Zamora contacted de Soto. Because the FMLN were unable to get U.S. visas during that era, it was decided to arrange a secret meeting in Canada between the leaders of the FMLN and de Soto on December 6. The timing was important because there was a meeting of the Central American presidents planned for December 8 at which they hoped to have the presidents announce the new role of the United Nations in the region. The result of contacts with the two sides, which was formalized at the Central American meeting two days later, was that the UN would take-up the role as intermediary, utilizing the "good offices" of the Secretary-General to get the talks going.

The Secretary-General and de Soto knew that they would need the leverage that could only be provided by countries willing to take on the issue. They were searching for a way to create a group of countries that would act as a kind of support for the Secretary-General. Ambassador Diego Arria, Permanent Representative of Venezuela to the United Nations during this period, gives the inside story from the point of view of the Friends in his chapter in this volume.[3] It was vital for the success of the negotiations between the parties to ensure that the impartiality of the Secretary-General was not compromised, and to counterbalance attempts at manipulation of the Secretary-General's efforts by one or another member of the Security Council acting as an ally for only one of the parties to the conflict—for example, the U.S. support for the Salvadoran government. Loss of impartiality would lead to the defection of one or both of the parties from the negotiations.

The Secretary-General felt that what was needed was a group that would offset the political weight of the Security Council. The United States at that time was still an ally of the Salvadoran government and took sides with the government rather than maintaining impartiality. The Security Council might have played too dominant a role in pressuring the Secretary-General to favor the government and thereby risk his impartial status. While U.S. support of the Salvadoran government was essentially bilateral, U.S. views were well-known and compromised the impartiality of the Security Council. The United States did apparently complain that some members of the Secretariat (de Soto) were pro-FMLN and the Secretary-General had to discuss this with the U.S. president at the time.[4] In fact, if the Secretary-General needed protection from pressure, it was more directly from the United States rather than from the entire Security Council.

It was considered by de Soto at the time that the Secretary-General might borrow a device that is frequently used in intergovernmental bodies, which is the notion of "friends of the chairman" or "friends of the president." Frequently, when there is a standoff on an issue and it is clear that a small negotiating forum is needed in order to achieve results, the chairman might simply gather a group of friends. There is no commitment placed on any participant. However, the chairman will choose the members carefully so that he will have inside the room all those whom he feels need to be a party to any deal that might be struck. The chairman retains a certain deniability to the extent that he can always say that he was just meeting with a "group of friends." One can imagine many occasions whereby agreements that could not have been achieved in a formally constituted group or in a large gathering such as the 191 members of the General Assembly can emerge from such a format.

On El Salvador, Secretary-General Pérez de Cuéllar, with his staff, formed a three-level diplomatic strategy: (1) one level was the parties to the conflict, the government and the FMLN; (2) the second was a group of very interested states, namely, the United States, the Soviet Union, and Cuba; and (3) third were countries not directly interested but who wanted to support peace in the region and who could strengthen the position of the Secretary-General, the "Group of Friends." The Nordic countries were also consulted but played a less direct role. The original members of the Group of Friends were Colombia, Mexico, Venezuela, and Spain. The first three countries were also the original members of the Contadora group along with Panama. Panama was not included because it was decided by the Secretary-General not to include any Central American countries in the Friends. If one Central American nation were included, then it would be hard to exclude others; and the others were too directly involved in the conflict to be impartial. Also, in December 1989, the United States had invaded Panama to remove President Noriega and the country was still in crisis over that event.

When the Central American presidents met on December 8, 1989 at the summit meeting in Costa Rica, they requested that the Secretary-General help them obtain the cooperation of countries outside Central America whose assistance in the process was necessary to make it work. Simultaneously, the Secretary-General was requested by the parties to offer his "good offices" in mediating the conflict. With these requests in hand, the UN had the authority it needed to move ahead.

The Group of Friends were already committed to finding a peaceful solution to the conflict, and all four had openly expressed a commitment to removing the conflict from the entanglements of the East–West rivalry. The United States had viewed the rebels as a threat in the spread of communism and Soviet influence within the Western Hemisphere. And, in truth, the rebels had been receiving Cuban and Soviet support. But the friends believed that the conflict grew out of poverty rather than ideological differences and wanted to prevent the war from becoming a large-scale regional war with more weapons pouring in from both major superpowers.

Each of the countries played an important role both in maintaining the consensus of the group and in offering something unique to the process. Mexico was important because the FMLN had had a kind of asylum in Mexico and therefore it was a place that they could meet with relative confidence. Colombia had been faced with internal conflict itself and was concerned to see that a peaceful solution would be achieved. Colombia, who was serving on the Security Council during this time period, had been instrumental in ensuring that the Secretary-General was given the mandate by the Security Council to use his "good offices." As Arria has described, Venezuela's president was particularly active. He would contact the guerrilla leaders, summon them to Caracas, and talk directly to them. He would also call-up the president of El Salvador and talk with him. There was some concern at times by the Secretary-General that the Venezuelan president might take over the process through his highly active role. But the Secretary-General and his staff kept in close touch with the Venezuelan president to brief him, consult, and prepare talking points. Spain was also a key player due to President Felipe González's influential activism in the region.

Mexico and Venezuela claim that their support was considered unconditional. Both countries had such close ties with El Salvador that they seemed to have a kind of tacit authority, perhaps even a moral authority. For example, both Mexico and Venezuela, which are oil-producing countries, had long-standing agreements with all the Central American and Caribbean countries regarding the sale of oil, beginning in the mid-1970s, called the San José Program. Venezuela would sell oil to El Salvador, for example, at current market prices, but then the Venezuelan Investment Fund, a publicly owned facility, would open a credit account with El Salvador equivalent to 30 percent of its oil bill. These funds could then be used for development projects. The plan lasts for fourteen years, with a seven-year grace period and seven more years to pay it off at very low interest rates. Mexico has a similar program, also called the San José Program. But both countries never used these programs as negotiating tools during the brokerage that they performed as Friends or at any other time during the peace process.[5]

What Is the Function and Purpose of a "Group of Friends of the Secretary-General"?

In a speech given by Secretary-General Boutros-Ghali in New Zealand in May 1995, he explained:

> The increasing complexity of operations has led, on the political side, to the intensification of peacemaking efforts. Thus, a new concept, that of "Friends of the Secretary-General," "International Conferences," or "Contact Groups" means that, while the United Nations peacekeepers are on the ground, intense diplomatic efforts continue, with the many parties to a conflict, in order to reach a political settlement. The increase in cooperation with States on such a basis serves three purposes: first, it serves to impress upon the parties to a conflict that the international community is directly concerned with a solution to the conflict. Second, it provides a mechanism for conflict resolution which complements the efforts of the Secretary-General. Third, it provides one more channel for multilateral action by Members States. It serves to reinforce the principle that all are concerned in the work of the United Nations.[6]

As the Secretary-General explained, the Group of Friends is an important tool to ensure that the parties to a dispute are kept well aware that the international community, through the consensus of key Member States, is focused on the issue. The idea, according to members of the UN Secretariat who have worked with the Secretary-General in support of various friends groups, is to use more than one country to exert pressure and present a common view that represents the international community as a whole. On his own, the Secretary-General, as the head administrator of the UN, cannot pressure state parties to act. His abilities are extremely limited without the backing of key Member States to exert pressure. He needs the Member States to take that initiative for the Organization. The Group of Friends offers the Secretary-General some "comfort space" in which to take action with the backing of key members. The main purpose of the Group is to keep a specific peace process on track and to try to harness rival would-be mediators to work in the same direction rather than at cross-purposes. It can prove to be extremely difficult to find a solution to a conflict if a number of actors are trying to carry on separate mediation efforts simultaneously with the parties involved. A Group of Friends can coordinate those efforts into one ongoing process.

Members of the Group might contact or meet with one or all of the parties and apply pressure or probe for keys to a solution, always keeping in close touch with the office of the Secretary-General. It might be described as "mediation within a mediation process." Some members of the Group may be more active than others; for example, in the Salvadoran peace process, the very active role played by President Carlos Andrés Pérez of Venezuela.

The Group can be used during the negotiation process prior to reaching a formal agreement or it might be used to aid in the implementation of an agreement after the parties have found some common ground but are dragging their heals. The advantage that a Member State provides is that of leverage. Representatives of the country that is one of the Friends can contact one of the parties to the conflict and offer incentives or clarify potential repercussions in order to push the process forward. A Friend can also invite one or more of the parties to its capital for a round of serious talks to probe for solutions. In the Salvadoran case, both Mexico and Venezuela as Friends invited the parties to their countries to meet and carry-on negotiations. In this sense, a head of government can facilitate negotiations by supplying a venue for dialogue and can deliver or withhold rewards in a way that the Secretary-General cannot.

The language in an agreement is often very general in nature and needs further clarification when it comes time to implement its provisions. An agreement also needs to be translated into practice in a way that is faithful to the spirit of the agreement and acceptable to the parties. This requires a continued process of negotiation among the parties with the help of the Secretary-General and the Friends who keep in contact with the parties to ensure that implementation is staying on course. Pressure from the Group of Friends can be essential here for keeping the peace process from breaking down. For example, the agreement on El Salvador called for the parties' military forces to withdraw to confined areas. The government forces were to return to their garrisons and the FMLN to camps. However, the agreement did not contain a map specifying the location of the camps. Some of the camps ended up in areas where there was not enough available drinking water or in areas that were subject to flooding. UN agencies had to coordinate efforts to alleviate these problems and were aided by donor support through the Friends and others—for example, Norway. Failure to establish adequate camps for the FMLN already had slowed the process and could have derailed it altogether.

There is often a key leader within the Group, one who can apply leverage and pressure and encourage an intransigent party to see the "wisdom" of complying with the terms of the agreement. A certain amount of carrot-and-stick diplomacy can be carried out by a Member State, which the Secretary-General would be unable to undertake himself. In the case of El Salvador, the Mexican government through its Permanent Representative to the UN, Ambassador Jorge Montaño, and President Pérez and Venezuela's Ambassador to the UN Arria were personally engaged in the process. They would contact the Salvadoran government or invite the rebel leaders for discussions. President Pérez personally invited the parties to Caracas to pressure them to move forward.

The Friends were also important in El Salvador during the implementation stage in various ways, which included pressing the government to comply with the military-reform provisions and pressing the FMLN to demobilize its guerrilla fighters as agreed upon in the final settlement. For example, the United States, who became a Friend in what was referred to as the "Four Plus One," provided funds for judicial reform and training for the new national police. In addition, the United States came to the aid of the demobilization process when it began to break down. In the agreement, it was stated that a land-distribution plan had to be implemented. The FMLN forces were threatening not to turn in their weapons until this plan was underway.[7] To support this part of the agreement, the United States provided money to the loaning institutions in El Salvador in order, in turn, to provide loans to those eligible to purchase small plots of land. Spain provided a large police contingent along with financial and technical support for the new national police. Mexico, Venezuela, and Colombia also provided police contingents.[8]

However, it is extremely important, if the mediation is to work, that the group and all its members are perceived by the parties to be impartial and that their actions are not viewed as taking one side or the other. If a Friend is seen to be taking sides, then the process is likely to break down; without impartiality, the parties would lose confidence that the negotiations would serve them fairly. They may decide that they can do better by returning to fighting to achieve their goals. It can be a delicate balancing act; outsiders may view the Group of Friends as having a stake in the outcome. However, the key here is the perceptions of the parties and the careful orchestration that is done behind the scenes by the Secretary-General and his staff to ensure that impartiality is maintained during any interaction with either side.

In addition to keeping the process on track and presenting a common policy on the issue, the Group takes on a number of other functions. It meets and prepares language for resolutions that are being considered by the Security Council or in the General Assembly. In some cases the Secretary-General, after having been in close contact with the group, prepares a draft of the language for its response. Then the Friends become a vehicle to deliver and support the resolution, using their weight to persuade other Member States to join the effort. In other cases, the Friends have been instrumental in directly preparing draft resolutions and encouraging consensus. Because they are focused on the day-to-day events surrounding the process, they are generally considered to be the best informed and most engaged members. Their view is generally accepted by other Member States who may not be following the issue as closely. By not taking sides, the Group of Friends is only interested in restoring peace so that relations within the region can be normalized. Its involvement in the process, as explained above, will only be productive as long as the parties are willing to accept its role as intermediary. Through these activities the Group of Friends provides another "channel for multilateral action by Member States"[9] ancillary to the more formal UN bodies.

In their capacity as concerned Member States, the Group of Friends can fill another very important role. The Secretary-General touched upon this additional function in his speech in May 1995:

> The complexity of peacekeeping operations of the second generation is such, that, in recent years, we have been confronted with a new type of problem: how to terminate a mission. Typically, two possibilities should be considered. First, when, as in Cambodia, a mission has fulfilled its mandate, and the country is at peace, the issue of terminating the mission arises. Some governments, understandably, are reluctant to have the mission continue at full strength. But a continued international presence is necessary to complete peace-building, to ensure that the country does not slide back into conflict. . . .
>
> The second possibility is that the mission has not fulfilled its mandate. . . . Thus, in Somalia, a group of nations, among them the United States, the United Kingdom, and Italy helped the pullout of United Nations troops.[10]

When peacekeeping troops have left the country and the UN is no longer involved in a major way, the Group of Friends can offer the Secretary-General and the Organization a means of preventing conflict from erupting again by continuing to mediate disputes and offering incentives to the parties to continue to manage the peace. The "Group of Friends on El Salvador," for example, continue to meet and offer its assistance to the Secretary-General as needed. A subsequent Group of Friends on Guatemala, which emerged out of the Friends on El Salvador, also continues to meet.

The Group of Friends of the Secretary-General on the question of Haiti has also continued to offer support. A letter signed by the Friends of Haiti, including the signatures of Ambassador Cárdenas (Argentina), Ambassador Fowler (Canada), Ambassador Merimée (France), Ambassador Tejera-Paris (Venezuela), and Ambassador Albright (United States), which was circulated as an official document of the UN on April 17, 1995, underlined their "firm support for President Aristide and the Government of Haiti [and] the importance of immediate and sustained international assistance in supporting the Haitian people through international financial institutions and bilateral and multilateral programmes." The letter also stated that "the Friends join the Secretary-General's call of 23 March for Member States to contribute to the creation of an adequate police force in Haiti and to the international police-monitoring programme."[11] This sustained support offers the United Nations a low-cost yet ongoing mechanism carried out by a group of members who are sincerely concerned with the maintenance of peace within the country in question.

What Countries Form the Group of Friends of the Secretary-General?

The groups generally have about three-to-six members and tend to have at least one country who is a member of the Security Council. They usually are constituted in response to a crisis in a particular country where the UN is involved to some degree and often where there is an ongoing UN operation. There are usually some countries that represent the region concerned—a major power and, at times, the former colonial power. The following is a list of Groups of Friends of the Secretary-General on:

- *El Salvador* (began December 1989): Colombia, Mexico, Spain, Venezuela, and, behind the scenes, the United States; referred to as the "Four Plus One."
- *Haiti* (began approx. January 1993): Canada, France, United States, and Venezuela; later joined by Argentina and then by Chile as these countries replaced each other on the Security Council.
- *Western Sahara* (approx. April 1993): France, Spain, United Kingdom, United States, and later, Djibouti, Cape Verde, and Venezuela.
- *Georgia* (approx. December 1993): a self-constituted group referred to as the "Friends of Georgia" rather than the "Friends of the Secretary-General"—France, Germany, Russia, United Kingdom, and the United States.
- *Guatemala* (approx. January 1994): a self-constituted group referred to as the "Friends of the Guatemalan Peace Process"; to act as Friends of the Secretary-General is only part of their activity—Colombia, Mexico, Norway, Spain, United States, and Venezuela.
- *Suriname* (1994): Brazil, The Netherlands, United States, and Venezuela.
- *Afghanistan* (1994): called the "Friends Group on Afghanistan," a self-constituted group including Iran, Pakistan, Russia, Saudi Arabia, and the United States. This grouping did not work, and another group was formed called the "Six-Plus-Two," consisting of China, Iran, Pakistan, Tajikistan, Turkmenistan, Uzbekistan, plus Russia and the United States. Other groups on Afghanistan include the Group of 21 and the Afghanistan Support Group formed in 1996 of the primary donor countries to Afghanistan.
- *Tajikistan* (approx. May 1995): Afghanistan, Iran, Kazakhstan, Turkey, Turkmenistan, United States, and Uzbekistan.
- *Friends of Rapid Reaction* (September 1995): Canada, The Netherlands, plus 22 other countries.
- *East Timor* (1999): called the "Core Group on East Timor," was gathered outside the UN framework—Australia, Japan, New Zealand, United Kingdom, and the United States.
- *Kosovo* (1999): called the "Group of Friends of Kosovo."
- *Guinea-Bissau* (2000): called the "Friends of Guinea-Bissau."
- *Central African Republic* (2001): called the "Friends of the Central African Republic."

It is interesting to note the approximate three-year gap in constituting Friends groups between the years 1995–96 and 1999, when groups on East Timor and Kosovo were formed. This reflects a disillusionment with the process during those years, as many conflicts remained unresolved. The crises of East Timor and Kosovo apparently reinvigorated the need to go back to a means of leverage that had worked in the past and could play a role in keeping the peace process on track.

A Group of Friends forms most easily when something similar has already been in existence. For example, the Group of Friends on El Salvador evolved largely out of the Contadora process and the countries that had supported that effort (adding Spain but not including Panama). However, becoming a member of the Group of Friends gives these countries a specific role to play within the larger UN system, provides a support mechanism for the Secretary-General, and offers stability to the group that membership, as such, provides. It is important that the members are like-minded and have the political will to stick with the issue. Maintaining a like-minded or common approach is essential so that the Friends act according to the same principles when applying pressure upon the parties. It would be detrimental to the process if each Friend was putting pressure on the parties to behave in a different manner. A Group of Friends most likely cannot form if the members are too far apart on the issues; for example, the Contact Group on the former Yugoslavia was not a Friends group because its members held different views on the outcome of the conflict (the United States siding with the Bosnian Government, Russia siding with the Serbs).

When Did the Phenomenon, of the "Group of Friends of the Secretary-General" Begin?

While the name "Group of Friends" originated with the Salvadoran peace process, the concept of drawing support for the Secretary-General through the formation of a small group of key Member States seems to have appeared earlier, under Dag Hammarskjöld, during the Suez Crisis in 1956:

> [I]t seemed natural to him [Hammarskjöld] that the matter should be brought before the Security Council under Article 37 of the Charter with the single aim of using the Council to invite a restricted number of member nations to set up a committee on the Suez question that might explore ways and means of the three objectives mentioned by Egypt. If the committee could agree on something, the results might be submitted to the Security Council, which might then pass them on either to all the users of the Canal or to the General Assembly, where all the users were represented.[12]

The first peacekeeping operation, the United Nations Emergency Force (UNEF), was created as a result of this crisis. Close collaboration between the United States, Canada, and Hammarskjöld at the time produced the concept of using troops donated by Member States to establish and patrol a buffer area between the conflicting parties. The support group that Hammarskjöld had created during this period may have played a role in formulating and implementing the first peacekeeping operation. The group continued to meet under Secretary-General U Thant, and he consulted with them before taking the decision to withdraw UNEF I in 1967.[13]

Secretary-General Pérez de Cuéllar also seems to have used this mechanism on other occasions without calling it specifically a "Group of Friends." Concerning Namibia, there had been, starting in 1977, a self-created group of Member States later referred to as the "Contact Group." It was comprised of five Western powers, including the three Western permanent members of the Security Council plus two nonpermanent members serving at the time, Canada and West Germany. Secretary-General Pérez de Cuéllar began to interact with this group during the late 1980s. While a contact group is similar to a Group of Friends, working as Member States who offer support for a peaceful solution, it differs in one major way: a Group of Friends operates in coordinated support of the Secretary-General and his efforts much as "friends" might do. A contact group is less cohesive and may take independent initiatives separate from the Secretary-General. A member of a contact group may seek a specific solution in line with its own interests.

Another group of Member States came to the aid of Namibia at a crucial period after the UN Namibia operation was established but was still not fully deployed (in 1989). A crisis developed when SWAPO forces crossed the border into Namibia threatening to disrupt the peace process. A secret emergency meeting of a handful of Member States (Angola, Cuba, South Africa, the Soviet Union, and the United States) took place in Namibia and brought the process back on track by intervening between the parties. During the peace operation in Cambodia in 1992–93, the Special Representative of the Secretary-General, Yasushi Akashi, met regularly with a group of Member States called the "Core Group."

How long a Group of Friends might stay in existence and continue to meet depends on the members and the issues involved. The Group of Friends of the Secretary-General on El Salvador still meets from time to time, as does the Group of Friends of the Secretary-General on Haiti.

How Do the Group of Friends Function?

The way the Group of Friends functions takes on a triangular dimension with the following pivotal apexes of activity: (1) New York; (2) the field (in the country in question); and (3) the capitals of the members of the group. The Friends are constituted in New York but usually have a counterpart activity in the field. There seems to be a flow of activity among the ambassadors of the group who are in the country where the operation is taking place then back to their capitals, and also to and from the ambassadors and the Secretary-General in New York.

The group itself physically does not always have to meet. Contact may take place by telephone or one-on-one between the members or with the

Secretary-General. Sometimes they may want to meet but cannot. They may work better by not coming together. Members of the group may not want to be seen working with another member for reasons outside this particular issue due to political sensitivities. However, for some groups, meeting as a whole is essential in order to develop and maintain a consensus. These meetings generally take place in New York among the ambassadors to the United Nations from the Member States and the Secretary-General. Meetings are primarily held in New York when consensus needs to be developed within the Security Council on the drafting of a resolution or the formulation of policy or to meet individually with the parties in the dispute.

Members of the group can also meet in the field where the UN operation is established. These meetings tend to take place after an agreement has been reached between the parties to the conflict and implementation is under way. These discussions are held with the Special Representative of the Secretary-General and the ambassadors to the country in question from the members of the Group of Friends. Hence the group can actually be active in many places. If the Secretary-General is traveling and the need arises, he may call a meeting together of the Group of Friends by meeting with their ambassadors in whatever country he might be visiting. This is one of the very useful aspects of this particular mechanism. The Secretary-General, on a visit to France, convened a meeting with the Group of Friends of the Secretary-General on Haiti, for example, and met in Paris with a representative of the French government and the other ambassadors to France from the group.

Policy decisions, however, are made back in the capitals of each of the members involved; the ambassadors report information back to their capitals. Ideas can come from any side of the triangle, but decisions generally are made by the governments. An ambassador from a small country may have more leeway to make policy decisions on his or her own. However, the ambassadors from the larger countries will get directions from, or at least confer with, their home governments. The ambassadors are appointed by and serve their governments and must take their direction from government leaders. So the link to the capitals is essential, particularly when governments may be asked to apply leverage and then be able to deliver on any promises made to the parties. In El Salvador, Spain contributed resources to the camps where demobilization of the military factions took place. The camps were suffering from a lack of funding and demobilization was in jeopardy. This information was transmitted from the field to Madrid and funding was made available to continue with the demobilization process.[14]

Problems arising in the field could be conveyed by the Special Representative to the local ambassadors who in turn might contact their capitals. Simultaneously, the Special Representative could be in contact with the Secretary-General in New York who could call an emergency meeting of the group, could meet with them individually (which is often the case), or could reach them by telephone. New York can be a useful venue because all the members are in close proximity and can meet with the Secretary-General very quickly and easily. Also, New York has the advantage of allowing discussions to take place invisibly. Diplomats are often reluctant to make a symbolic statement by traveling to another country for a meeting.

The UN Secretariat can also play a key role in this mechanism by providing background information and supporting the work of the special political advisor to the Special Envoy or Representative of the Secretary-General on the country in question. These political advisors have been within the Office of the Secretary-General or from the Department of Political Affairs and serving at the regional division (or desk) for the country in question. The special advisor reports directly to the Envoy or Representative of the Secretary-General and not to an under-secretary. A special political advisor may have language and diplomatic skills that enhance the negotiating process and may travel for the Secretary-General, or his Envoy/Representative, when needed. For example, Alvaro de Soto of the Secretariat played an important role in assisting the successive Special Representatives to El Salvador (Iqbal Riza, Augusto Ramirez-Ocampo, and Enrique ter Horst)[15] and provided an important continuity to the process when these Representatives replaced one another. On Haiti, Francesc Vendrell played a significant role in assisting Special Envoy Dante Caputo, who was also assisted by Nicole Lannegrace of the UN Department of Political Affairs. Lannegrace continued on to assist Special Representative to Haiti Lakhdar Brahimi when Caputo resigned.

Other Groups Similar to the Group of Friends but Have Not Taken on That Name

There have been and are other groups of Member States that have taken on a similar role as the Group of Friends but have not been called by that name. For example, on Angola there is the "troika" that consists of Portugal, Russia, and the United States. The Contact Group on the former Yugoslavia was not a Group of Friends of the Secretary-General; it was not created to help the Secretary-General on this issue. The word "contact" here is an accurate description of its function: The members were in contact with the parties to try to find a solution, but the group itself did not have a common view on the situation or how it should be resolved. It did not proceed with the kind of consensus that depicts the Group of Friends. In Bosnia, those in the region had such strong interests in a particular outcome that they did not trust one another and therefore were not able to form a Group of Friends. They blamed one another for the conflict: Germany was blamed for recognizing break-away states too soon; the United Kingdom was blamed for not wanting to take strong action; Russia was blamed for supporting the Serbs; and the United States was blamed for being pro-Muslim and not committing troops to UNPROFOR while calling for NATO to bomb the Serbs. Each member had its own interests and did not have a unanimity of purpose with the others. The effect of the Contact Group was minimal and the United States, with pressure from France, ended up taking the lead in bringing about the Dayton Accords that signified the end of the war.

The front-line states on apartheid and Namibia also worked as a pressure group of Member States—in this case with some effective results. These African Member States are those who border the countries at issue. They stayed with the process, continuing to keep the issue alive at the United Nations and pressuring the parties to end the conflict. A support group of Member States also kept in close touch with the UN operation in Mozambique. On Cambodia, the group of Member States that kept the UNTAC process on track was referred to as the "Core Group." The members of this group were Australia, France, Indonesia, Japan, Thailand, and other ASEAN countries, and later the United States. The group was used when momentum stalled to put pressure on the parties. The meetings took place in New York, but the members also met regularly in Cambodia with Special Representative Akashi.

The key to the success of these groups, whether they are specifically linked to the Secretary-General or not, is being able to maintain: (1) a unanimity of purpose; (2) impartiality in dealing with the parties; (3) a will to stay with the process; and (4) the capability to deliver incentives, or threats, when the parties need a push. The advantage of the Friends of the Secretary-General is that the group can benefit from the impartial reputation the "good offices" of the Secretary-General holds and from the coordination and consensus that the Secretary-General and his staff can orchestrate to keep the process moving forward.

Under What Circumstances Is a Group of Friends Formed or Not Formed?

In order to form a group certain conditions are needed. First, it is necessary to have credible players: those in the region who don't have a national stake in the outcome that favors one party over the other or a tainted history in the region that cannot be overcome. It is helpful to have one or two credible players outside the region who have the capacity to apply pressure through power or by offering resources, for example, the United State's loans to El Salvador for land reform, and Spain's significant contribution to military and police observers in El Salvador. Second, it is important to have countries who have enough political will to take on the issue, stay with it through various crises, and who are in consensus with one another and the Secretary-General. And third, there has to be a legitimate contact inside the target country to deal with on a consistent basis and to provide consent. In Somalia, there was no government to deal with; and in Burundi the government told the UN to stay out.

A Group of Friends will *not* come together for various reasons. First, a group will not form if there are no countries who can trust one another or who can reach consensus on a common policy, for example, countries that might be interested in being engaged in the issue who are looking for a particular outcome to the conflict that might favor one side or the other or serve their own interests rather than the interest of peace (problems that arose with the contact group in Bosnia). Second, a group won't form if the crisis comes at a time when the key members are already overloaded or feel that they should not get involved in a hostile situation, for example, as in Burundi. And third, a group won't form if there is no one in the crisis country to deal with and Member States are not prepared to mount the necessary means to deal with the situation by force, uninvited.

It was difficult to rally support in Rwanda to stop the genocide because countries were hesitant to get involved in the midst of hostilities. The Security Council had been unable to take speedy action. France was the only nation willing to deploy troops to Rwanda during the crisis; even though other countries had histories of interests in the region, there was no one else willing to intervene and therefore there was no capacity to form a group. As with France in Rwanda or Nigeria's involvement in Liberia, a country with an interest in the region may be especially willing to intervene. While they may provide the needed assistance in a crisis, the international community needs to be careful that the interested intervener is not pursuing its own hegemonic goals at the cost of the country in crisis. The trade-offs here are complex.

If a group cannot come together to apply common pressure on a specific issue, the Secretary-General will try to keep an informative process going and to keep the dialogue alive by continuing to meet with key ambassadors to the UN and by being in close contact with UN agencies to encourage preventive action.

A USEFUL LEVERAGE TOOL

The Group of Friends of the Secretary-General is a mechanism that is emerging as one of the more useful tools available to the Secretary-General. The Friends offer him the ability to take action through the members of the group in a way that would otherwise be impossible. The group can use leverage on the parties to a conflict, help mediate, and develop common ground among Member States in the United Nations. They help develop and implement peaceful solutions to conflict, and prevent the return to conflict by continuing to watch over the peace process. The group can also maintain pressure on the parties to adhere to the terms of an agreement and mediate future disputes after the United Nations has withdrawn its operation from the field. It seems that this innovative mechanism holds promise for aiding the UN in preventing a return to violence in areas of crisis.

While the Group of Friends can be, and has been, a very useful tool, it has not always worked, particularly when members of the group are unable to maintain a consensus or separate their own interests from the peace process. The Friends of Tajikistan is a case in point; one of the Friends—Afghanistan—has been deeply embroiled in a war of its own until recently when U.S.-led forces ended Taliban rule.

The concept has been viewed by a few members of the UN with skepticism. Some members sitting on the Security Council have viewed these groups somewhat negatively, seeing them as being highly undemocratic.[16] At that time, the Friends of El Salvador and the group on Haiti were both active. In addition, during that period, Groups of Friends formed on Western Sahara, Georgia, and Guatemala. The skeptical members, who were serving on the Security Council at the time, felt that the entire Security Council should be involved in the work of the Groups of Friends, not just an elite few. They were angry that the groups met privately and refused to discuss with the other members of the Security Council what they were doing. A few Council members who were not in the Groups of Friends resented that drafts of resolutions were presented to the Council as a finished product. They felt that what the groups were doing, in fact, was the role that the entire Security Council should play, being an institution within the United Nations that was designated to handle these kinds of issues. They particularly resented that just at the time, after the end of the cold war, when the Council was finally capable of taking action, these elite groups were usurping that role and marginalizing the work of the legally constituted bodies. Their concern increased as the number of the Friends groups began to multiply. These members requested that the work of the Friends be made more open and available to the entire Security Council. These requests later led to greater communication between the groups and Security Council, and those who had been highly critical of the process now feel that the procedure is evolving in a positive direction, being more open and democratic.[17]

UN members recognize that it is useful to have a clearing house for mediation. They also recognize that countries that have leverage can play a useful role from time to time by doing some "heavy arm twisting" when parties to a conflict have become intransigent. But there was a concern that these Groups of Friends were not acting in a manner that was accountable to the Security Council or the General Assembly and were thus bypassing these institutions.[18] The negative reaction to the formation of Groups of Friends as elitist will have to be reckoned with by the Secretary-General if the groups are to function in a positive way within the larger context of the Organization. This can be done through greater communication to the Security Council and/or the General Assembly. While it is fair to ask Friends groups to be in communication with the Security Council, efforts to curtail the use of Friends by accusations of elitism are counterproductive to the goals of the Organization—namely, international peace and security.

The Role of the Friends at Each Stage of the Process

The Negotiations. Friends groups can be very useful during the negotiation process to achieve a peace agreement. On El Salvador, the Friends were engaged in the negotiation process on almost a daily basis. They took on the task of writing draft resolutions for the Security Council and reviewing reports by the Secretary-General on the situation. By that time both Venezuela and Spain were on the Security Council, which facilitated this arrangement.

In addition to writing draft resolutions, Friends have hosted a number of the negotiating sessions. For the situation in El Salvador, these lasted several weeks and went on all day and even into the early hours of the morning. Mexico hosted most of the meetings, but whichever country was involved, it paid for everything, including hotel, meals, staff support, security, and so on. It also paid and arranged for the transportation and visas for the guerrillas who did not have government resources or airplanes to take care of these needs. The host country held official meetings with the two parties and the UN in attendance, and it also held secret meetings where it covered all the expenses. President Pérez on at least one occasion, having been frustrated by the slow pace of negotiations, sent airplanes to transport the parties to Caracas so that he could introduce his own plan. It was not accepted, but the gesture *did* seem to get the process going again. In addition, while Venezuela was brokering the agreements with the government and the rebels, President Pérez invited the chief of staff of the military of El Salvador to Caracas for a two-day meeting with the chiefs of staff of the Venezuelan military to discuss how the Venezuelan armed forces had reformed into a professional army that supported a democracy.[19]

Later, in 1991, when the negotiations on El Salvador moved primarily to New York, the Friends would meet with each delegation separately, primarily at the Mexican Mission to the United Nations. First, one side would come in, for example, the government delegation that generally consisted of President Cristiani's Chief of Staff Oscar SantaMaría, head of military operations Colonel Mauricio Earnesto Vargas, Minister of the Interior Colonel Juan Martinez Varela, David Escobar Galindo, and Rafael Hernán Contreras. They would meet in the conference room with all the Group of Friends present and discuss their position. Then when they had departed, and with some time separating the two meetings, the other delegation would arrive, in this case the representatives of the FMLN. The FMLN members generally were military commander Shafik Hándal, Salvador Samayoa, Roberto Cañas, Miguel Sáenz, Joaquín Villalobos, and two women, Ana Guadalupe Martínez and María Marta Valladares (also known as Nídia Diaz). The Friends would then convey the positions of each side to the other party and the issues were discussed. The delegation would then leave to discuss their response and the process would continue the next day.

In general, the Friends did not offer solutions but only conveyed the positions of each side. UN officials would also attend these meetings and would hold their own meetings with the parties. The United States did not join these meetings, but was kept informed and on occasion the Friends would meet at the U.S. Mission to the United Nations to brief the Americans.

Friends can also intervene and, in the El Salvadoran case, on at least two occasions did. One intervention took place in September 1991 during a series of meetings in New York. The parties had reached an impasse over how to reform and reconstitute the new police force—a critical part of the negotiations—and it was feared that the process was breaking down. The disagreement was over whether to allow any of the previous military police to continue to serve in the new civilian force. If none of them were allowed to remain, it would take perhaps two years before El Salvador would have a new police force in operation. The United States also was concerned about the issue of law and order because of this possibility of having no deployable trained or experienced police during the transition period. What the Friends proposed was that for a two-year transition period a certain number of the currently serving National Police as well as an equivalent number of FMLN ex-combatants could enroll in the new police academy. But the two groups together could not exceed the total number of new police who would make-up the student body of the new academy. In other words, at least 50 percent of the new civilian police would have to be people who had never served in either the military or the FMLN and after two years all recruits would have to be new members. Later, during the implementation of the agreement, the ratio became 20 percent government, 20 percent FMLN, and 60 percent new recruits. The Friends proposal became a part of the agreement and broke the impasse.[20] The other intervention by the Friends of El Salvador took place in December 1991, a few days before the end of Secretary-General Pérez de Cuéllar's tenure, which is explained in detail by Diego Arria in chapter 3 of this volume.

The Implementation Stage. During the implementation stage the center of activity switches to the country under concern, rather than New York. At that time, the Friends work with the Special Representative of the Secretary-General headquartered in the country, utilizing at that point the ambassadors in the capital from the Friends' countries. The responsibility of the Friends at this stage is to oversee the implementation of the points in the agreement within the established time-frames. In El Salvador, complaints by the FMLN fell into several categories: (1) the reform of the police—that certain military units had been illegally folded into the new police force; (2) the distribution of land met with innumerable delays; (3) compensation for those injured during the war had not taken place fully on either side; and (4) modifications in the judicial system were being delayed. This is only citing a few of the complaints. If the FMLN had made these in New York at the Friends' meeting at the Mexican Mission, the

Mexican ambassador would then contact the embassy in El Salvador and ask them to verify the complaints. If the complaints were substantiated, the ambassador would contact his government. Then the Mexican president or his foreign minister would contact President Cristiani directly and explain the situation. Generally, this process achieved results and hence implementation would move ahead.

The Salvadoran government side had two major complaints during the implementation stage, one having to do with the discovery that the FMLN had been secretly hiding large numbers of weapons contrary to the agreement. The Friends put pressure on the FMLN to relinquish the weapons and in some cases that occurred. But the military was still not completely satisfied that all the weapons were turned over. It was pointed out that after the agreement was signed, FMLN weapons started turning up in Guatemala and other parts of Central America.[21] The second major complaint by the Salvadoran government focused on the release of the report by the truth commission. The agreement called for the creation of a truth commission to be established as an independent investigative body. The Secretary-General proposed the names of persons to head the commission and then they were approved by the parties. The three commissioners were Belisario Betancur from Colombia who served as the chairman, Reinaldo Figueredo Planchart of Venezuela, and Thomas Buergenthal of the United States. All three were from the Friends Plus One countries. Their report is very detailed and lists people by name along with the crimes they committed. Before the report was to be released, information was leaked that names were going to be cited in the report, many of them of military officers and some high-ranking government officials. The government complained to the Friends, who conveyed these to the commission; they did not make a recommendation to the commission, respecting the independence of that body. The report was released with the names. Shortly after it became available, the Salvadoran national legislature passed a law granting amnesty to everyone listed in the report.

During the implementation phase the Friends countries can also provide personnel. In El Salvador, they provided police personnel to train and help the interim police force and provided peacekeeping troops to the UN operation, ONUSAL (the United Nations Mission in El Salvador). The Spanish contributed significantly to the reorganizing of the entire justice and security systems and provided some funds for their implementation. The United States played perhaps the largest role in providing resources for the implementation and funds for the loans needed in the land-distribution plan. A fund was also created to support the implementation process, with Venezuela making the first contribution of $100,000 to the fund, which was followed by other Friends and members of the UN.

The Follow-up Stage. As the UN operation winds down and most of the provisions in the agreement have been achieved, the role of the Friends diminishes and the Security Council may no longer be seized of the issue.

The matter may be passed to the General Assembly where the Friends group can continue to monitor the situation and review reports made to the Assembly on the country in question.

In interviews with the parties to the conflict in El Salvador and with a number of the Friends, there was general agreement that the relationship had been intense and operated on a nearly daily basis. One of the Friends described in this way:

> Who clinched the deal? The United States. Who supported the deal politically and made it possible to clinch the deal? The Friends. And who created the ground work to be able to conduct the two-year-long process of negotiations, the patience, the perseverance? De Soto and his team. That is a major truth. Each one played its role.[22]

The Group of Friends of the Secretary-General on Haiti

The Group of Friends of the Secretary-General on Haiti was begun during the tenure of Secretary-General Boutros Boutros-Ghali. The Secretary-General in December 1992 had named Dante Caputo, former minister for foreign affairs of Argentina (and former president of the UN General Assembly), to be his Special Envoy to Haiti. A few weeks later, in January 1993, the Secretary-General of the Organization of American States (OAS), which had been seized with the issue since the Haitian coup in September 1991, also named Caputo as his Special Envoy.[23] The fact that he was from Argentina gave him a link to the Latin Americans in the OAS that was very useful. Francesc Vendrell, a member of the Secretariat, was appointed by the UN Secretary-General to assist Caputo. Vendrell, who had worked with de Soto on El Salvador and knew from close experience the functioning of the Group of Friends on El Salvador suggested to Caputo that the same be done for Haiti.

Secretary-General Boutros-Ghali agreed to the idea to form a Group of Friends as had been suggested by Caputo and Vendrell and carefully chose the members: Canada, France, the United States, and Venezuela. Canada, the United States, and Venezuela are all members of the OAS, which had been playing a key role in trying to restore democracy to Haiti and was still actively involved. Canada also had business interests in Haiti and was very involved in the country. It was thought that it would be important this time for the United States to be a direct member. With the Group of Friends on El Salvador the United States had remained on the periphery, particularly during the beginning. However, regarding Haiti, the United States was much more directly affected by the Haitian refugee problem and it was felt that it would be better for the United States to meet directly with the others in the group to hear their points of view. The United States had ties to the military in Haiti that could be useful but that also needed to be balanced by those who were sympathetic to Haiti's ousted president, Jean-Bertrand Aristide. France was chosen as a member of the group because of its long ties with the country and their common language. Venezuela was a key member of the group as well. It had given asylum to President Aristide when he fled during the coup.[24] The ambassador from Venezuela to Haiti, Elsa Bocceciampi, was a very dynamic woman and was extremely helpful to Aristide. Also, Venezuela was a member of the Security Council at the time and had played an important role in the Group of Friends on El Salvador.

Venezuela was the only member of the Friends of El Salvador other than the United States (who had joined later) to also be a member of the Friends of the Secretary-General on Haiti. Venezuela has a little-known but historic tie to Haiti. Haiti had financed Simon Bolivar's war of independence for Venezuela from Spain at a time when Haiti was a prosperous country. Also, Venezuela's ambassador to Haiti had been actively engaged in the democratic transition in that country and was well-connected within the diplomatic community there. While the coup was underway, Ambassador Bocceciampi notified President Pérez of Venezuela, and he and his chief of staff were immediately on the telephone to Bernard Aronson of the United States and the chief of staff of Canada's Prime Minister Mulroney. In Port-au-Prince, the ambassadors of France, Canada, the United States, and Venezuela (all who eventually became the Friends) went to the Haitian military headquarters to try to negotiate the release of President Aristide, who had been captured during the coup. The four ambassadors were able to secure his release and, although he had been badly beaten, managed to get him to the airport. The United States had contacted President Pérez and asked if he would send an airplane for Aristide. When Aristide arrived in Caracas at about 2:30 A.M., the ambassadors to Venezuela from France and Canada along with Pérez's chief of staff were there to greet him. President Pérez treated him as a visiting head of state and provided him with the president's guest-house (with staff) for his stay during the next three months.[25] So from the beginning of the crisis these four countries had demonstrated that they were significantly concerned to become directly involved and take action.

Prime Minister Mulroney became immediately actively engaged in the process and contacted President Mitterrand of France and President Bush to encourage them to take on the role of members of the Group of Friends. President Pérez was also heavily involved and Ambassador Arria immediately began to pressure the Security Council to receive President Aristide at a formal meeting in New York. There was resistance in the Security Council by members who viewed this as a domestic issue and did not want the Council to become involved. Nonetheless, Aristide was allowed to give an informal presentation to the Council.

By January 1992 Venezuela was on the Security Council along with permanent members France and the United States. So by that time three of the four Friends were members of the Council. The Friends served much the same function on Haiti as they had on El Salvador in terms of keeping the Security Council advised of the matter and writing draft resolutions.

When Venezuela went off the Security Council and was replaced by Argentina, Argentina joined the Group of Friends, with Venezuela staying on. This happened again when Argentina ended its term on the Council and was replaced by Chile, which then also joined the group, becoming, finally, six members. It was important to maintain the Latin American link to the OAS within the Security Council but then not to lose the effectiveness of Venezuela and later Argentina once they were off the Council. Also, it would have been undiplomatic to drop them from the Group once they were no longer on the Council.

The group worked primarily in New York, but the ambassadors in Haiti also met with the Special Envoy there. Sometimes the meetings took place at the ambassador level, at other times at the staff level. This flexibility of venue and participants adds to the viability of the Friends mechanism. The United States also had its State Department coordinator for Haiti, Lawrence Pezzulo, working closely with Special Envoy Caputo.

There was a consensus among the group on a policy towards Haiti—namely, to restore democracy. The group was trusted by other UN members, with some exceptions, to devise a strategy for handling the crisis. They were well-informed, following events on a day-to-day basis, and were the most interested in finding a solution. Also, it was important to have continuity and have all negotiations on the issue go through one body, in this case the United Nations Group of Friends. It would have been disruptive if several countries were working at the same time or at cross-purposes to mediate the crisis. The Group of Friends not only kept the issue focused at the UN, but also became the focal point and clearinghouse for all negotiations.

It was important to the Secretary-General and to the process that the Haitian military was not given the possibility of playing one country off another. Because of the Haitian military ties to the United States, through the CIA, it might have had an opportunity to gain U.S. support and resist pressure to accept the return of Aristide. Having the United States in the Group of Friends and participating in a unified policy to return democracy to Haiti weakened the Haitian military's ability to manipulate the peace process. In other words, it was very important to maintain a common front among the group members. Caputo kept in constant touch with the members of the group, and they met frequently as a group. On occasion, if the Secretary-General or Caputo as his Special Envoy wanted something said to the parties, it would be done by the Friends as representing the consensus of the international community.

Like the Friends of El Salvador, the Friends of Haiti helped to prepare drafts of Security Council resolutions. Their input was pivotal, because without their support, it would have been very difficult to implement any decisions coming out of the Security Council. For example, if sanctions called for by the Security Council were to be effective, as in Security Council Resolution 841 (1993) adopted on June 16, 1993, it was essential that the Group of Friends be participants from the beginning. The Group of Friends helped to promote the idea of sanctions to the Security Council and the other members. The OAS (especially the Caribbean countries) and Caputo had supported sanctions early on as a way to pressure the military, but the United States had not been in favor initially. Once sanctions were approved by the Security Council, it was then essential that the Friends keep the other members engaged during the implementation phase. For the most part, consensus was maintained throughout the process. Maintaining that consensus was possible because the Friends in general wanted the same thing—which was not true, for example, for the Contact Group in Bosnia. But it was important for the key players to keep up their steady support during the process. They also had to play an important leadership role for the other Member States within the UN.

Friends of the Guatemalan Peace Process

While this chapter does not go into great detail on the Friends of Guatemala, some reference should be made here because of its relationship to the Friends of the Secretary-General on El Salvador. The group began in 1994, initially at the request of the president of Guatemala who had contacted the presidents of Venezuela, Mexico, and Colombia, asking that they form a Group of Friends of the President of Guatemala. His request had not been as Friends of the UN Secretary-General, but as Friends of the President of Guatemala. The presidents called their ambassadors to the UN and asked them to go to Guatemala to meet with the president.

Ambassador Arria of Venezuela and Ambassador Tello of Mexico went to Guatemala and met there with the ambassadors to Guatemala from Norway and Colombia. In meeting with the president, it was explained that the group could not be simply "Friends of the President," because they would be seen as taking sides with the government, which would destroy their effectiveness in dealing with the guerrillas. The ambassadors preferred that they be "Friends of the Secretary-General" to preserve impartiality. A compromise was struck and they agreed to be called "Friends of the Guatemalan Peace Process."

However, the ambassadors believed that if they were to be effective, they would need to meet immediately with the guerrilla leaders. Because the Guatemalan rebel leaders lived in Mexico, the ambassadors flew directly from Guatemala to Mexico City. Mexico's Deputy Foreign Minister Rosario Green hosted the meeting between the ambassadors and the rebel leaders. The meeting went on for several hours, the purpose of which was mainly to convince the rebels that the Friends were impartial and did not represent the interests of the president. In the end, the rebels accepted and the process began.[26]

The negotiation process continued much the same as it had on El Salvador, but most of the meetings took place in Mexico, with that country covering the bulk of the costs. In the case of Guatemala, it was a matter of *what* should come *first* on a long list of issues: a cease-fire, disarmament, the integration of guerrillas into civil society, land reform, Indian rights, and human rights. Once an agreement was reached as to the main issues that had to be included in the peace agreement, then it had to be decided which should come first.

The first agreements to be resolved were on human rights and then on indigenous peoples. This is similar to the pattern set by the Salvadoran process. A practical solution had to be reached to put an end to abuses of human rights. The impunity of the Guatemalan authorities became a critical issue. Once the human-rights agreement was resolved and signed, it was a clear indication to the guerrillas that the negotiations would continue until a final peace agreement could be reached. The Friends continued the process through the signing of the final agreement in December 1996 and function now in a similar way as the Friends on El Salvador did for the implementation phase.

The Friends of Rapid Reaction

While most Friends groups focus on a country in crisis, the mechanism has also been adopted to apply leverage on a particular issue; for example, developing a rapid-reaction UN capability. In various reports, the Secretary-General had asked Member States to explore the possibility of developing a rapid-reaction or rapid-deployment capability, particularly in the aftermath of the tragedy in Rwanda. The "Friends of Rapid Reaction" was formed during the period of the General Debate of the General Assembly in the fall of 1995, the fiftieth anniversary of the UN. The Canadian government, whose General Romeo Dallaire had been the UN force commander in Rwanda[27] during the crisis, had developed a report released in September 1995 titled "Towards a Rapid-Reaction Capability for the United Nations." The Canadian report, produced with the support of the Canadian government, stimulated the formation of a group of like-minded countries who developed a consensus based on many of the concepts in the report. The co-chairs of the Friends of Rapid Reaction were Canada and the Netherlands. The group had an additional 22 members, which include all the Nordic countries, representation from the G-77 (Group of 77, which represents countries from the developing world within the United Nations), as well as other supporting Member States.

The rapid-reaction group purposefully did not include any of the five permanent members of the Security Council. Politically, it was considered by the co-chairs to be better if the United States and other permanent members were not seen to dominate the process. Also, because the United States had been delinquent in paying its assessments during that period, many countries did not want to join any group of which it was a member. For a time, there appeared to be widespread anger at the United States for withholding its payments, leaving the UN in the worst financial crisis of its

50-year history. The group kept in communication with the five permanent members, however, essentially through the Military Staff Committee, which continues to meet, albeit at the colonel level. The group also consulted regularly with the UN Secretariat in the Department of Peacekeeping Operations (DPKO).

The Friends of Rapid Reaction[28] represented an expansion and evolution of the Friends concept. While earlier groups were centered around a crisis within a country or region, this Friends group was focused on an operational reform of the United Nations. Its mandate was significantly different and its role is, therefore, changed from the small, tight groups that meet in confidence and carry-out sensitive diplomatic negotiations. This group was much larger—24 members—instead of the usual three to six. The purpose here was to develop a broad consensus and to build the means to launch the project.

The consensus of the group seemed to be fairly broad, which was basically that: (1) the UN should have a rapid-reaction capability; (2) the Member States would loan officers to establish and maintain an operational-level headquarters located in New York that would be responsible for planning and for advance preparations; (3) the UN, when needed, would be able to assemble from Member States a multifunctional force of up to 5,000 military and civilian personnel and rapidly deploy it under the control of the operational-level headquarters; and (4) forces would be provided through the standby arrangements that have already been established with most UN countries, stating what troops and equipment could be made available to the UN as needed on a case-by-case basis.

Members of the Friends of Rapid Reaction[29] had good representation from various regions of the world including Latin America, Africa, and Asia as well as Europe, all of whom were in agreement.[30] They also worked with DPKO. The advantage to DPKO is that this operational headquarters could be deployed immediately and intact into the field and would not require that DPKO would suddenly be required to shop around for military officers to send on mission. DPKO would also not have to give up its own staff to go into the field and could continue its role of arranging the logistics for deployment and liaising with the Secretary-General and Member States through the UN headquarters in New York. DPKO now has a staff of about 600, only some of which are military officers; the rest are support and planning staff. With now some 14 UN operations in the field, DPKO cannot afford to lose officers to a sudden crisis situation.

The rapid-reaction headquarters would have about two hundred officers from different countries. These would be on loan from their governments for a two-year period during which they would be under the authority of the UN. The one issue on which the governments would retain control would be that an officer on loan would be expected to fulfill the role that had been agreed upon initially by his government. If the officer's duties were changed, his government would retain the right to recall the officer if it did not approve of the reassignment.

There was a great deal of initial optimism about the implementation of the rapid-reaction plan, but momentum waned when some Member States from the developing world feared that the force would be used most often in the Third World and might violate the sovereign rights of the country involved. There was also some backlash against the formation of the Friends group because a few troop-contributing countries that had not been invited to join the group were angry about being excluded. The Friends thought that they would have the headquarters in operation in about two years, but this was slowed by differences within the General Assembly.[31] The Member States had planned to cover all the costs, with no costs to the UN. This could be an advantage at a time when the UN is under budgetary stress.

By 2002, consensus on creating a rapid-reaction headquarters had accumulated and a sufficient critical mass had been created to overcome the previous obstacles due to the continued work of the Friends to build-up support. Sensitivities on issues of sovereignty by some members of the Non-Aligned countries were counterproductive to the needs of other countries, particularly in Africa, that were often in need of rapid deployment on humanitarian grounds. Now, many in the Non-Aligned are supportive of the rapid-reaction movement, understanding that if the United Nations does not have this capacity, then developed countries in the North will step-in to fill the vacuum. If the UN is involved, then troop-contributing countries from around the world will participate and the equipment that can be provided by Northern countries will be utilized by all members. The first steps have been taken to create an operational headquarters in New York for rapid deployment, with equipment storage and logistical support in Brindisi, Italy. At the same time, the Danish had been creating what is called the "Stand-by High Readiness Brigade (SHIRBRIG)."[32] This is a international brigade trained and ready to be deployed and work in cooperation with the Canadian/Dutch plan for the operational headquarters. The first test of this mechanism has been the recent deployment of SHIRBRIG to Ethiopia. The Friends group was instrumental in building support for this new mechanism, which demonstrates that these kinds of groupings of Member States can be used for issues other than country-specific crises.

Conclusion

The formation of a Group of Friends of the Secretary-General (or similar Groups of Friends) has become a useful tool when a consensus is needed to move a process forward to resolve an intransigent problem. It offers the Secretary-General and the United Nations a mechanism for taking action to resolve an issue through the support of a group of like-minded Member States in a way that would otherwise be more difficult for the Secretary-General to do without the backing of Members States who can offer leverage. The Group of Friends helps keep the process on track, channels mediation through one consistent source, helps formulate policy, and applies pressure on the parties to a conflict to cooperate in implementing an agreement. The Friends offer the UN and Secretary-General a clearinghouse to coordinate different channels of mediation and a sounding-board to try out different ideas.

At a time when the Security Council is seized with numerous global issues, a Group of Friends along with the Secretary-General can specialize on a specific issue and carry out the needed information-gathering and policy-preparation for the rest of the members, forming a kind of "expert committee." One of the advantages of this mechanism is its versatility. Ambassadors anywhere in the world as representatives of the members of a Group of Friends can meet when needed to keep the process moving along. The personalities of these actors is important. Active leadership can keep the process on track, but a player who tries to dominate the action and take initiatives outside the consensus of the Group can spoil the efforts to achieve a peaceful solution.

As was seen with the Friends of Rapid Reaction, this tool can also be used to support the implementation of a new concept or structural reform and is not limited to dealing with a country or region in crisis. It offers the members of the UN, whether on the Security Council or not, a greater role in the functions of the Organization. Where there is sufficient will by the group, it can stay with an issue and maintain an ongoing presence after the United Nations has officially ended its mission. There are times, as discussed above, when a group cannot be formed, and there may be times when a group will not be effective.

Also, it is important to take into account the negative reaction by some members to the formation of what they may view as elite groups that operate outside the legitimate bodies of the Organization without some kind of formal accountability. Guidance by an impartial Secretary-General is very important so that self-selected Member States do not band together to promote a solution that serves their interests and ignores those of the parties involved. However, this innovative mechanism continues to grow and evolve. Adjustments can be made, as they already have been, to make the Friends more effective and acceptable to the other members of the Security Council and the UN as a whole. It would be useful to examine in further depth additional cases to see when and why this mechanism works or not. In the meantime, it has clearly emerged as another useful tool of leverage for the Secretary-General as he seeks to resolve conflicts and prevent the parties involved from returning to violence.

NOTES

1. Secretary-General Boutros Boutros-Ghali, "Global Leadership after the Cold War," *Foreign Affairs* 75(March/April): 86.

2. Interviews were conducted during March and April 1996 and again in May and June 1997 with United Nations officials in the office of the Secretary-General

and in the Department of Political Affairs. Another round of interviews was conducted by the author in El Salvador in June 1997 with the parties to the conflict. In August and September 1997 the author met with some of the Friends, including Mexico and Venezuela. There is very little, if anything, written on this issue and therefore the majority of the information gathered had to be from interviews with people who have been directly involved with the Friends groups.

3. Ambassador Arria in his chapter explains that the first efforts to form the Friends took place in the fall of 1989 during the General Assembly. From his point of view, that was true; he did not know at the time the role that the others were playing.

4. This information was gathered from an interview with a former political advisor to Secretary-General Javier Pérez de Cuéllar.

5. This fact was maintained in interviews with Ambassadors Tello and Albin of Mexico, Ambassador Arria of Venezuela, and Beatrice Rangel.

6. Press Release, May 1, 1995: "Secretary-General Addresses Institute for International Affairs and United Nations Association of New Zealand." United Nations document number: SG/SM/5624.

7. On 30 September 1992, FMLN informed the United Nations that, in order to maintain the link in the original timetable between the key undertakings of the two parties, it would suspend demobilization of its forces until new dates had been set for the start of the transfer of land and other aspects of the agreement that had fallen behind schedule <http://ralph.gmu.edu/cfpa/peace/html.onusal>, 4.

8. Information gathered from an interview with a member of the UN Secretariat closely associated with the mission in El Salvador; interview at the UN on October 2, 1996.

9. UN document: SG/SM/5624.

10. Ibid.

11. UN document S/1995/306, April 17, 1995.

12. Brian Urquhart, *Hammarskjöld* (New York: Harper & Row, 1972), 163.

13. U Thant, *View from the UN* (New York: Doubleday, 1978), 224–27.

14. Internet: <http://ralph@gmu.edu/cfpa/peace/html.onusal>.

15. Ibid.

16. This information was gathered from an interview with a representative of one of the Member States on May 7, 1996.

17. Ibid.

18. Ibid.

19. Ironically, this same military was involved in an attempted military coup to overthrow Pérez in 1992, using some of the officers who had served in the peacekeeping operation in El Salvador, according to the interview with Ambassador Arria.

20. This information was gathered from interviews with UN officials associated with the process.

21. This information was gathered through interviews conducted in El Salvador in June 1997 with the parties.

22. This a quote from Ambassador Arria, who was Venezuela's ambassador to the UN during this period, from an interview conducted with him in New York on September 5, 1997.

23. <http://ralph@gmu.edu/cfpa/peace/html.unmih>.

24. John Tessitore and Susan Woolfson, eds. *A Global Agenda: Issues Before the*

50th General Assembly of the United Nations (New York: UNA-USA/University Press of America, 1995–96), 25.

25. Interview with Rangel.

26. This information was gathered through interviews with Ambassadors Arria and Tello.

27. By Resolution 872 (1993), the Security Council established the United Nations Assistance Mission for Rwanda (UNAMIR). It was composed of 2,459 military personnel and 60 civilian police observers.

28. Later, the name "Friends of Rapid Reaction" was changed to "Friends of Rapid Deployment" or FORD.

29. The representatives to the meetings are generally the military attachés to the missions.

30. "UN Ready to Establish a Military Crisis Team," *International Herald Tribune* (July 22, 1996); Barbara Crossette, "At the UN, a Proposal to Speed Aid During Crisis," *New York Times* (July 21, 1996): A9.

31. This information was gathered through an interview on April 9, 1996 with a member of a mission to the UN who supports the rapid-reaction project.

32. Deployment of SHRBRIG is still subject to parliamentary approval on a case-by-case basis and is therefore not under the control of the UN for immediate deployment. For more information, see <www.shirbrig.dk>.

CHAPTER EIGHT

Leveraging Obstructionist Leaders

DONALD C. F. DANIEL AND BRADD C. HAYES

In the first half of the 1990s, civil conflicts and man-made humanitarian disasters proved so disturbing that outsiders felt compelled to intervene. Often authorized by the UN Security Council, national governments dispatched soldiers and civilians to crisis regions to labor alongside international civil servants and relief workers. Appropriately labeled "complex contingencies," these interventions were fraught with difficulties, not the least of which was securing the cooperation of the indigenous groups or factions competing for control of parts or all of the country where the intervention was taking place. Rival faction leaders regularly obstructed the interventionists when they concluded that doing so advanced their cause.

This chapter analyzes the obstructionist leaders problem and suggests ways and perspectives for using leverage when dealing with it. Its conclusions reflect written firsthand accounts, secondary analyses, and the remarks of practitioners assembled at three workshops dedicated to the topic. The practitioners were active or recently retired civilian officials and diplomats from the United Nations, national governments, and nongovernmental organizations (NGOs) as well as UN military-contingent commanders from several nations.[1] Drawing on their experiences, they offered perspectives and recommendations about how to think about and respond to obstructionists.[2] All unattributed citations in this chapter are from these workshops.

We begin with generalizations about faction leaders and the contexts that contribute to their behavior. We then outline strategies and options that interventionists have for dealing with obstructionist behavior. Contrary to our initial intent, we eschew recommending strategies and sequencing of options. The workshops led us to conclude that it is feckless to do so because the details of each case too often are devilishly significant. One participant put it succinctly when writing from the perspective of an operation as a whole: "Each humanitarian effort must have its own plan that is carefully fashioned according to the unique circumstances of each emergency."[3] The preceding chapters of this book reinforce this view. We offer instead guidelines that first address the mindset with which interventionists should approach leadership recalcitrance. The guidelines constitute starting points and filters as the outsiders sift through the facts of a situation and consider possible responses. Nested within these guidelines are more specific and overlapping recommendations that focus primarily on using leverage to preempt problems. The high priority that experienced practitioners gave to preemption was another unexpected result of our workshops.

FACTION LEADERS AND THEIR ENVIRONMENT

Characteristics, Types of Factional Leaders, and Their Susceptibility to Leverage

Practitioners describe faction leaders as tough and authoritarian, having little respect for open, democratic, political practices. All are obviously willing to employ force to secure personal or group values. Most are corrupt, and those who are not may well tolerate venality or employ corrupt practices. While some are driven by ideologies that call for ethnic dominance or the building of a socialist society, most seem motivated by material wealth, political power, and/or security for themselves and their entourage. They are almost always viscerally disinclined to respect the demands of outsiders unless doing so suits their interests. Living in an environment whose inherent insecurity is compounded by civil strife, they are hypervigilant to threats to their well-being from within or without their faction. They instinctually mistrust outsiders who urge compromise for the sake of peace and those with whom they would have to compromise to achieve it. Many seem inimical to any compromise and see an opponent's willingness to do so as reason to expand their own goals rather than make reciprocating concessions.[4]

Factional leaders fall into different categories that can affect their sensitivities and how they should be approached. One basic division is between incumbent government leaders, those formally recognized as being in charge prior to the outbreak of civil strife, and challengers, those vying for that recognition. The former often benefit from their official status when dealing with interventionists, invoking sovereignty as a reason for noncooperation with outsiders, who after all are intervening in the nation's domestic affairs.[5] Conversely, challengers can be as sensitive to their perceived legitimacy and status vis-à-vis the incumbents. For example, one factor conditioning the attitude toward mediation of the rebel Renamo group in Mozambique was its contention that "the mediators favored [its] Frelimo [opponents] by 'regarding the talks as being between a group of guerrillas and a government rather than between two political parties who have been at war for fifteen years.'"[6] In short, that leaders highly value their legitimacy can be significant when dealing with them.[7]

Ideological and ethnic avatars can be expected to be inflexible if outsiders demand that they repudiate part of their code or the achievement of their vision, such as an independent or socialist state. Many would rather go down with flags flying than admit that achieving their goal is no longer worth the fight. Civilian politicians may be especially sensitive about their links to the masses or their movement's rank-and-file, while military bosses or dictators tend to be more narrowly concerned with the well-being of the army and maintaining troop loyalty. As long as oligarchs or junta members view themselves as mutually dependent, they weigh developments for their impact on the collective while remaining sensitive to the distribution of power within their group and to the rise of anyone with Caesar-like ambitions. Guerrilla or insurgent leaders are often driven by ideological principles but "overthrowing the incumbent group is their chief raison d'etre."[8] They can be expected to accept hardship and be patiently inflexible as long as they believe there is progress to be made. Overlapping with the guerrilla leader is the Weberian charismatic warlord who rises to power by virtue of his heroism, success in battle, skills as a commander, or other exceptional qualities that draw fighters to recognize and accept him as the leader.[9] He is primarily a military figure or operates principally in an analogous hierarchical system that complements or solidifies his position. Charismatic warlords were certainly not the norm in the 1990s, and they contrast particularly sharply with what can be termed the "self-serving warlord."[10] Motivated by greed or power, he is an anti-hero determined to control a country or region "by brute force and cunning."[11] Exactly the same can be said for crime bosses, except that their motivation is more explicitly economic. Figureheads or titular leaders may simply be the spokesmen for an oligarchy or junta, or they may front for larger groups because they present a more acceptable image to outsiders than the real leader or leaders. They may take direction from a puppet-master who avoids the limelight altogether. He may have a personality quirk, fear for his life, otherwise benefit personally from remaining in the shadows, or simply be a *persona non grata* (possibly a declared war criminal) with the international community. Alternatively, he may publicly down-play his influence, such as Paul Kagame did in Rwanda right after his group assumed power. Before becoming president, he first served as vice president and minister of defense, in order to play-up the image of a democratic movement both to his own people and the international community.

While some of the above categories seem mutually exclusive, most are not, and as circumstances change, leaders can shift from one to another.

Any individual leader, furthermore, could fall under several at one time, including those that would seem incompatible. For example, while ideologically driven guerrilla or charismatic leaders may turn to criminal activity to finance their movement, outsiders may question the dominant motivation. Aristide portrays himself as a friend of the poor, for example, but there are those in Haiti who feel betrayed by his movement if not by him personally because of alleged links with drug interests that have become evident in the last few years.[12]

The Context Surrounding an Obstructionist

The massive domestic instability that justifies international intervention is usually caused by a rising sense of insecurity among leaders, committed followers, or the masses as to their ability to meet basic needs.[13] These can be material (food, housing, medicine, clean water, energy, and education), psychological (individual and group recognition, autonomy, well-being, fairness, and justice), or physical (personal or group security). A sense of insecurity rises when permissive conditions and catalysts come together.[14] The principal permissive conditions include mounting economic problems, increased political repression, and/or heightened social discrimination. Whether economic, political, or social in nature (or a combination), the changes strike at a people's basic needs and raise their sensitivity to threats to their well-being. Existing historical antagonisms encourage them to be particularly alert to threats that could emanate from traditional rivals. Such conditions may not be enough, however, to generate the outbreak of widespread conflict.

Just as sparks can cause an explosion in a volatile environment, catalytic events can ignite domestic strife. They can range from a contextual sea-change such as the collapse of a command economy, to premeditated human intervention like the April 1994 presidential assassinations that preceded the genocide in Rwanda. Premeditated human intervention by domestic elites is probably the most frequent catalyst.[15] By virtue of being the elite, the stakes for them can be high, and they can presumably get the masses or those who physically control the instruments of power (guns, money, goods and services, the media, and symbols) to do their bidding.[16]

While instability may often be attributable to elites from at least one side of the factional divide, it is important to note that they do not operate in a vacuum. They relate symbiotically with domestic counterparts, rank-and-file followers, the general public, and external supporters. These partners can significantly influence what leaders do. Domestic partners play their role in the relationship by looking to leaders for direction and aid in fulfilling their own material, psychological, or symbolic needs. Leaders do their part by manipulating symbols, controlling rewards and supplies, applying violence, providing protection, and representing the entire group. These symbioses can make leaders insecure, particularly since periods of rising instability can cause a diffusion of power in a society and provide opportunities for new aspirants to power.[17] Thus, unless leaders rule strictly by terror and fear, they look to their partners for affirmation of their elite status. If they are insecure about their domestic partners, they may "lead" by following. If they are insecure where they stand with external partners, they may hesitate taking steps that could (further) alienate them. Thus, whether faction leaders move toward moderation or destabilization, they are not alone.

Finally, the outbreak of conflict too often resembles the release of the bottled genie, for it seems far more difficult for leaders to end a conflict than to begin it. It is generally accepted, for example, that by the early 1990s both sides in the Mozambique civil war were near exhaustion and looking for a way out, but even then outsiders needed constantly to push-and-pull them to resolution. They were unable to come to closure on their own.[18] From the point of view of outsiders wishing to turn faction leaders toward cooperation, there are many perverse features to the broader set of circumstances influencing those leaders.

Factors Militating against Moderation and the Successful Use of Leverage

At least ten factors work against outsiders who are trying to influence factional leaders. Two concern the nature of war as a mechanism to resolve disputes. The first of these is that the expectation or reality of violence usually causes (potential) victims to consider responding in kind and can almost guarantee a loss of objectivity in favor of a "we"-versus-"they" mind-set instead. The second and closely related factor is that, once any war breaks out, it often has its own logic that allows termination only after one side has won or both have exhausted themselves. As one faction kills or maims its opponents and seizes or destroys what is important to their material and psychological needs, it generates anger, rage, and mental instability among the victims that clouds their perceptions and judgments. While some victims lose their ability to cope altogether, other becomes seized by desires not only to recover their losses but to revenge them as well. Total subjugation of one's opponents is the only outcome that can justify the suffering brought on by the war. Even after the shooting has stopped, residual anger and mistrust may limit the ability of far-sighted leaders to move toward reconciliation.

A third factor is the nature of civil wars. Participants have good reason to predict that loss would not only be humiliating but catastrophic. Those in charge can expect to be hunted down by the winners and condemned by their own side as responsible for the defeat. If the war does not lead to partition, losers face the possibility that they and future generations will be second-class citizens, forced to dance, and possibly die, to the winner's tune. Partition may be the best hope to protect group autonomy, but it could involve displacement and would mean having to settle for whatever the victor allows. In other words, the stakes of personal survival, group autonomy, and quality of life could not be higher. Compounding the above concerns for a leader is a fourth factor: civil wars breed independent operators or inspire a sense of independence among subordinates, further heightening his sense of insecurity. With the metaphorical crown resting so uneasily upon his head, a leader fears revealing his weakness by committing to policies he cannot be certain of implementing.[19]

Even worse for a leader prone to compromise is a fifth factor, the fear he will be criticized as weak and outbid by ambitious opportunists. Such aspirants can drive incumbents toward (further) extremism and make compromise seem like a sell-out. As with earlier factors, zero-sum thinking becomes the norm and total victory the goal. Leaders of all factions (and especially the one who catalyzed the conflict to begin with) may feel especially vulnerable if they try to end it without having something to show for all the sacrifices suffered by their people.

A sixth factor is that external threats to a group from opposing factions as well as from interventionists provide its leaders with a major opportunity to cement their positions as the masses react by rallying around the flags they wave. The Allied bombings aimed at forcing Serbia's hand in Kosovo initially caused the Serbs in Belgrade to intensify support for the Milosevic regime. Thus, incumbents may have a personal stake in increasing or maintaining tension, but this situation can also, of course, work against them by reinforcing negative effects, such as the rise of alternative leaders and ambitious opportunists.

A seventh factor is that factional leaders and their cronies can benefit economically as well as politically from the continuation of conflict. With control of an area comes the power to tax, levy fees, and share in the profits from the sale of resources such oil (as in the Sudanese and Angolan civil wars), diamonds (as in Angola and Sierra Leone), timber (as in Cambodia), or illegal drugs (as in Afghanistan). Their control of transit routes also means that they can profit even from internationally imposed embargoes, since government or faction leaders are usually well-positioned to engage in smuggling or, for a fee, enable others to do so.

An eighth factor is that more than just leaders can benefit from the continuation of chaos and instability. Margaret Joan Anstee, the Special Representative of the Secretary-General for Angola, narrates how Jonas Savimbi, the now-deceased UNITA rebel leader, described his men as having "an identity and self-respect while they were active in UNITA's forces, a sense of being 'someone'; so how would they fare when ejected into an unknown world of anonymity?"[20] No doubt some enjoyed bullying others or operating in an environment where their gun sustained swagger as well as material support. Criminals thrive in an atmosphere where law and order is inherently weak and where credit and basic goods are scarce. In addition, their economic clout and lack of scruples in carrying out deeds that others shy from can cause leaders to seek them out as partners. Alongside combatants and criminals are profiteers, arms dealers, and employees of aid organizations, such as "drivers, secretaries, warehouse guards, programme staff, liaisons with authorities, who may find their survival threatened by the cessation of conflict and the resultant withdrawal of emergency assistance."[21] Any group leader must consider that these and similar constituencies may well turn against him if his pursuit of peace threatens their instability-based life-style.

A closely related ninth factor is that many obstructionists have extremely limited world views. Not only are their life-styles circumscribed, so are their views of how the world actually functions. Pol Pot spent twenty years in the jungle before taking control of Cambodia, and Foday Sankoh, Sierra Leone's rebel leader, had never seen a skyscraper until he attended negotiations in Cote d'Ivoire. For most of their lives they have been the center of their known universe and have lived in a world that fosters meglomania on one hand and paranoia on the other.

Finally, hurried attempts by international-community representatives to forestall additional deaths from hunger and disease can lead them to implement solutions that benefit obstructionist leaders and thus contribute to continued problems in the long run. The relief effort in Somalia, for example, encouraged the merchant class to rob relief supplies, which corrupted their natural instinct for law and order. It also reinforced the power and wealth of armed warlords at the expense of the clan elders, who had traditionally stabilized Somali society. Relief organizations paid outrageous fees in money and goods to warlords to operate in "their" areas, obtain their protection, and rent their warehouses and office space. By doing so, the aid agencies enriched the leaders personally, financed their war efforts, and provided them with resources they could use to reward the loyalty of their minions.[22]

In sum, there is no paucity of factors for inducing pessimism about the ability of outsiders to positively influence recalcitrant leaders. To consider them collectively is to realize how difficult the problem can be; but while success may not be achievable in all cases, it is in some.

Strategies to Keep Pessimism in Check

Even the somber history of peace support in the last ten years shows that outsiders have sometimes positively used leverage to influence obstructionists. The reasons for success vary and usually involve taking advantage of timing and employing positive and coercive inducements, and particularly looking to the situation in which obstructionists find themselves. The inherent insecurity that attends the life of (most) faction leaders often provides outsiders a starting point to influence them, but it is a twin-edged reality. While increasing a leader's insecurity could cause him to become more obdurate for fear of seeming weak, it could also make him more cooperative if outsiders have an opening either to markedly harm his interests or, conversely, to reassure him that he and the group he represents will be better served by turning toward moderation. The record of success in the 1990s, in this regard, is checkered at best. Some operations, such as in Cambodia, Mozambique, and Eastern Slavonia, were successfully concluded; and, even in the midst of failing cases, such as in Somalia or Bosnia, there were numerous instances when representatives of the international community succeeded in getting obstructionists (at least for a short time) to change their behavior. Which way things go could well depend on what outsiders do and how and when they do it.

There are five general strategies that interventionists can follow (more if they pursue a mixed or hedging strategy).[23] At any given point in time, the decision to follow a particular option must depend on the type(s) of leader to be confronted and the circumstances in which he is found.[24] The five general strategies are:

First, working *with* obstructionist leaders. Options under this strategy include:

- Negotiation to accommodate reasonable demands
- Appeasement
- Assurances
- Bribery
- Taking charge at critical junctures.

Second, working *on* an obstructionist while continuing to accept him as authoritative. Options here encompass:

- Diplomatic entreaties and public criticism
- Socialization (i.e., coaxing him into the norms of stabilizing behavior)
- Plucking his feathers; that is, subtly or indirectly changing the underlying conditions that prop-up the leader through measures such as:
  - —cutting back or redirecting the flow of resources controlled by the interventionists and going to the obstructionist and his followers
  - —appealing to the populace and to those who physically control indigenous social, economic, or cultural resources
  - —building up alternative leaders
  - —urging a leader's external partners to use their influence on him
- Coercive inducements (i.e., sanctions and demonstrations of force)
- Seizing or destroying an obstructionist's assets such as a radio station or "illegal" arms cache.

Third, working *against* an obstructionist leader to neuter or remove him. This strategy can involve techniques mentioned directly above, plus:

- Isolating him
- Attacking his legitimacy
- Arresting him for trial.

Fourth, working *above* or temporarily superseding an obstructionist could involve:

- Hoisting him on his own agreements
- Establishing an international transitional governing authority
- Resorting to a joint executive authority made-up of representatives from the indigenous parties.

A final strategy might be to abandon the field either by:

- Withdrawing permanently or
- Withdrawing until conditions are ripe.

Interventionists must choose from the above strategies and options those that best apply to the situation at hand. The almost infinite variety of situational possibilities precludes recommending here which strategies or options to utilize and when. Nevertheless, distilling the wisdom of experienced practitioners does yield decision guidelines for interventionists anticipating or confronting recalcitrance.

Guidelines for Dealing with and Leveraging Obstructionists

These guidelines focus on the mind-set with which interventionists should approach obstructionists and on actions they should undertake to preempt or limit problems before they begin. The first mind-set guideline goes to the core of the obstructionist leader problem: outsiders must internalize that dealing with civil-conflict leaders means engaging in *recurring* contests of wills. Intervention in civil wars is not for the faint of heart. Whether they be substantive (such as which faction will control a strategic location) or symbolic (such as how donated food will be distributed), new issues will continually arise as old ones are dealt with, and old ones re-surface to be dealt with again. Prevailing against an obstructionist on one day does not prevent him or his civil-war opponents from causing problems on the next. Indeed, the record is replete with leaders ignoring pledges. Experienced practitioners advise that "nothing is permanent" when dealing with obstructionists.

Hence interventionists must commit to complete their mission as long as there is realistic hope for success; otherwise they invite obstructionists not so much to wait them out as to hurry their departure by deliberately making their life difficult. This may be the most crucial of all the factors in interventions that aim to get the parties to abide to a social contract governing their coexistence. It makes a significant difference if indigenous leaders know that outsiders will monitor and support implementation of any stabilizing agreements and actively oppose foot-dragging.[25] To announce exit dates independent of reaching stability goals is to abdicate leverage.

A third guideline advises against overreaction. Because the stakes are so high for indigenous leaders, outsiders should expect them to be more-or-less obstructionist and should realize that what they regard as recalcitrance—including the violation of agreements—may be viewed by the leaders concerned as what anyone would do to protect personal and group interests. This is particularly true when it comes to implementing tension-reduction measures between highly distrustful opponents.[26] In addition, what a leader does and how he does it may reflect his culture. In Somalia, for example, UNITAF officials found that an agreement among Somalis was not necessarily viewed by them as a commitment; rather, it "might mean a desire to appear cooperative, or that the elements in the agreement were not utterly unacceptable and might be implemented under certain circumstances. It rarely meant what the United States understood formal top-level agreements to mean."[27] Thus, outsiders must generally avoid simplistic dichotomous judgments about a leader's cooperation or obduracy. They must be sensitive to the richness or granularity of the context surrounding a leader before rendering judgment.

In addition, what worked in a previous case may not apply in another even if it is similar in many respects. The details are devilish and interventionists must attend to them. They must obtain as much knowledge as possible about each leader's background and personality, his objectives and likely moves, his inner circle, the group or faction that recognizes him as leader, the sources of his power and the identity of his domestic and international supporters, and his vulnerabilities including the rivals for his position. In particular, practitioners have recorded that "understanding the local political dynamic was imperative in order to avoid unnecessary pitfalls and maximize both popular and factional support."[28] Such information must complement knowledge about the local culture and peoples including their history, daily habits, value systems, norms, concept of time, negotiating styles, and, as noted in the above paragraph, views on verbal and written assent. Also important, and to some practitioners no less critical than insight into the local political dynamic, is understanding the local economy, the role that leaders play in it, and the profits they generate from it. The gathered information should be sifted not only for what it reveals about a leader per se but also for determining whether the true source of problems is in fact the leader or the people around him, neighboring governments in league with him, a Diaspora depending upon him, or economic partners profiting with him.

Notwithstanding the above guideline, interventionists must expect that their information will often be *highly* imperfect and that they will probably never fully understand all the factors at play. Practitioners advise that "uncertainty is the norm when dealing with faction leaders." Intelligence analysts explain that good information about the leaders and the crisis region is often hard to come by. One reason is that both the leaders and the regions were not previously of high interest in either political or academic circles. Another is that civil-war factions tend to be excellent at masking their internal political dynamics even from their own followers and masses. Unless outsiders have highly placed informants or are able to intercept privileged communications, they are reduced to primitive Kremlinology for deciphering exactly what is happening and why.[29]

Compounding the problem is that leaders may not have immutable motives. Not only may these shift, but leaders may also deliberately embark on contradictory two-track policies in order to retain flexibility or confuse outsiders. It is not unusual for leaders to plead that, as much as they personally wish to cooperate, circumstances, fear of strengthening a rival for power, a need to respond to alleged provocations, negative supporter reactions, or the like, force them to be obdurate.[30]

The implications of acting on imperfect information means that interventionists should proceed cautiously when going beyond humanitarian aid to bring about structural changes in states undergoing civil conflict. While empathy for innocent victims of a conflict can trigger an understandable desire to champion reform and prevent further hardship, the aim to alleviate immediate suffering is best kept separate from attempts to solve how contending parties should live with one another or select who their leaders ought to be. This is not to say that urging specific reforms should be eschewed, but that it should follow well-informed judgment grounded in experience. The going-in attitude of interventionists whose (initial) mandate is only to alleviate hardship should be: "Feed and then feel your way" as to whether and how to pursue societal reform. As much as possible, whatever is decided and done should reflect what the indigenous majority wants, not what outsiders want for them.[31] Such an attitude does not mean, however, abdicating to indigenous leaders the power to decide what the interventionists can or ought to do. Whatever the mandate and associated agreements worked out with the factions, however, interventionists should regard them collectively as a foundation, as opposed to a restrictive ceiling for getting on with what needs doing in light of conditions of the day. The presumption should be that what is not expressly forbidden is allowed as long as it can be linked back implicitly if not explicitly to the mandate and other controlling documents.

Finally, it is imperative, practitioners say, to anticipate and head-off problems before they arise—otherwise the intervention will almost certainly fail. This admonition is the thread running through more specific and overlapping guidelines concerning preemption.

The sine qua non for preempting obstructions is being credible to and receiving the respect of indigenous leaders and peoples; anything less invites opposition. There are five precepts subsumed within this guideline: "front-load for success," seize the initiative on arrival, preserve and enhance your legitimacy, never promise what you cannot deliver, and always deliver what has been promised.

To "front-load for success" one must recognize how critical initial impressions of an intervention are to indigenous peoples and leaders. Interventionists must arrive with proper personnel and material resources. Their mandate must set objectives that are clearly understood by mission personnel as well as by the indigenous leaders with whom they will interact. It must give them the authority to demand the elimination of obstructions and to force the issue when they are not. Rules of engagement for the military contingent must be appropriate to that authority and based on prior agreement among the interventionists about how to handle contingencies. Lack of agreement may be reason enough to forestall an intervention, since indigenous leaders will surely exploit differences and hesitancies among the outsiders.

Front-loading should apply as much to the civilian as to the military side of an intervention aimed at long-term stabilizing change. Experienced practitioners are (nearly) unanimous in the view that when planning such interventions, the international community has generally been too focused and reliant upon the military dimensions. Whether a High Commissioner or Special Representative of the UN Secretary-General, the civilian leader constantly interacts with indigenous leaders, but, as was the case with Carl Bildt, the High Representative in charge of implementing the civilian elements of the Dayton Accords, too often he or she arrives understaffed, underfunded, and overly dependent on unenthusiastic and sometimes resistant soldiers to carry-out basic police, crime-fighting, electoral support, humanitarian, and mission-coordination functions. Relief organizations fill-in some of the needs but staunchly oppose control by any other than their own headquarters. Even when the military element successfully employs force to implement the mandate, the civilian mission leader may remain woefully limited in ability to impress indigenous leaders and the populace that promised goods and services can be delivered.

Upon arrival, interventionists must seize the initiative to shape first impressions and forestall expected challenges. To some leaders, the start of an intervention is exactly the time when the outsiders, who may still be sorting themselves out, are particularly susceptible to challenges that test the limits of what they will allow.[32] In other interventions, the start is a period where uncertain leaders and war-weary peoples are receptive to being told what to do and expect the interventionists to assert authority and show the way. A valid criticism of UNTAC, for example, was that many Cambodians expected and/or desired that it act more decisively than it did when it arrived on the scene.[33] If interventionists have no plan or seem pusillanimous, then the indigenous leaders are emboldened to fill the vacuum themselves and thereby put outsiders to the test.

Once on the scene, the interventionists must also tend to their perceived legitimacy. Humanitarian-aid organizations are legitimized by virtue of their goals and reputations, but this is not the case with others, including military contingents, that deploy to protect aid delivery. For them, the best *external source* of legitimacy today may be the endorsement of the United Nations Security Council; the best *inside source* is how they behave. Once in place, interventionists should consult with leaders at all levels, make clear to them and to the populace that they will be guided by and apply the mandate and agreements impartially, and avoid subjecting the citizenry to unnecessary hardships.

Maintaining a perception of impartiality can be particularly difficult if sanctions or coercion are applied against only one party, and special efforts may have to be made in this regard. Within seven days of the start of the IFOR (International Force used in Bosnia after the Dayton Accord) operation, for example, IFOR dismantled 40 Bosniac and Serb military positions and checkpoints in Sarajevo, 20 for each side.[34] In Somalia, UNITAF's headquarters' physical proximity to Aideed's led some to believe that there was a special relationship with him, an impression that Aideed fostered. Those rumors were laid to rest, at least temporarily, after UNITAF struck one of his weapons-storage compounds that had fired on U.S. Marines despite many warnings. UNITAF, however, had to carefully balance "its raids on Aideed's weapons caches with similar raids on those belonging to . . . other factions."[35]

To retain credibility and respect, interventionists should abide by two other maxims that effectively define what it means to be credible. One is never to promise what cannot be delivered, and the other is always to deliver what has been promised. Even implied promises can wreak havoc. Take for example the unfortunate name given the initial UN operation in Bosnia: United Nations Protection Force. The implication was that the UN was there to protect victims of aggression. The reality was that UNPROFOR was there to protect the relief effort. The result was almost immediate disillusionment with the operation. The UN compounded this problem when it assigned the term "safe area" to locations where the Serbs were not to conduct operations. So few UN forces were assigned to those areas that they hardly constituted a deterrent to Serb operations against the areas and later capture of some.[36] Unmet expectations breed resentment in those hoping for the best, and sneers from those who would do ill. In particular, bluffing is risky, if not stupid, and repeated bluffing is a slippery slope to failure.[37]

Beyond activities that enhance credibility and respect are other guides for preempting obstructions. One is arriving expeditiously after the decision to intervene has been made. One reason is heading-off (further) large-scale population movements, since displaced people, especially the young, are open to the blandishments of opportunistic camp or militia leaders and may become dependent upon them for basic food and security.[38] Expeditious arrival is also relevant if it occurs in the aftermath of an agreement wherein the indigenous parties agree to outside intervention. It could also forestall a leader changing his mind, imposing new, crippling conditions, or pursuing last-minute initiatives (such as seizing additional territory) that run contrary to what the interventionists are supposed to accomplish.

Once in place, the interventionists must speak with one voice to the leaders and their publics, and they must continually coordinate their efforts and (planned) responses to contingencies.[39] Not to do so invites a leader to play-off one intervening partner against another. Obstructionist leaders know that each national contributor to the intervention worries about casualties, costs, divisions of labor, and questions of national pride such as usually attend command-and-control decisions. While on-scene personnel regularly resolve these issues on the day or by agreeing on standard procedures, there are often underlying political differences dividing the capitals that faction leaders can exploit.

Complementing the need to speak with one voice is paying attention to what the people in the crisis area are being told. Specifically, interventionists must limit the ability of indigenous leaders to incite local hostility against the mission, since popular opposition is an obstruction that is usually insurmountable. In Bosnia, SFOR (Security Force that replaced IFOR) found that it needed both to shutdown the Pale Serb's television channel as well as pressure the Croats to take rabidly nationalist news programming off the air.[40] In addition to shutting-down protagonist media, interventionists must carry out a public-relations campaign that preempts false and inflammatory propaganda. A media campaign should also indicate the source of outside aid, for while interventionists may have to work with a leader to distribute it, they must be careful lest he take undue credit for the benefits it provides. UNTAC found it beneficial in Cambodia to deploy a broadcasting capability and to distribute portable radios in order to keep people objectively informed about events in general as well as its aims, activities, and plans relative to administration and the election.[41]

Preempting popular hostility also requires something more fundamental: providing the people with a stake in peace. They must be given concrete reasons to support the intervention even when their leaders call on them to rally round. As often as not, common citizens are inclined to support interventionists when they first arrive. Certainly the victims of war are eager to see an end to the fighting as long as they have hope that a better life will result. An intervening military force can help; its presence and its active efforts to provide general security can calm local fears—a prerequisite for buttressing popular willingness to take risks in the interest of peace.

In addition, the extent to which both the civilian and military elements of the intervention restore basic services, provide medical aid, reopen transportation routes and the like can cause the public to conclude that the intervention should not be obstructed. The military contingent should view such undertakings as mission-enabling and not as mission-creep, especially before civilian organizations can fully take over. Commanders of military contingents have allowed how they sought to broaden the benefits of projects done to carry out their military mission to the surrounding population. Roads and bridges once repaired were used by the locals as well as by their own soldiers. Electricity restored to power military systems and associated equipment also helped average citizens to get on with their lives and restart the economy, and, where possible, improve local conditions for all groups. During the IFOR operation, the United States "distributed . . . grants evenly among projects in the [Bosnian] Federation [region] and [in] the Republic of Serbska. . . . It had the dual effect of building a store of goodwill and proving that the United States was not there with any ulterior or exploitive motive."[42]

The task of structurally improving a torn society falls mainly to the civilian side of the intervention mission. Too often in past cases, however, it has been strapped for resources. Practitioners call for providing civilian leaders with "walking around money" that they judge could produce large benefits if wisely used. Past efforts to raise such funds in Haiti and Rwanda, for example, involved "passing the hat" among mission personnel and foreign embassies—a hardly edifying practice. However obtained, discretionary money would allow the quick purchase of critical equipment, repair parts, and laborers to bring water, electrical, transport, and like systems on-line. It can also directly help to "drive a wedge" between a recalcitrant leader and the rank-and-file through the temporary hire of former combatants and others to clean-up the rubble of war and re-establish and maintain basic services. Not only would the employed be doing socially useful tasks, but their jobs could lessen their dependency on a leader's largess, limit their availability for leader-inspired mischief, and possibly reduce their susceptibility to calls to lash out against outsiders—be they the intervening force or other factions.[43]

Giving people a lasting stake in peace may also require (re-)instituting systems of governance, police, and justice, but even without the pressure of time these are difficult tasks for outsiders to bring off (as evidenced, for example, in the myriad problems still plaguing efforts to provide Haiti with a workable police and objective judiciary). The fall-back is to provide people with enough respite from war and enough restoration of basic services as to allow them to get on with putting their lives together and developing their own alternative economic, educational, medical, and local-governing systems responsive to their concerns. These can be the first steps toward a new stability. In a quite interesting paper focusing on "cultures of peace-building that are instituted by peoples living in the midst of war," Carolyn Nordstrom writes of what people can do when they have the opportunity. In Mozambique, for example, "traditional authorities and spontaneous civilian groupings variously decided on their own to do everything from establishing peace zones . . . to protecting their communities from the excesses of troops and renegade bands of ex-military preying on the unarmed population."[44] At about the same time farther north, "normal Somalis," writes Walter Clarke, "were striving against mighty odds and a lot of [warlord] firepower to reinstate local authorities, create self-help groups, open schools, reopen farms, and shops, and restore community services."[45]

Implied in several guidelines already presented is the need to co-opt and work with mid- and low-level officials with some analysts viewing mid-level leaders as particularly important for moving a group toward stability.[46] A survey of military officers serving in UNPROFOR concluded that the "best chance for creating and maintaining consent is to bring the management of a conflict beneath the level of top leaders."[47] If a top leader is accommodative, working with his subordinates will reinforce that spirit and may help to minimize his using lower-level resistance as an excuse for not getting things done. Conversely, if he is himself resistant, co-opting his subordinates could be very important should interventionists adopt the option of building-up alternatives to him.

Finally, interventionists should understand that regardless of how impartial they try to be, what they do will affect the leadership situation. They enhance the political status and legitimacy of an individual vis-à-vis alternative leaders and the populace when they treat him as a leader, and particularly when they work through him or give in to his demands. They can also enhance his economic clout when they purchase goods and services that he controls. This control may be obvious and direct, as occurred in Mogadishu when international agencies purchased protection and rental spaces from the warlords, or indirect as may still be occurring in Bosnia and Croatia. According to a NATO official, the intervening powers may be spending as much as $40 million a year in leasing costs from landlords who front for the governing parties.[48] The consequences are positive only when they help a cooperative leader or influence him to be cooperative. The darker side of legitimacy was demonstrated, however, during the Rwanda crisis when relief agencies permitted deposed Hutu leaders to distribute supplies, with deadly consequences.[49] The aphorism, "Be careful whom you empower," summarizes the views of many practitioners.

CONCLUSION

Interventionists will determine on the day whether and how, for instance, they will reassure or appease an obstructionist on the one hand, or pluck his feathers on the other. The guidelines and maxims offered in this chapter are intended to help them make those decisions as well as to suggest ways whereby interventionists can head-off obstructionism in the first place. It is testimony to the difficulty of the obstructionist-leader problem, however, that even the guidelines and maxims are themselves not easy to apply because of internal tensions. Two important guidelines are to be sensitive to the granularity of context and tending to devilish details. A third guideline warns the interventionists that their information will probably be highly imperfect. There is tension as well in simultaneously feeling one's way while also seizing the initiative or in encouraging interventionists to co-opt lower-level officials while also being careful about whom they empower.

Such tensions are not contradictions, however, and should not paralyze decision-making. Rather, they highlight the need for interventionists to consider two final guidelines. Because the tensions and the inherent factual uncertainties confronting interventionists leave considerable room for judgment and choice, interventionists must avoid "excessive focus . . . on what is theoretically desirable rather than what is politically and practically feasible."[50] They must also continually revisit and revise their decisions as new information becomes available and conditions change. Policy-makers, particularly those in the field who must be prepared to act on a daily basis, should have an array of leveraging instruments at their disposal, but need, in addition, the contextual understanding of how and when to use the leverage that is available to them.

Notes

1. Our research, including two of the workshops, was supported by a grant from the United States Institute of Peace. The first workshop was arranged with the cooperation of the Council on Foreign Relations and took place on 17 June 1998 at the headquarters of the Carnegie Endowment for International Peace in Washington, D.C. The second workshop took place at the Naval War College on 9 October 1998. The third workshop was supported by a grant from The Widgeon Foundation and was conducted at New York University on 8 October 1999.

2. Preliminary research published in Donald C. F. Daniel and Bradd C. Hayes, "Dealing with Obstructionist Leaders," *Civil Wars 1*(3) (autumn 1998): 65–94.

3. Andrew S. Natsios, "Each humanitarian effort must have its own plan that is carefully fashioned according to the unique circumstances of each emergency. "Humanitarian Relief Intervention in Somalia: The Economics of Chaos," in *Learning from Somalia: The Lessons of Armed Humanitarian Intervention*, ed. Walter Clarke and Jeffrey Herbst (p. 94) (Boulder, CO: Westview Press, 1997). See also Beatrice Pouligny, "Peacekeepers and Local Social Actors: The Need for Dynamic, Cross-Cultural Analysis," *Global Governance 5*(4) (Oct.–Dec. 1999): 405–6.

4. See Stephen John Stedman, "Spoiler Problems in Peace Processes," *International Security 22*(2) (fall 1977): 10–11, 14–16. See also Nicholas Sambanis, "Peace-Makers or Peace-Spoilers? United Nations Peacekeeping under Uncertainty," unpublished paper, 25 September 1998. Sambanis focuses on the "strategic problem" posed for peacekeepers of having to deal with insincere parties who manipulate the peace process. Sambanis wrote the paper when he was a Ph.D. candidate at Princeton's Woodrow Wilson School. See as well Dennis C. Jett, *Why Peacekeeping Fails* (New York: St. Martin's Press, 1999, 61–63), where he raises

the issue of "leadership styles" such as "unifying," "noncooperative," and "introverted." Unfortunately, concept of style remains very broad and inchoate and thus of limited practical utility.

5. See Barry H. Steiner, *The Varieties of Collective Preventive Diplomacy: Great Power Approaches to Intrastate Ethnic Conflict*, report prepared for the United States Institute of Peace in connection with grant SG-79-94 (Long Beach: California State University, Long Beach, 1 July 1998), 9–10.

6. Cameron Hume, *Ending the Mozambique War: The Role of Mediation and Good Offices* (Washington, DC: U.S. Institute of Peace Press, 1994), 105. The imbedded quotation is from a Renamo "report" on the peace talks.

7. Ibid., 74. The mediators during the Mozambique negotiations, for example, "husbanded very carefully their limited ability to influence the parties by conferring or withholding symbols of legitimacy from proposed solutions."

8. Charles King, *Ending Civil Wars*, Adelphi Paper 308 (Oxford: Oxford University Press for the International Institute for Strategic Studies, 1997), 41.

9. Max Weber, *Economy and Society*, ed. Guenther Roth and Claus Wittich (Berkeley: University of California Press, 1978), 1:244; see also 2:1142. The charismatic warlord, as described here, is very similar to Susan Woodward's references to "tribal warlords," which she also attributes to Weber. See her "Failed States: Warlordism and Tribal Warfare," *Naval War College Review 52*(2) (spring 1999): 62. In her focus on tribal warlords, she argues that this category does not fit what was happening in places such as Bosnia and Somalia in the 1990s. Our workshop participants would generally agree.

10. John Mackinlay, "War Lords," *RUSI Journal* (April 1998): 29.

11. Andrew S. Natsios, "Commander's Guidance: A Challenge of Complex Humanitarian Emergencies," *Parameters* (summer 1996): 51.

12. This was the opinion of several well-informed observers that one of the authors (Daniel) spoke with when in Haiti in April 1999. They felt betrayed because they had put their hope in Aristide whom they regarded as possessing charisma.

13. See Herman C. Kelman, "Social-Psychological Dimensions of International Conflict," in *Peacemaking in International Conflict: Methods and Techniques*, ed. I. William Zartman and J. Lewis Rasmussen (p. 195) (Washington, DC: U.S. Institute of Peace Press, 1997).

14. Michael E. Brown, "The Causes and Regional Dimensions of Internal Conflict," in *The International Dimensions of Internal Conflict*, ed. Michael E. Brown (p. 571) (Cambridge: MIT Press, 1996).

15. Ibid., 582, table 17.3. See also B. Blechman, W. Durch, W. Eaton, and T. Stukey, *Effective Transitions from Peace Operations to Sustainable Peace, Final Report* (Washington, DC: DFI International, September 1997), 20.

16. While many lament the deep-rooted nature of the ethnic differences in Bosnia, Carlos Westendorp, the High Representative charged with implementation of the Dayton Accords, claims that the ethnic divisions in Bosnia are "created by power elites to preserve their power." As quoted in "The Balkans Survey," contained in *The Economist* (24 January 1998): 7.

17. See Daniel Byman, Kenneth Pollack, and Matthew Waxman, "Coercing Saddam Hussein: Lessons from the Past," *International Security 40*(3) (autumn 1998): 125–48.

18. This is a central theme of Hume's book (note 6).

19. Woodward, 61.

20. Margaret Joan Anstee, *Orphan of the Cold War: The Inside Story of the Collapse of the Angolan Peace Process, 1992–93* (New York: St. Martin's Press, 1996), 55.

21. Mary B. Anderson, *Do No Harm: Supporting Local Capabilities for Peace through Aid, Local Capacities for Peace Project* (Cambridge, MA: Collaborative for Development Action, 1996), 12.

22. Natsios, 86.

23. Detailed descriptions of these strategies and options can be found in Don C. F. Daniel and Bradd C. Hayes, "Dealing with Obstructionist Leaders," *Civil Wars 1*(3) (autumn 1998): 65–94.

24. A framework for facilitating decision is found in ibid.

25. See Barbara F. Walter, "Designing Transitions from Civil Wars: Demobilization, Democratization, and Commitments to Peace," *International Security 24*(1) (summer 1999): 127–55; and Walter, "The Critical Barrier to Civil War Settlement," *International Organization 51*(3) (summer 1977): 335–64. See also Fen Osler Hampson, *Nurturing Peace: Why Peace Settlements Succeed or Fail* (Washington, DC: United States Institute of Peace Press, 1996), 210.

26. See John L. Hirsch and Robert B. Oakley, *Somalia and Operation Restore Hope: Reflections on Peacemaking and Peacekeeping* (Washington, DC: United States Institute of Peace, 1995), 99. See also Mats Berdal, *Disarmament and Demobilisation after Civil Wars*, Adelphi Paper 303 (Oxford: Oxford University Press for the International Institute for Strategic Studies, 1996), 20–23.

27. Hirsch and Oakley, 57. On the issue of written agreements, workshop participants advised against "signature obsession." Major-General Lewis MacKenzie noted another issue in Bosnia: "As had become routine after a VIP visit, the city was ablaze with fighting all night. I began to develop the theory that the military on both sides associated such visits with a possible cease-fire or outright end to hostility. That being the case, they wanted to gain as much territory or carry out as much revenge as possible, before the status quo was locked into place by some agreement. I made a mental note to discourage VIP visits in the future" (*Peacekeeper* [Toronto: HarperCollins, 1994, 463]).

28. Hirsch and Oakley, 157–58.

29. Stephen Stedman noted that the SRSG in Cambodia, Asushi Akashi, "told aides of his fear that Hun Sen had only tenuous control over hardliners, who if pushed too far, would rebel against Hun Sen and return to war. Akashi's staff, however, believed Hun Sen to be firmly in control of his followers." Stedman, 33. See also 23–30.

30. Anstee, former Special Representative of the Secretary-General in Angola, reported that both President dos Santos and his rival, Jonas Savimbi, insisted that their personal desire for peace and cooperation had to be tempered by the "internal resistance" they faced within their own factions. Anstee, 109.

31. There are Haitians who lay at least part of the blame of Haiti's failure to move toward stable self-government to policies of the interventionists. As one put it: "It is no longer a democracy struggled for by the Haitian people. Today it's the United States and the international community that are wanting to build *their* project." Statement of Camille Chalmers, head of the Haitian Platform for the Promotion of Alternative Development, as quoted by Dan Coughlin, "Haitian Lament: Killing Me Softly," *The Nation* (March 1, 1999), as found at <http://ebird.dtic.mol/

Feb1999/s1999021haitian.htm>. Emphasis added. One of the authors (Daniel) traveled to Haiti and can testify to a pervasive sense among many people in their speech and in cartoons that the international mission has gone off-track and is trying to impose a system on the Haitians.

32. Durch claims that "credibility with the local parties is established, or lost, according to experienced hands, in the first six weeks of a new operation." William J. Durch, "Running the Show: Planning and Implementation," in *The Evolution of UN Peacekeeping: Case Studies and Comparative Analysis*, ed. William J. Durch (p. 64) (New York: St. Martin's Press, 1993).

33. Trevor Findlay, *Cambodia: The Legacy and Lessons of UNTAC*, SIPRI Research Report No. 9 (Oxford: Oxford University Press for the Stockholm International Peace Research Institute, 1995), 113–16.

34. Admiral Leighton W. Smith, Jr., "The Pillars of Peace in Bosnia," *NATO Review* (July 1996): 13.

35. Hirsch and Oakley, 57.

36. To be fair to the Serbs, the Bosniac military had an unfair advantage in that it could use the "safe areas" for sanctuary.

37. "[H]ypernationalist leaders [as in civil conflicts] can be expected to call bluffs, and . . . bluffing tactics usually don't work with an adversary who has . . . called earlier bluffs." David Callahan, *Unwinnable Wars: American Power and Ethnic Conflict* (New York: Hill and Wang, 1997), 143.

38. It is often the case that large popular displacements occur so early on in a crisis that they are a *fait accompli* by the time an intervention can be mounted.

39. Antonia and Abram Chayes and George Raach point out that the speed and complexity of developments on the ground require that controlling authorities such as in the UN Secretariat or the Security Council should "radical[ly] decentraliz[e] operational responsibility *to the field* with agreement to cooperate fully ther to develop an integrated approach—together with adequate delegation of authority to do so." Antonia Handler Chayes, Abram Chayes,and George Raach, "Beyond Reform," *Global Governance 3*(2) (May–August 1997): 118. Emphasis in original. See also 135.

40. "A precarious peace," *The Economist* (24 January 1998): 8. In Rwanda, Major-General Romeo Dallaire longed for the ability to shut down the vituperative media that fomented that country's genocide. R. A. Dallaire and B. Poulin, "UNAMIR: Mission to Rwanda," *Joint Force Quarterly* (spring 95): 70.

41. James A. Schear, "Beyond Traditional Peacekeeping: The Case of Cambodia," in *Beyond Traditional Peacekeeping*, ed. Donald C. F. Daniel and Bradd C. Hayes (p. 257) (London: Macmillan Press, 1995).

42. Major-General William L. Nash, "The Year of Living Creatively," *Armed Forces Journal International* (November 1997): 42–43.

43. Ibid. USAID in Bosnia "provided $5 million to execute more than 100 projects aimed at rebuilding local infrastructure using demobilized soldiers—in effect, a jobs program that contributed directly to the protection of American soldiers and helped Bosnia recover from the ravages of war."

44. Carolyn Nordstrom, "The Eye of the Storm: From War to Peace—Examples from Sri Lanka and Mozambique," Reprint Series 13:PR:15 of the Joan B. Kroc Institute for International Peace Studies (Notre Dame, IN: University of Notre Dame, n.d.), 99, 102. See also Pouligny, 412–14.

45. Walter Clarke, "Failed Visions and Uncertain Mandates in Somalia," in Clarke and Herbst, 13.

46. John Paul Lederach, *Building Peace: Sustainable Reconciliation in Divided Societies* (Washington, DC: U.S. Institute of Peace Press, 1997), 33, 40, 42; and Timothy D. Sisk, *Power-Sharing and International Mediation in Ethnic Conflicts* (Washington, DC: United States Institute of Peace, 1996), 84.

47. Wolfgang Biermann and Ole Frederik Ugland, "Lessons Learned in the Field," in *UN Peacekeeping in Trouble: Lessons Learned from the Former Yugoslavia*, ed. Wolfgang Biermann and Martin Vadset (pp. 87–88) (Aldershot, UK: Ashgate Publishing, 1998). See also Pouligny, 410–12.

48. Mike O'Connor, "Political Parties in Bosnia Get Millions in Rent for NATO Bases," *New York Times* (13 October 1998): A10.

49. Donald C. F. Daniel and Bradd C. Hayes, with Chantal de Jonge Oudraat, *Coercive Inducement and the Containment of International Crises* (Washington, DC: U.S. Institute of Peace Press, 1999), 139.

50. The words are from Mats Berdal, *Whither UN Peacekeeping?*, Adelphi Paper 281 (London: Brassey's for the International Institute for Strategic Studies, 1993), 75. Berdal argues persuasively that both the academic and policy elements of the peace-support community suffered from that excessive focus. This was a prescient conclusion that helps explain many of the difficulties that later surfaced in peace-support operations.

CHAPTER NINE

Challenges in the Exercise of Leverage in Peacekeeping

CHRISTOPHER COLEMAN AND ANDREW GRENE

ADAPTING TO CHANGE

Two major changes, witnessed in the last decade, have redefined peacekeeping and will continue to do so for the foreseeable future. These two changes are fundamental to understanding the objectives of peacekeeping operations and the leverage required to achieve them.

The first, by now very familiar, is that the nature of conflict has changed. We are rarely faced with purely interstate violence anymore. But neither are we dealing with internal conflicts. Rather, conflicts today are a confounding mix: their core is essentially internal, but they are complicated by the cross-border involvement of state or nonstate actors. And their consequences can quickly become international, because of destabilizing refugee flows as well as factions pursuing each other regardless of where the border lies.

This has demanded the adoption of a new strategy of peacekeeping, which can be summed up in very broad terms as the "institutionalization of politics." Conflicting interests are inherent in any society, and United Nations peacekeeping operations do not presume to remove conflict from the societies that they are trying to assist. Rather, they seek to remove those conflicts from the battlefield and to facilitate the use of legitimate institutions, in such areas as elections, human rights, or law enforcement, so that all constituencies have, and feel that they have, meaningful political and economic access. Much of the task of today's operations, therefore, is to assist the parties to strengthen existing institutions, or even to create new ones. This is the rationale behind multidimensional operations, and, at the far end of this spectrum, those interim administration operations in which the United Nations actually governs while indigenous institutions are being developed. The "institutionalization of politics" is also the exit strategy for today's peacekeeping operations, since it promotes the emergence of conditions in which the peacekeeping operation can withdraw and expect to leave behind a country that will remain at peace.

The second major change to which we have had to adapt is the decline in the old-fashioned leverage that peacekeepers could draw upon in order to push parties to abide by their commitments and to respect the peacekeepers who were monitoring them. Until the end of the cold war, peacekeeping operations rarely exercised leverage directly. Whenever negotiation and persuasion failed, the next step was to report violations to UN headquarters in New York. At that point, after a quiet call from the Secretariat, the great powers could be counted upon to exercise influence on their respective client states. They did this, usually behind the scenes, because they did not want the conflict to escalate to a level where the superpowers might be dragged into a direct confrontation. The leverage at their disposal was based on economic- and military-assistance programs, which could be manipulated up or down. With the end of the cold war these programs dried up, as superpowers disengaged—and the leverage dried up with them.

Today, the political support and behind-the-scenes leverage of Security Council members continues to be essential—but it is not enough, for two reasons. First, Council members may or may not be the states with the most influence over the parties. (For this reason, additional ad hoc political frameworks have been created, such as the so-called "contact groups" or "Friends of the Secretary-General.") And second, external, state-to-state influence may not do the job, especially since some of the players are nonstate or substate actors having no direct relationship with external states. Today's conflicts are characterized by weak borders and overlapping ethnicities; they are often driven by tensions between ethnically or religiously based communities, whose rivalry has been inflamed by uneven distribution of wealth or opportunity; leaders may stoke such tensions for personal gain, and may receive significant support from outside parties and/or the private sector; and chains of command may be blurred or uncertain. In response, today and in the future, peacekeeping operations must have their own source of leverage that they can directly utilize in the field. They must focus not only upon political leaders, but also upon field commanders, individual combatants, and the general public.

Leverage in the field includes the ability of the operation on the ground to convince key actors that the benefits they can obtain through peace outweigh those they can gain through continued conflict, or that the cost of disruption of a peace process is too high to pay. The first two forms of leverage identified below have long been part of peacekeeping but merit reconsideration in light of recent developments. The remaining four have gained prominence as distinctive features of peacekeeping over the past ten years. Many of these observations and recommendations, however, could be usefully applied, in various degrees, to all operations, including "traditional" ones based primarily on a military component backed by a limited mandate to stabilize a conflict situation.

Forms of Leverage

Moral Authority as the Witness for the International Community

A key form of leverage upon which peacekeeping operations have traditionally relied is their unique stature as the eyes and ears of the international community and as a symbol of the international community's will. The universal character of United Nations peacekeeping confers "moral authority." While this remains a crucial asset in peacekeeping, it can be of less value in circumstances in which a state has splintered into multiple factions and/or law and order has generally broken down and some elements operate without any apparent reference to international norms and standards to which state actors are expected to conform. As shown in Rwanda and Srebrenica, some of today's combatants ignore the moral stature of an operation, especially if it has no physical capacity to back it up. Moral authority will remain an essential element in the leverage of a peacekeeping operation but alone cannot provide operations with the clout they need; other means of leverage will also be required.

Military Capability to Reassure and to Deter

Another key form of leverage in today's peacekeeping operations is provided by the military component. Its role is *not* to shoot its way into accomplishing a mandate; this is not the job of a peacekeeper. However, military credibility is vital in peacekeeping today and it represents a key form of leverage in two ways: First, the presence of an international military component may help provide a sense of security and thus persuade belligerent commanders in the field or ex-combatants to engage in disarmament and demilitarization so that a peace process can advance. If any of the parties believe that disarmament leaves them vulnerable, they won't disarm. They must perceive the peacekeeping force as sufficiently strong to protect them against cheating by the other side.

Second, even when a relatively solid political agreement exists, a peacekeeping operation may require deterrent capacity to reduce the likelihood of challenges to its mandate and an ability to respond to such challenges when necessary. Regardless of the quality of the peace agreement, we much expect one group or another to want to test the international community's will as manifested in the peacekeeping operation. If the peacekeeping contingent shows up looking small and weak, it's inviting trouble. If, on the other hand, it arrives quickly (an important part of credibility), with strength and obvious determination, it invites respect. A credible deterrent capacity, in such circumstances, is fundamental to success.

If the peacekeepers are not credible, the parties can quickly lose faith in the peace process, which then begins to fall apart.

The behind-the-scenes dynamics involved in drafting a Security Council mandate often reveal much about the degree of consensus that exists on the exercise of leverage, especially the use of force. Informal consultations among Council members prior to their adoption of a resolution will generally expose any fault lines. In what is by now the best-known example, UNPROFOR, at least one Permanent Member was ambivalent, to say the least, with regard to the use of force against the Serbs while another Permanent Member consistently pushed for resolutions authorizing such force as a means of protecting Bosnian Muslims (but was willing to back-up its words with troops). The well-known result was a series of contradictory mandates that were conspicuously missing authorization of the force levels required to implement them.

Apart from members of the Council wanting to protect a traditional ally or fellow member of an identity group from Council-authorized enforcement, there is always an additional "fault line" apparent or just below the surface of Council negotiations. It is the still-unresolved tension between the principle of nonintervention in the internal affairs of sovereign states on the one hand, and the recognition that, overwhelmingly, war in today's world has major "internal" dimensions that must be addressed. This issue has been sidestepped, to a certain extent, with the authorization to use force when necessary to ensure freedom of movement in the accomplishment of the mandate. Boothby's chapter on UNTAES in this book (chapter 5) provides a good example of how such authority can be utilized effectively when a mandate is matched with an effective force (i.e., one that is cohesive, well-armed, -led, -trained, and -equipped and guided by clear rules of engagement).

Beyond these political and conceptual concerns, there are practical issues that are also rooted in political realities. The elements required for an effective military component in today's peacekeeping operations include well-trained and well-equipped troops who can deploy quickly, who have access to force multipliers such as communications equipment and vehicles, and who have appropriate financial support. A Council agreement on paper with regard to the use of force, enshrined in an unambiguous and internally consistent mandate, is far from sufficient. Who will supply the military assets, including personnel, required for success?

The resolution authorizing UNAMSIL (Sierra Leone), for example, was clear. UNAMSIL, among its other responsibilities, would protect civilians within the limits of its capabilities, in its area of deployment. No disagreements from Member States on this issue could be detected in the informal consultations leading up to the authorizing resolution. However, those pushing the hardest for such a mandate were conspicuously unenthusiastic about contributing forces for its implementation. The results are by now well-known. A rather weak force was deployed, with some contingents arriving without the basic equipment and training required of them. UNAMSIL looked weak and vulnerable and it was predictably tested as a result. It did not initially withstand the test; the operation faced a major crisis as violence erupted and the peace process unraveled.

The Brahimi Panel report, seeking to address just this sort of problem, suggests that Council resolutions should be kept in draft form until such time as the Secretary-General confirms that governments have committed the requisite forces. In theory, at least, this would shift the responsibility back to the Council, to use its influence to secure troop contributors to implement its decisions. This would be an improvement, because the Council's influence far outweighs that of the Secretary-General, who has very little leverage with which to persuade governments to send their forces to faraway lands. Whether the Council will implement this recommendation, and, if so, what the practical impact will be, remains to be seen.

Positive Incentives

In pursuing a strategy of political institutionalization as described above, forms of leverage other than a credible deterrent capacity—leverage that can be exercised at the field level—are also necessary. Peaceful politics, and the reconciliation upon which a functioning political system must be based, cannot be imposed. Other forms of leverage, in particular noncoercive forms, have therefore been developed. The first is *positive incentives*—the concept that by providing relatively low-cost benefits, particularly to those in middle- and lower-level positions in a hierarchy, an operation can dilute the appeal of continued fighting and help pave the way for progress towards peace.

A good example of using positive incentives can be found in the area of disarmament and demobilization. Even when leaders sign agreements, rank-and-file combatants are often reluctant to lay down their arms. This may, of course, be driven by concerns over threats to their physical security. It may also reflect concern over losing a way of life. Combatants may have been recruited as child soldiers and now, as young adults, may have never known anything but fighting. They may have missed out on formal education altogether. They have no prospects of earning a living. They fear a loss of status, of the deference that is accorded them when they walk into a village carrying a gun. It is necessary to address these concerns, offering them a reason to join in the peace.

In these types of cases, positive incentives have taken the form of demobilization packages and support for reintegration. The demobilization package consists of food, clothing, and, in some circumstances, a bit of cash to sustain them while they get their feet back on the ground. Reintegration support involves education, job training, and counseling, and, in some cases, "microcredits," so that former combatants can look forward to a successful life off the battlefield.

In tragedy, we must find the beginnings of opportunity. Within the tragedy of a war-ravaged country and its devastated economy, the incentives we have described cost a modest sum of money by international standards but can provide a meaningful opportunity to a recently demobilized combatant.

Within the process of disarmament, demobilization, and reintegration, positive incentives have proven to be useful and cost-effective sources of leverage. However, the availability of the necessary resources has sometimes been problematic. In this context, the Secretary-General proposed in his report on the role of peacekeeping in DDR (S/2000/101) that the Security Council should consider demobilization exercises, or at least their initial stages, as eligible for support from assessed contributions for the operation; the report recommended a similar provision for seed money for "quick-impact projects." Both of these recommendations were once again placed before the international community in the Brahimi Panel report and remain under consideration.

Enabling Resources

Another form of noncoercive leverage, which will remain essential in coming years, could be called "enabling resources." They are different from positive incentives. In the case of enabling resources, the persons we are trying to influence already want to abide by their commitments, so we do not have to persuade them of anything. However, they lack the capacity to do what is required.

A classic example of this is the transformation of a guerrilla army into an effective political party. If this process fails the guerrilla side will be incapable of pursuing its interests and those of its constituents in legitimate politics. In those circumstances, they will have little incentive to remain in the peace process and will face many temptations to return to the battlefield. In operations such as those in El Salvador and Mozambique, the mobilization of enabling resources—technical assistance, training, a kind of crash course in democratic politicking—has proven to be one of the keys to an enduring peace.

Engaging the Private Sector

Another form of leverage, essential now and in the future, has to do with the links between factional armies and the global economy. The ability of a peacekeeping operation to advance a peace process and persuade local actors to abandon violence exists within the broader context of resources generally available within the conflict area. In the past, private businesses have at times undermined a peace process, sometimes unwittingly, by facilitating unregulated exploitation of a country's natural resources and eroding a legitimate government's authority. Where foreign military-assistance programs have become far less readily available (as noted above), factions are nonetheless acquiring the wherewithal to fight through the use of export commodities: gems and timber in Cambodia, diamonds in Angola and Sierra Leone. Traditional political leverage is undermined proportionately, since combatants have an independent capacity to obtain funds and an incentive to prosecute violence.

There are several ways to sever this link: one, of course, is economic sanctions. Depending on the type of commodity, these can be very difficult to enforce. A fortune in diamonds can be carried out by one individual. Other commodities would be operationally easier to intercept. For example, the logging roads along which the Khmer Rouge exported timber out of Cambodia were well-known and easily spotted. What is operationally easy, however, may be politically impossible, especially when important external partners in the peace process turn out to be economically complicit with one or more of the factions. Thus sanctions are one possibility but not always a practicable one. Their potential and limitations continue to be reviewed by the Security Council.

A second way to sever this link—one that may ultimately prove more promising—is to go further up the chain. If we go up high enough, we are likely to find a major commercial enterprise that has a big interest in maintaining a positive market image, especially among consumers in the West. Engaging such enterprises proactively, so that they can become (and be seen to become) part of the solution rather than part of the problem, may be a promising avenue of leverage to be further explored. Corporate codes of conduct, and public watchdogs to monitor behavior, could be a useful part of this.

Because of its moral stature and its ability to reach a global public, the United Nations can help deter misconduct by setting standards and by publicizing it where it occurs. Where private businesses have undermined a peace process the United Nations can publicly identify culprits, as was done by the Security Council's panel of experts on sanctions in Angola; even before publication of the report, concerns over negative publicity led to new kinds of self-regulation by the International Diamond Manufacturers' Association. This experience could be built upon and further avenues to publicize misconduct, either by the Council or the Secretariat, could be explored.

At the same time, the United Nations is well-placed to engage the business community as a partner and catalyst for progress in peacekeeping operations. Where the lack of economic activity within a postconflict area can threaten a peace process, the engagement of private business as an employer and source of economic and technical advancement may help promote recovery from conflict. Businesses may bring technology, capital, entrepreneurial skills, and tax revenues to a postconflict environment. Again, it is worth exploring how the United Nations could seek to give positive exposure to those businesses that have made helpful investments in areas emerging from conflict.

Thus far, the international community has developed only limited experience and understanding of this dimension of today's conflicts. Effective action to pursue these means of promoting change will require cooperation within the United Nations system; with various NGOs (nongovernmental organizations); with Member States; with the private sector; and with academia.

Power of Communication

A final form of leverage that will be important to future successes in peacekeeping is the power of communication with the population living in the mission area. This is not a luxury but an operational requirement—a form of leverage to ensure that the peace process holds, and a "multiplier" of many other forms of leverage that are discussed here.

The role of public information was identified as an element of peacekeeping as far back as 1956 with the creation of UNEF (United Nations Emergency Force), which included a component that dealt with media correspondents. In today's operations, however, public-information components focus not only upon the international media, but also upon combatants and the general public in the host country.[1] As noted above, the strategy of today's peacekeeping operations is often based upon the development of effective institutions through which all constituencies can pursue their interests. This can only work if the people are actively engaged and made a part of the process; if not, they will have no faith in the outcome, and this lack of faith will quickly become a self-fulfilling prophecy.

Moreover, in the types of conflicts we have described in which power and authority are fractured, we often deal with individuals and communities who do not respect or even recognize the ostensible leaders who have made commitments to the international community. The peacekeeping operation, therefore, must be able to communicate with the population directly, explaining why we are in the country, what we expect from them and their leaders, and what they may expect from us. Peacekeeping operations must also have a capacity to hear their views directly. A good relationship cannot be achieved in the absence of effective, *two-way* communication.

This is a form of "soft leverage" that must be developed much further than has been the case so far. This requires greater technical backstopping capacity within the Secretariat, as recognized by the Brahimi Panel report. It also entails developing a good understanding of the issues at stake for the local population, and of its perceptions of these issues, which in turn requires stronger links between the Secretariat and others outside the diplomatic world, including in particular anthropologists, scholars, and academics.[2]

CONCLUSIONS

The nature of conflict and distribution of power in the world have changed dramatically in recent years. National and international institutions seeking to manage and resolve conflicts are struggling to adapt to these changes. The traditional forms of United Nations leverage for conflict management and resolution (based primarily on the exercise of influence by states upon other states within a legitimate multilateral framework) are no longer sufficient to the task.

State-to-state leverage is still important, though states in a position to use that leverage in any given case do not necessarily belong to the Security Council. As a result, political frameworks have been developed, such as core groups, contact groups, and groups of friends. These adaptations are also insufficient. In contrast to traditional circumstances, leverage must be exercised in the field directly. When it has been possible to do so, important elements have included a credible military capacity, positive incentives, enabling resources, and public communications. But much remains to be done before peacekeeping operations can make full and effective use of these concepts.

All of these issues must be tackled with an awareness of the bigger questions affecting peacekeeping, relating to the nature of the mandates themselves, the end to which a peacekeeping operation is "effective," and the long-term impact of peacekeeping operations—their legacy is one, five, or ten years after their withdrawal. The answers to these questions, as much as or more than its short-term effectiveness, will determine the contribution of United Nations peacekeeping.

Notes

1. A thorough discussion of this issue can be found in Ingrid A. Lehmann, *Peacekeeping and Public Information: Caught in the Crossfire* (London: Frank Cass Publishers, 1999).

2. A useful study of this issue is a discussion paper by Thant Myint-U and Elizabeth Sellwood on "Knowledge and Multilateral Interventions," published by the Royal Institute of International Affairs (also known as Chatham House), London, 2000.

PART THREE

Conclusion

CHAPTER TEN

Leveraging for Success

JEAN KRASNO, DONALD C. F. DANIEL,
AND BRADD C. HAYES

RESPONDING TO THE CHANGING ENVIRONMENT

United Nations peace operations have become more complex since the inception of peacekeeping, when the first United Nations Emergency Force (UNEF) was deployed in 1956 to form a buffer zone between the warring parties. Now UN operations do more than just keep factions at bay. With greater cooperation on the UN Security Council and the end to East–West competition over spheres of influence, there is much more effort on the part of Member States to try to address the root causes of conflict and build sustainable peace. These efforts to construct sustainable peace mean that a complex orchestration of measures are brought into play. The UN now requires a large basket of instruments that can be made available to those who are charged with bringing about successful solutions. In response to this changing environment and the new opportunities for the UN to build peace, we endeavored to examine cases in such a way as to shed light on how leverage can be used to bring about changes in behavior and compel action toward agreement and compliance with UN peace mandates.

THE COMPLEXITY OF LEVERAGE AS A CONCEPT

This project set out to study two aspects of leverage: first, to examine how leverage is brought to bear on parties to a conflict to end the fighting and accept UN assistance and/or intervention, and second, to probe for examples of how leverage was used to pressure the parties to comply with UN mandates once agreement was reached. In comparing the results of the case studies, we concluded that understanding compliance meant examining the integrated effects of sources of leverage. However, the study revealed that sources of leverage are more complex than we had originally anticipated and also more difficult to classify into neat categories. Some were more obvious, like the use of troop deployment or the imposition of sanctions, but others involved more elusive intangibles like trust, prestige, and moral authority. At first, it may seem that combining such unlikely factors as military deployment, trust, and legal leverage into one category would be like lumping together apples, oranges, and even cumquats; nevertheless, all can be used to leverage behavior.

Instruments of leverage appear to range along a continuum, albeit overlapping at times, from hard leverage like the use of or threat to use military force at one end of the spectrum, to soft leverage, exemplified by intangible qualities such as trust at the other. Some sources of leverage such as information appear to fall into both hard and soft categories. For example, on the one hand, dissemination of information via radio in the field to the public affected by a UN operation in order to facilitate its cooperation can be considered as concrete, hard leverage. However, the negative quality of misinformation or the positive quality of the truth may be considered to be more subjective and harder to quantify. Yet these subjective factors *do* matter in influencing behavior.

What we hope to describe here is kind of salad bar array of instruments of leverage that players involved in the peace process can choose from and combine in useful packages when an opportunity offers itself. It becomes important then to include in this selection not only the more traditional tools, but also the invisible qualities that also compel behavior. The complex nature of integrated leverage means not only that there are many factors to examine, but that influential sources of leverage may change over time as circumstances change. It is not only a question of who has leverage to offer, but also who is open to respond to that leverage at any given point in time. This can apply to the belligerents and their external supporters and those that internally undergird the warring parties, including their leaders and followers. This requires good information gathering and analysis, but the fact is that most often this information is imperfect. In trying to grapple with the concept of leverage and its explanatory power in analyzing success stories, we found it useful to look separately at these two components: (1) instruments of leverage; and (2) those players who use and orchestrate leverage.

THE COMPONENTS OF LEVERAGE: INSTRUMENTS AND PLAYERS

Instruments of Leverage

Military Force. The deployment of military troops is the most visible aspect of most peace operations. Nevertheless, *using* force and *showing* force are two distinct qualities, albeit ones that are interlinked. The cases elaborated in the preceding chapters demonstrate that the UN needs to ensure that adequate force is available. Bluffing is no substitute when adequate force is not available. Force size has always been a point of contention between the UN Secretariat staff and members of the Security Council. The staff is interested in providing an operation with enough resources to enhance its chances of success, while some Security Council members, who have to pay the tab, are often eager to get by on the cheap. In chapter 1, Mats Berdal documents that inadequate troop deployment did little to deter attacks on safe areas or deter the Bosnian Serbs from taking UN peacekeepers hostage. Berdal warns that in the midst of civil war, as in Bosnia, a symbolic military presence alone does *not* provide leverage. He instructs the United Nations not to hand-over leverage to the belligerent parties by being vulnerable to hostage-taking, which not only happened in Bosnia but was repeated in Sierra Leone in May 2000.

The Bosnia lesson led to a reevaluation of troop strengths, and those lessons learned were applied to UNTAES as Derek Boothby, in chapter 5, so aptly conveys. Although UNTAES was manned at a lower level than the UNDPKO staff recommended, it was given its own considerable military resources besides having an implied relationship with NATO that conveyed the impression to anyone who might confront the operation that there was ample force waiting just over the horizon.

Another lesson learned is to deploy the force quickly, front-load a visible military presence. Having the appropriate number of highly visible troops arriving on schedule gives the SRSG (Special Representative of the Secretary-General) on the ground the leverage he or she needs to keep the other components of the operation moving forward. Anyone familiar with UN operations knows that troops are normally deployed at a glacial pace. Arguments over the budget and force levels for Namibia led to delayed deployment that almost destroyed the mission. UNTAES forces were available within three months of its mandate's passage, which was lightning speed for a UN operation. Following the crisis in East Timor, the Australian-led force arrived in a matter of weeks. Although this force was authorized by the UN Security Council, it was not considered a UN force. However, the speed of deployment by the Australians during the Timorese crisis demonstrates that it can be done quickly.

In chapter 4, Dirk Salomons points out that the slow deployment of troops in Mozambique created fears of renewed insecurity, but their final arrival also showed that setbacks can be overcome. An example of the devastating effects of slow deployment is Namibia, where lack of a UN presence in the north on April 1 left a vacuum in which over 300 people were killed, almost derailing the operation. The most devastating example is, of course, Rwanda, when Security Council members continued to meet and discuss the crisis but procrastinated while some 800,000 civilians were brutally slaughtered. In the end, the French deployed Operation

Turquoise under Security Council authorization but after most of the genocide had already taken place.

UNTAES clearly demonstrated successfully that a peace operation must have the necessary strength to respond with force when challenged. However, UNTAES had the advantage of coming after the peace agreement at Dayton. UNPROFOR had no such advantage. The UN has to have the capacity, if attacked, to resolutely strike back. This requires not only the military capacity to strike, but a good understanding of the force and will of the opposing recalcitrant party or parties. Salomons makes clear that having the right level of UN troop force provides the parties with the sense of security needed to disarm. They need assurances that they will not be vulnerable to attack. The right level of force presence as a deterrent can make the actual use of force unnecessary. This also requires that the troops are highly visible.

Economic and Financial Tools. Whether expressed as punishments in the form of sanctions or offered as inducements, economic factors are important leveraging tools. The threat of continued UN-authorized economic sanctions against South Africa was a tool that both SRSG Ahtisaari and his deputy, Legwaila, used when pressuring South Africa to comply with various measures needed to make the elections in Namibia "free and fair"—the key phrase that would enable the Security Council to lift sanctions. But perhaps more important than sanctions were financial factors such as the ability to borrow in international markets and to receive direct investments. This was an element in South Africa's eventual compliance.

It was also a useful threat in dealing with the Indonesian leadership after the "consultation" erupted into violence. This pressure brought to bear by international financial institutions like the IMF eventually succeeded in bringing about the necessary Indonesian permission to allow the Australian-led force to enter East Timor and end the violence. In order not to violate the country's sovereignty (an important UN norm), the Security Council needed the Indonesian government's consent before it could send troops. Indonesian leaders finally responded to the financial leverage because their economy, already weakened by the Asian economic crisis, needed outside financial assistance in order to avoid collapse. While international financial institutions can provide carrots or sticks, donors' conferences, even thought they are ad hoc, can jump-start the process by infusing funds and demonstrating international support.

Bilateral incentives can also come into play in making available what can be termed "enabling resources." The Friends of El Salvador provided economic support for the peace process by financing most of the meetings between the parties. Member States can also be "on call" to provide funds in a crisis. Knowing that the Italians would produce the resources needed to keep Renamo leader Dhlakama on board, even when he realized he would lose the elections, saved ONUMOZ at a critical juncture. Providing the SRSG with a little "walking around money," as Salomons recommends, can also make an immediate impact when he or she sees areas of need. These funds can enable him to act quickly to save a situation from turning ugly. Pay-outs for military officers and other military/guerrilla fighter personnel can assist demobilization by smoothing the way to retirement of offering a bridge for the transition into civilian life.

Nonfinancial Constraints or Sanctions. Embargoes on arms and other items as well as travel bans can also be very useful leveraging tools. However, arms embargoes may backfire. In Bosnia, the arms embargo left the two sides unevenly armed, and it was not until there was an equalization of military power that a stalemate could be achieved and the Serbs, fearing further territorial losses, were willing to negotiate seriously. Embargoes can also be informal rather than mandated by the Security Council. As Diego Arria points out in chapter 3 on the El Salvador case, Cuba and the Soviets agreed not to continue to support the FMLN with arms and the United States made it clear to the Salvadoran government that it was no longer going to provide millions of dollars of aid to its military. This informal embargo encouraged both sides to realize that they were not going to win the war.

The Power of Information. For an operation in the field to be successful, the UN needs the capacity to get its message across to the local people who must participate in compliance. Simply because national leaders have worked out an agreement, does not mean that local consent can be assumed. Misinformation can destroy a mission. Good relations with the public can be cultivated by sponsoring various forms of media. For most operations, radio broadcasts reach the greatest number of people. Newspapers are another good way of communicating operation objectives and making the truth known. In some limited areas such as Eastern Slavonia where most households have televisions, UN access to television-broadcasting equipment would be more effective. No UN operation, however, has ever been funded or provided with television equipment. Having to rely on locally controlled broadcasting systems can leave the UN hostage to the manipulations of uncooperative parties. In Namibia, for example, it had to rely on SWABC, which was controlled by South African sympathizers and consistently spread misinformation about the UN and other political groups. It was only a few weeks before the elections that the UN was able to correct this problem. UNTAES Administrator Jacques Klein took control of a similar situation by exerting forceful leverage successfully and in so doing, closed down a source of misinformation that could have undermined the UN operation there.

Information also needs to be shared among UN personnel and internal communication must be ongoing. Those opposing an international mandate will work any means they can find in order to undermine the operation. These include "seams" between troop contingents, seams between agencies or groups involved such as NGOs, and those between the field and headquarters. Interpretation of the mandate must be consistent and clearly conveyed to all contingents and the public. For example, communicating a proactive interpretation of the mandate is significantly different than conveying a more narrow interpretation—that of self-defense applied to UN troops alone. These differences in communication can undermine the operation. UN personnel need to be operating under the same instructions on policy implementation at every level. In Bosnia, the public assumed that the "protection force" was there to protect civilians, but the narrow interpretation of the mandate—self-defense of UN troops—was the operative standard. Had that been understood, the cynicism may not have been as intense and civilians would not have place false trust in the peacekeepers.

International public opinion can often be favorably employed. First, it can be used to persuade leaders that have an internationalist bent to change their behavior or bend to the will of the international community. And second, it can be used to help maintain support for the operation among donor countries and within the Security Council where decisions on the operation are made.

Legal Leverage. Legal leverage or legal authority overlaps in many ways with politics and moral issues. For a peace operation the UN must look to a number of legal instruments, and the pivotal legal instrument for each specific operation is the Security Council mandate. That becomes the law for the operation during its existence. However, mandates, as we know, can be, and usually are, ambiguous. Nevertheless, too much specificity in the mandate can be a bad thing. Making the mandate clear, but leaving specific implementation details vague, provides the Special Representative of the Secretary-General with the maximum amount of flexibility. Boothby insists that the mandate should be used as a floor, not a ceiling, and it should be implemented innovatively. An ambiguous mandate may be a political necessity in order to achieve agreement among the members of the Security Council, particularly the five Permanent Members (P-5). The danger in ambiguity, however, is that it may reflect significant differences in how the implementation of force is interpreted, as was seen in Bosnia in particular, with unfortunate results. Legal instruments do not exist in a vacuum, however, and are highly susceptible to politics. In general, political maneuvering creates the laws to begin with, and even after a legal agreement is drawn up, it will be subject to political manipulation.

Judicial interpretations, tribunals, and courts must also be included in the "toolbox" of legal instruments that are available. Recalling the Namibian case, the UN sought legal authority for the Namibian cause from the International Court of Justice in The Hague and lost both times. It was not until there were changes in judges on the Court that a ruling was made in favor of Namibian independence. The two prior Court rulings emboldened the South Africans by making their case appear just. On the other hand, the second negative ruling also emboldened the UN General Assembly, in exacerbation to take stronger action, unilaterally declaring Namibia's independence and establishing the Council on Namibia and a number of other mechanisms under UN auspices that strengthened SWAPO's leveraging position. The UN tribunals on both the former Yugoslavia and Rwanda represent attempts to establish accountability for atrocities carried out in those countries and address issues of impunity. However, even these efforts only deal with small numbers of perpetrators, and it will remain to be seen as to whether they will deter such future crimes. Yet, these may represent instruments of leverage that will strengthen over time.

The Internalization of International Norms. Linked to the abovementioned discussion on legal authority is the concept of the internalization of legal norms. In chapter 6, Mark Quarterman points out that President Habibie of Indonesia had internalized international norms more than others in the Indonesian leadership, which made him more willing to comply. This is a factor that needs further study.

Making Use of Local Groups and International NGOs. Local groups such as churches or community organizations can be used to leverage compliance and implement the provisions of the peace operation. The leverage may work both ways, in that local groups may use the UN to achieve peace and reconciliation just as the UN uses them for the same end. Jacques Klein used local groups and community functions like market day to foster confidence-building and reduce tensions. The Namibian Council of Churches facilitated much of the repatriation of refugees and worked with the UN to educate the population on voting. Sant'Egidio was pivotal in bringing about the peace agreement in Mozambique and handing off the implementation of the agreement to the UN. On the other hand, the inability to achieve the compliance of local extremist groups can undermine the operation. Where compliance is impossible, other leverage may need to be brought to bear to manage local militias or at least to isolate them. The UN can also work integratively with nongovernmental organizations like Doctors Without Borders and with UN agencies like UNHCR, UNICEF, UNDP, and others. These organizations can be particularly useful in the demobilization and reintegration of soldiers after years of fighting.

Moral Authority. A number of instruments of leverage are harder to concretize. The remaining factors fall into this category. One of the most recurring is *moral authority*. For example, the momentum that was carefully constructed by SWAPO and the African Group in the UN was heavily dependent on the moral nature of their cause—to free Namibia from South Africa's brutal grip. In the East Timor case, the UN's role in allowing the people to decide on independence for themselves was based on years of accumulated moral outrage at the repressive treatment of the East Timorese by Indonesia's military. With this moral backing, the UN was able to act quickly when Habibie opened a small window of opportunity for action to be taken. Member States were supportive of UNTAET because of the strength of the moral case and were willing to overlook what could have been interpreted as interference in a sovereign state. Moral considerations were also a key factor in placing human rights at the forefront of the peace process in El Salvador.

Moral considerations can have a negative side as well. Member States wanted to look like they were taking action to aid a humanitarian crisis in Bosnia but were actually unwilling to provide the necessary support for the operation. The result was moral humiliation for the UN and Member States who were blamed for letting Serbs overrun UN forces and carry-out genocide in the safe areas. This humiliation has deeply hurt the UN, which clearly wants to avoid being on the wrong side of the moral issue in the future. This may make it easier to leverage Member States for adequate resources when they are reminded of the lessons learned in Bosnia.

Trust. Trust is another intangible that plays into leverage in many subtle ways. Parties emerging from conflict need to be able to have confidence that the UN and the SRSG are trustworthy and will not betray them. Rebel groups are particularly vulnerable and need to trust that they will be both secure and brought through the process as equal partners before they can demobilize. In giving up their arms and disbanding their forces, they give up their primary source of leverage. Trust between the parties and the guarantors is essential, but trust among the key players within the international community is also important. The Friends or any leveraging group of Member States have to demonstrate trust in order to maintain a focus on one common outcome—peace. In Bosnia, the parties to the conflict did not trust the UN and the major powers did not trust one another. Even when there is basic agreement, a primary role of the SRSG is to cultivate trust throughout the process. Losing it can have devastating results. Trust can also be found in unusual places, as with the lay group Sant'Egidio. Credibility derives from trust, and both involve keeping promises and only making promises that can be kept.

Impartiality. The UN's greatest asset is its impartiality. Whether it is Namibia, Mozambique, El Salvador, or East Timor, the UN has to carefully guard its perception as an impartial mediator and peacekeeper. The status of the Organization is bound-up in its stature as a body that represents the common good. If it is perceived to take sides, the other party or even Member States and donors may opt out. Impartiality is deeply intertwined with trust. The parties need to *trust* that the UN will remain impartial.

However, during the 1990s the UN became entangled in situations where one side was clearly more at fault and the nature of UN impartiality had to change, particularly when the party at fault was carrying out acts of genocide and ethnic cleansing in clear view of the United Nations. The Organization could no longer protect its moral authority and be impartial toward both parties. In these cases, the UN had to abandon impartiality toward the guilty party in order to enforce the mandate and not let itself be manipulated by those who would violate its provisions. Berdal instructs the UN not to remain impartial in the face of aggression; this only encourages the perpetrators to hold the impartiality card as leverage over the UN while continuing to abuse the situation.

Once belligerents understand that the UN is going to be consistent, they will adjust their behavior to comply or suffer the consequences. All actors involved may prefer for the UN to be trusted to enforce the mandate, even if it means taking action against on side or the other, rather than to play a hands-off role that in the end favors the intransigent party. Even the noncomplying party may have more respect for an SRSG who can be trusted to enforce the mandate, no matter who is thwarting the UN's efforts. Nevertheless, Member States with troops on the ground may still prefer the UN to refrain from punishing a perpetrator in order to keep their soldiers from becoming directly in the line of fire. This presents a serious dilemma for troop contributors, but in the long run, the disgrace of allowing genocide to go unchecked may force Member States to reconsider their short-run policies. The Dutch government was forced to resign in spring 2002 when a report was released that clearly implicated the Dutch UN contingent with Serb mass killings during the fall of the Bosnian safe areas.

Impartiality is essential for mediation. Negotiators can successfully use the perceived impartiality of the UN, or a lay group like Sant'Egidio, to leverage agreement between parties who would not turn to any other would-be mediator who was perceived as being partial. The success of the Group of Friends on El Salvador was that both parties perceived them as being impartial. In fact, the UN and the Friends were their last hope for peace when all else had failed.

Prestige. The UN, Friends groups, other Member States, and even nongovernmental organizations like Sant'Egidio can gain prestige by successfully assisting the peace process. This can provide incentives to keep the players engaged. The awarding of the Nobel Peace Prize to East Timorese Bishop Carlos Belo and independence leader Jose Ramos Horta was an important leveraging factor, conferring credibility and prestige to those that supported the cause. Prestige can be used as a tool in other ways. The location of peace talks such as inviting the parties to New York and even to the residence of the Secretary-General, as Pérez de Cuéllar did, can create a kind of prestigious environment that encourages agreement. The spotlight of attention that location affords may be very useful.

The removal of prestige or the threat to bring about international humiliation can also act as leverage to bring about a change in behavior. A country threatened with becoming an international pariah, such as South Africa had become, can suffer not only from a lack of esteem but also from the economic and social stigmas associated with this kind of condemnation. The fear of failure on the part of the UN and the humiliation that can bring, like the cloud cast over the Organization by the fall of the safe areas, can also induce the UN and its Member States to act more proactively to prevent disgrace. Hence the fear of losing prestige can offer its own kind of leverage.

Social Pressure and Personal Contacts. Personal contacts can be an important tool. The ability of President Pérez of Venezuela to pick of the telephone and call the president of El Salvador or FMLN leaders was key at important critical moments in applying leverage to one party or the other. Also, the desire of a country's leaders not to be socially ostracized can bring them to the negotiating table, and an intervention that conveys the proper message with a personal touch over the telephone or in person can be just what is needed.

Exposure and Accountability. Accountability and the exposure of condemned behavior is another important tool. UN observers have taken on this role, but other entities can also be given this task. Monitoring the South African police by UN CivPol eventually achieved results. The UN considered this so important in Namibia that it increased the number of CivPol members from 500 to 1,500 within a few months. UNTAES also showed that the potential exposure by UN observers deterred bad behavior. In East Timor, prior to UNTAET (which was deployed after the crisis), the UN mission was not allowed to have troops or CivPol in the field. Nevertheless, the UN team facilitated observers by creating an environment for the media who then took on that role for the international community. Formal reporting to an authoritative body like the Security Council would have offered the UN mission a more consistent and trustworthy source of information and accountability than the more ad hoc reporting of the media. In the end, reporting of events has to land on somebody's desk in authority who wants the process to succeed or at least does not want to be humiliated by its failure.

International Players That Use Leverage

Member States. Christopher Coleman and Andrew Grene explain in chapter 9 that the end of the cold war changed the dynamics of major-power leverage on client states. In some ways, this has weakened the ability of the UN to turn to the major powers for help, but it has also opened the door for greater UN activity where previously it had been relegated to dealing only outside, or at the fault lines of, East–West spheres of influence. Nevertheless, the major powers continue to have a key role to play and are the ones that supply most of the leverage available to the UN, the Secretary-General, and the SRSG in the field. If a major power is involved, it will normally ensure that its forces are adequately protected and that the operation will have the support necessary for success. The major powers can also facilitate economic incentives, have influence with the IMF and World Bank, encourage direct investment, and offer aid packages. An increased number of operations has been assigned to a lead-state such as Operation Turquoise conducted in Rwanda by France, the Australian-led coalition in East Timor, and the British-led operation in Afghanistan that was later taken over by Turkey and then Germany.

All UN peace operations require enabling resolutions from the Security Council. Therefore agreement (or nonagreement) among the members of the Council is key to launching a successful operation. While the UN in the last decade has not witnessed the veto to the same extent as it did during the cold war, the power of the veto shadows every discussion on the Council. A P-5 member only has to say that it doesn't like the language here or there, and the language will often be changed. The nonpermanent members have the power of the block veto if they can garner seven opposing votes, but they rarely exercise this because of bilateral interests with the major powers.

The United States is clearly the first among equals in the UN with its veto power, its obligations to pay 25 percent of all peace operations, and its ability to provide logistics, transport, and other support to an operation whether or not it directly contributes troops. The United States also has considerable political clout. A visit made to General Wiranto during the crisis in East Timor by the commander-in-chief of the U.S. Pacific Command seemed to have had an effect. This was also linked to U.S. suspension of arms sales to Indonesia.

Depending on the case at hand, regional powers and other states can take on key roles as well. In addition to U.S. resources, other Member States contribute troops, equipment, and expertise, and a few also provide air- and sea-lift capabilities. Groups of Member States such as the Friends of the Secretary-General on El Salvador as described by Arria can also use their leverage as powers in the region or as committed players. These countries can have their own resources that impact on the parties. Front-Line States and the African Group at the UN also played that role in Namibia; Italy played a key role in Mozambique; former colonial power Portugal played an important role in East Timor, followed by the regional power Australia when force was needed. The Cubans and Soviets also played an important role in Namibia after April 1 by pressuring Sam Nujoma to withdraw SWAPO forces back to Angola, something he did not want to do, and preventing UNTAG from unraveling. Another key point regarding the major powers and other interested countries is that they should not operate as spoilers. By agreeing to support the peace process or at least not impede it, the Soviets (later the Russians) and the Cubans enabled the negotiations to succeed in El Salvador.

Member States' long-term commitment helps antagonists understand the need to cooperate. Announcing in advance an exit date can abdicate leverage to the belligerents who, in turn, can just conserve their resources to be unleashed as international troops wave good-bye on their departure. Hence, when the UN leaves, it's the staying power of Member States who are willing to continue to use leverage with the parties that can keep the peace until new government mechanisms become more inclusive. A lack of long-term commitment encourages intransigent parties to oppose and eventually outlast the operation. Friends groups of Member States, as described by Krasno and Arria, have played key roles by maintaining leverage with the parties even after the UN operation has ended.

The power of a Member State, particularly that of one of the major powers, is so implicit that a person representing the state embodies a symbolic, unspoken source of leverage, precluding the need even to mention military or economic strength. A strong personality like Jacques Klein representing the UN but nevertheless clearly an American, or Venezuelan President Pérez, can work that state-power value to its fullest extent.

The Important Role of the Special Representative of the Secretary-General. Personality matters! An SRSG is most effective when he or she has an international reputation or represents a major donor power and acts proactively; for example, that he or she expects cooperation and does not hesitate to compel it when necessary. Both Salomons and Boothby highlighted this point in their chapters. In addition, cultural difference need to be carefully taken into consideration in selecting the right SRSG for the job. While the highly deferential Yasushi Akashi may have worked well within the Asian environment of Cambodia, he may not have been the best choice in dealing with the Serbs in Bosnia during UNPROFOR. Both Ajello, the SRSG for ONUMOZ, and Ahtisaari, the SRSG for UNTAG, were consistently resourceful in their orchestration of leverage on a day-to-day basis with a complex array of parties and issues. Knowing exactly when to apply leverage and who and what you have to reinforce you is a true art. Ian Martin, the SRSG in East Timor, was certainly clever, but by not having any UN troops to call upon he lacked the means to address the violence perpetrated by the Indonesian militias. Selecting the right SRSG and providing him or her with the right instruments of leverage is essential.

THE UN AS A FOCAL POINT FOR THE ORCHESTRATION OF LEVERAGE

As Mark Quarterman so insightfully reveals, the UN can operate as the focal point for orchestrating leverage, acting as the center for a confluence of leveraging instruments. He uses the term "regime" to describe a set of loosely orchestrated factors that work toward a common goal, falling along a spectrum of weak-to-strong. *At its weakest,* the UN has no negative action to threaten the parties; it is not seized of the issue; Member States lack the will to apply pressure; transnational networks and actors are not mobilized; and the media is not covering the issue. *At its strongest,* the UN Security Council and/or General Assembly are seized of the matter and willing to apply coercive measures or inducements; Members States with influence apply bilateral pressure; transnational networks and actors are actively engaged; and the media is spotlighting events. Quarterman explains that most cases fall somewhere in between. The salience of each factor pitted against the cooperation or intransigence of the parties may allow international players to manipulate the relative application of the leverage tools available to the regime—in other words, try to ripen the process.

The UN, acting as the central hub of activity, can facilitate consultations. Its nearly universal membership means that countries have representatives in New York at almost all times of the year. Members can meet at any time in the delegates lounge, in the halls, or down the street at a local cafe to exchange ideas. They, of course, have to refer back to their capitals for the authority to take any action, but proximity at the UN is a tremendous advantage. Also, by meeting unobtrusively at the UN, countries can avoid what might be perceived as a symbolic visit to another country, something that might attract too much unwanted attention.

Coordinating leverage at the outset would most likely be better, but that may not always be possible. Quarterman points out that interlocking actors who work in tandem for the same purpose may not necessarily work in coordination but the outcome may still have beneficial effects. In some cases, it may not be possible to know what was the pivotal source of leverage and therefore we may only be able to see the integrated picture and not be able to rely upon the explanatory power of a single piece. Arriving at the wrong conclusion or looking for the one "silver bullet," as Berdal explains of the NATO bombing in Bosnia, may not be accurate and even could lead to wrong assumptions for future cases, such as in Kosovo.

An essential key to the successful implementation of a peace operation is matching the right instruments of leverage with the right players at the right time. This artistry comes in identifying all these factors and orchestrating their integration. The case studies in these chapters illustrate through example how this has been done well, and not so well, in the past. We hope to provide policy-makers with this institutional history, spotlight how tools of leverage can come into play, and offer some lessons learned. Salomons points out that luck cannot be learned, but timing and opportunity can be recognized and exploited. Speed and agility to respond are critical when a window of opportunity becomes available, not only to initiate a peace operation, but to keep the parties from reneging. Yet responding with speed and agility requires having the right instruments lined up on the table, finely tuned and ready for selective use in crafting the final product.

suggested bibliography

Akashi, Yasushi. "Managing United Nations Operations," in Wolfgang Biermann and Martin Vadset, eds., *UN Peacekeeping in Trouble: Lessons Learned from the Former Yugoslavia*. Aldershot, UK: Ashgate Publishing, 1998.

Berdal, Mats. *Disarmament and Demobilization after Civil Wars*, Adelphi Paper 303. Oxford: Oxford University Press, 1996.

Clarke, Walter, and Jeffrey Herbst, eds. *Learning from Somalia: The Lessons of Armed Humanitarian Intervention*. Boulder, CO: Westview Press, 1997.

Cohen, Ben, and George Stamksoki, eds. *With No Peace to Keep: United Nations Peacekeeping and the War in the Former Yugoslavia*. London: Grainpress Ltd., 1995.

Crocker, Chester, Fen Osler Hampson, and Pamela Aall, eds. *Herding Cats: Multiparty Mediation in a Complex World*. Washington, DC: U.S. Institute of Peace Press, 1999.

Durch, William J. *UN Peacekeeping, American Policy, and the Uncivil Wars of the 1990s*. New York: St. Martin's Press, 1996.

Hanlon, Joseph. *Mozambique, Who Calls the Shots*. Bloomington: Indiana University Press, 1991.

Hannay, Sir David. "The UN's Role in Bosnia Assessed." *Oxford International Review*, vol. 7, no. 2 (spring 1996).

Harlech-Jones, Brian. *A New Thing?: The Namibian Independence Process, 1989–1990*. Windhoek, Namibia: EIN Publications, 1997.

Hearn, Roger. *UN Peacekeeping in Action: The Namibian Experience*. Commack, NY: Nova Science Publishers, 1999.

Hume, Cameron. *Ending the Mozambique War: The Role of Mediation and Good Offices*. Washington, DC: U.S. Institute of Peace Press, 1994.

Johnstone, Ian. *Rights and Reconciliation: UN Strategies in El Salvador*, International Peace Academy Occasional Paper Series. Boulder, CO: Lynne Rienner Publisher, 1995.

Kelman, Herman C. "Socio-Psychological Dimensions of International Conflict," in I. William Zartman and J. Lewis Rasmussen, eds., *Peacemaking in International Conflict: Methods and Techniques*. Washington, DC: U.S. Institute of Peace Press, 1997.

Koh, Harold Hongju, "Why Do Nations Obey International Law?" *Yale Law Journal*, vol. 106 (1997).

Pérez de Cuéllar, Javier. *Pilgrimage for Peace: A Secretary-General's Memoir*. New York: St. Martin's Press, 1997.

Ratner, Steven R. *The New UN Peacekeeping: Building Peace in Lands of Conflict after the Cold War*. New York: St. Martin's Press, 1996.

Smith, Michael G., with Moreen Dee. *Peacekeeping in East Timor: The Path to Independence*, International Peace Academy Occasional Paper Series. Boulder, CO: Lynne Rienner Publisher, 2003.

index

about the editors and contributors

DIEGO ARRIA was a Visiting Diplomatic Fellow of the Council on Foreign Relations in New York and is a member of the Board of the International Peace Academy. He served as Venezuela's Ambassador to the United Nations from 1991 to the end of 1993 and was president of the Security Council in March 1992. He participated in the Group of Friends of the Secretary-General on El Salvador, Haiti, and Guatemala.

MATS BERDAL is a professor at King's College, London, of security and development in the Department of War Studies. He received his doctorate in International Relations from Oxford University in 1992. His publications include *Whither UN Peacekeeping?* (1993); *The United States, Norway, and the Cold War, 1954–1960* (1997); and, with David Keen, "Violence and Economic Agendas in Civil Wars: Some Policy Implications," in *Millennium: Journal of International Studies*.

DEREK BOOTHBY joined the United Nations in 1978 after serving as a career officer in the British Royal Navy. In the UN Department of Disarmament Affairs, he worked on issues of nuclear nonproliferation and conventional arms limitations and verification. Following the end of the Gulf War he helped to establish, organize, and implement UN weapons inspections in Iraq. In February 1996 he was appointed as Deputy Transitional Administrator of UNTAES.

CHRISTOPHER COLEMAN is senior political affairs officer in the UN Department of Peacekeeping Operations Africa Division. He is currently assigned to UNMEE, the United Nations Mission in Ethiopia and Eritrea. Prior to this position, he was acting special assistant to the Under-Secretary-General of Peacekeeping and chief of the Policy and Analysis Unit. Previously, he was director of Conflict Resolution Studies at the International Peace Academy. His publications include *Montego and Venata: A Simulation Exercise on Peacemaking and Peacekeeping in Secessionist Conflicts* (1993) and *The Salvadoran Peace Process: A Preliminary Inquiry* (1993).

DONALD C. F. DANIEL is a professor at Georgetown University and member of the core faculty in the Strategic Studies Program of the Walsh School of Foreign Service. Previously, he served at the National Intelligence Council in Washington, D.C., and held the Milton E. Miles Chair at the U.S. Naval War College where he was director of the Strategic Research Department, Center of Naval Warfare Studies. His publications include *Coercive Inducement and the Containment of Crises*, with Bradd Hayes and Chantal de Jonge Oudraat (1999), and "Is There a Middle Option in Peace Support Operations?" in *Managing Arms in Peace Processes: The Issues* (1996). He holds a Ph.D. in international relations from Georgetown University.

ANDREW GRENE is currently a political-affairs officer in the Asia and Middle East Division of the UN Department of Peacekeeping Operations (DPKO). Previously, he served in the unit on peacekeeping policy within the Office of the Under-Secretary-General for Peacekeeping Operations, and as Secretary for the General Assembly's Special Committee on Peacekeeping Operations. Prior to joining DPKO, he served in the Executive Office of the Secretary-General during the tenure of former Secretary-General Boutros Boutros-Ghali.

BRADD C. HAYES is professor and senior strategic researcher in the Decisions Strategies Department of the Center for Naval Warfare Studies, Naval War College (NWC). A retired U.S. Navy Captain, he served as the deputy director of the NWC's Strategic Research Department from August 1992 until his retirement in 1996. Prior to assuming that position, he was the strategy and policy officer for the commander-in-chief, U.S. Naval Forces, Europe. His publications include *Coercive Inducement and the Containment of Crises* with Don Daniel and Chantal de Jonge Oudraat (1999), and *Doing Windows: Nontraditional Military Responses to Complex Emergencies* with Jeffrey Sands (1998).

JEAN KRASNO is a fellow at International Security Studies, Yale University, and associate research scholar in the Department of Political Science at Yale. She was executive director of the Academic Council on the United Nations System from 1998 to 2003. She has also served as deputy director of the Yale-UN Oral History Project under James Sutterlin where she conducted a series of interviews with people who have been directly involved in crises involving UN peace operations. Her publications include *The*

United Nations and Iraq: Defanging the Viper with James Sutterlin (2003), and "Brazil" in *The Pivotal States: A New Framework for U.S. Policy in the Developing World* (1998).

MARK QUARTERMAN is currently chief of staff, Office of the UN Special Coordinator for the Middle East Peace Process in Jerusalem. Prior to this appointment he served as special assistant with responsibility for Asia and the Pacific in the Office of UN Assistant Secretary-General for Political Affairs. He was a participant in the UN-led East Timor negotiations between Indonesia and Portugal and served in UNAMET from May through December 1999. He holds a law degree from Harvard University.

DIRK SALOMONS is director, Humanitarian Affairs Program, School of International and Public Affairs, Columbia University. Prior to his recent work, he served in a wide range of management, peace-building, and policy-advisory functions in several organizations of the United Nations system, including FAO, UNAIDS, UNDP, and the UN Secretariat. He was the executive director for the UN peacekeeping operation in Mozambique (UNOMOZ). He holds a doctoral degree in comparative literature and sociology from the University of Amsterdam. His recent publications include *Recovering from Conflict: Strategy for an International Response* (2000).

LaVergne, TN USA
25 February 2011
217956LV00003B/26/P

9 780275 978839